Contents

What is this ethnographer's magic, by which he is able to evoke the real spirits of the natives, the true picture of tribal life?

—Bronislaw Malinowski (1922)

1

An End to Innocence

The Ethnography of Ethnography[1]

JOHN VAN MAANEN

There once was a time—some might say a dreamtime—when ethnography was read as a straight-ahead cultural description based on the firsthand experience an author had with a strange (to both author and reader) group of people. Those who wrote ethnographies may have had their doubts about what the adventure of fieldwork taught them and just how "being there" resulted in an ethnography, but few doubts surfaced in their written products. It seemed as if an ethnography emerged more or less naturally from a simple stay in the field. One simply staked out a group, lived with them for awhile, took notes on what they said and did, and went home to write it all up. If anything, ethnography looked like a rather pleasant, peaceful, and instructive form of travel writing.

For some readers of ethnography—myself included—the apparent freedom from rigid methodological rules associated with fieldwork and the blissful disregard that many ethnographic writers displayed for high-flying abstractions in their papers and monographs seemed to provide a wonderful excuse for having an adventurous good time while operating under the pretext of doing serious intellectual work. Certainly for me the ethnographer's way of knowledge appeared in this dreamtime to be less arcane, more concrete, and far more intimate and respectful than count-and-classify survey work or building and testing off-the-shelf theoretical models. All that was required, it seemed, was a steady gaze and hand, a sturdy and thick notebook, and plenty of time to spare.

No more. The master trope these days appears to be *J'Accuse!* Ethnography is no longer pictured as a relatively simple look, listen and learn procedure but, rather, as something akin to an intense epistemological trial by fire. Boon (1982), for instance, takes ethnography to task for its reliance on unquestioned cultural conceits ("ours" not "theirs"). Rosaldo (1989) sternly chides ethnography for its unwarranted claims of objectivity, whereas Clifford (1988) points to its inevitable but treacherous subjectivity. Clough (1992) indicts ethnography for its gendered silences and partiality. Denzin (1988) faults ethnography for its failure to abandon the scientific posturing associated with modernism or essentialism, and Said (1989) considers ethnography's link to the empire discrediting yet difficult to shed. For these reasons and more, the cultural representation business has become quite tricky. Nor does it seem to matter much whether one goes to the headwaters of the Amazon or to the corner tavern in search of others sufficiently different from one's self to ethnographically realize. Just what is required of ethnography today is by no means clear, and among its producers and consumers alike, restlessness is the norm.

Such restlessness, however, has not brought the enterprise down. And, like any other social practice, the techniques and results of ethnography—though to be fair, not so much its aims—have long been subject to question. The very term ethnography carries several meanings whose gradual and contested emergence must be appreciated to understand the current epistemological moans and groans. The trade has persisted over time not by pushing away critique but by absorbing it, thus maintaining certain ethnographic traditions by stretching them to embrace novel interests and practices. Some of these ethnographic traditions— notably those associated with fieldwork, the culture concept(s), and the pursuit of what is so often presented as the empathetic understanding of the other—are now so strongly articulated, so associated with recognized, hard, and intractable questions, and so enlivened by various interpretive strategies that deep or paradigmatic change is difficult if not impossible to imagine.

Broadly conceived, ethnography is a storytelling institution. It is one that carries a good deal of cultural legitimacy because its stories are commissioned and approved by the leading scientific and educational organizations of the day. Ethnography claims and is granted by many if not most of its readers a kind of documentary status on the basis that someone actually goes "out there," draws close to people and events, and then writes about what was learned *in situ*. It is, by and large, the ethnographer's direct personal contact with others that is honored by readers as providing a particularly sound basis for reliable knowledge. Put in cartoon form, an ethnographer is something of a Supertourist who visits a group of natives in their natural habitat and brings back the news of their way of life. This cartoon is, of course, a view of ethnography more common outside than inside ethnographic circles. Most ethnographers would offer a considerably more nuanced, sophisticated, and perhaps skeptical perspective on their trade. Nonetheless, these general understandings and expectations do play a part in what at any given time will be read as a proper ethnography.

The full measure of the ethnography industry includes the ceaseless production of authoritative monographs, exhaustive reviews of the literature(s), method manuals, encyclopedias of concepts and theories, meta-critical expositions, themed anthologies, experimental writings, annotated bibliographies, established and quasi-established journal publications, formal presentations of talks and papers presided over by a number of academic societies, and so forth. Little wonder that novelties and new directions can be readily absorbed.[2] Over long periods of time, everything may change, but from day to day, ethnographic practices seem much the same. In other words (my words), the center may not hold, but it appears rather formidable at any given time. This is especially true with the sense of vocational purpose or mission carved out and claimed as distinctive by those in the trade—to write about one culture in terms of another. Thus, even when ethnography is racked by debate—as it is today—it continues to remain ethnography so long as what is being debated is not whether or not the work should go on but how best to go on with such work.[3] Consider, in more detail, the scope and shape of contemporary ethnography.

Fieldwork, Textwork, and Headwork

In the most general sense, ethnography refers to the study of the culture(s) a given group of people more or less share. The term is double-edged for it points to both a method of study and a result of such study. When used to indicate a method, ethnography typically refers to fieldwork conducted by a single investigator—the fabled though slightly oxymoronic participant observer—who "lives with and lives like" those who are studied for a lengthy period of time (usually a year or more). When used to indicate a result, ethnography ordinarily refers to the written representation of culture. Contemporary students of culture emphasize the latter usage and thus look to define ethnography in terms of its rhetorical features such as the topical, stylistic, documentary, evidentiary, and argumentative choices made by an author and displayed in a text.

To understand the move toward rhetoric is to also appreciate three rather distinct activity phases or moments associated with ethnography.[4] The first moment concerns the collection of information or data on a specified (or proposed) culture. The second refers to the construction of an ethnographic report or account and, in particular, to the specific compositional practices used by the ethnographer to fashion a cultural portrait. The third moment of ethnography occurs with the reading and reception of an ethnographic text across various audience segments. Each phase raises distinctive and problematic concerns for the subjects, the producers and the consumers of ethnography.

By far the most attention within ethnographic circles has been paid to its first moment—fieldwork. This live-in form of social research is both a product of and a reaction to the cultural studies conducted in the mid to late nineteenth century (Stocking 1987, 1992). Early ethnography is marked by more than a little distance between the researcher and researched. The mostly British ethnographers of the day based much of their cultural representations not on firsthand study but on their readings of documents, reports, and letters originating from colonial administrators, members of scientific expeditions, missionaries, traders, adventurers and, perhaps most important, far-away correspondents guided by questions posed by their stay-at-home pen pals.[5] It was not until the early twentieth century that ethnographers began to enter and stay for more than brief periods in the social worlds of those of whom they wrote. The modern and more or less foundational form of fieldwork as advocated but not always practiced by Malinowski ([1922] 1961, 1-25) required of an ethnographer the sustained, intimate, and personal acquaintance with what the "natives" say and do—in today's vernacular, what "cultural members" say and do. Malinowski's marching orders for fieldworkers were characteristically blunt and to the point: "Find out the typical ways of thinking and feeling, corresponding to the institutions and culture of a given community and formulate the results in the most convincing way" (p. 3).

There is (and was), however, a good deal of variation in terms of just how a fieldworker goes about finding things out and, perhaps more critical, just how such gentle or hard-nosed detective work leads to a convincing written description of culture. In regard to fieldwork, current practices include techniques such as intensive and representative interviewing, working closely and almost exclusively with a few "key" informants, designing and administering local surveys, observing and participating in everyday routines and occasioned ceremonies engaged in by those studied, collecting samples of member talk and action across a range of social situations, and so on. Indeed, there is now an enormous literature designed to help novice or veteran fieldworkers carry out various forms of ethnographic research (e.g., Frielich 1970; Hammersley and Atkinson 1983; Spradley 1979; Werner and Schoepfle 1986).

Yet much of the good advise offered in fieldwork manuals defies codification and lacks the consensual approval of those who produce ethnographies. Fieldnotes, for example, are more or less *de rigueur* in terms of recording what is presumably learned in the field, but there is little agreement as to what a standard fieldnote—much less a collection of them—might be (Sanjek 1990). Moreover, how one moves from a period of lengthy field study to a written account based on such study is by no means obvious. Despite seventy or so years of practice, fieldwork remains a sprawling, highly personal, and therefore quite diverse activity (Kuper 1977; Lofland 1974; Stocking 1992).

The second moment of ethnography—"writing it up"—has by and large been organized and dominated by a genre called "ethnographic realism" (Clifford and Marcus 1986; Van Maanen 1988). It is, however, a genre that has itself undergone changes over time from a relatively unreflective, closed, and general ("holistic") description of native sayings and doings to a more tentative, open, and partial interpretation of member sayings and doings (Geertz 1973). Still, realism—for some quite defensible reasons—remains a governing style for a good deal of ethnography, descriptive, or interpretive (Jacobson 1991). The genre itself is marked by a number of compositional conventions including, for example, the swallowing up and disappearance of an author in the text, the suppression of the individual cultural member's perspective in favor of a typified or common denominator "native's point of view," the placement of a culture within a rather timeless ethnographic present, and a claim (often implicit) for descriptive or interpretive validity based almost exclusively on the author's own "being there" experience (fieldwork).

The most unapologetic realist styles foster an impression that ethnography is a clear, unmediated record of a knowable world. It is washed by a thick spray of objectivity. Aesthetic visions are downplayed because artful delights and forms are often seen by writers and readers alike to interfere with the presentation of what is really there in a given social world. Realism, of course, depends heavily on current cultural codes as to what counts as really real. Thus prevailing ideas as to the nature of the studied world and the acceptable kinds of explorable differences between "them" and "us" as well as the easy accessibility of the writing and its insistent certainty contribute to what might be called a Studio Portraiture form of realism—tightly framed, sharply focused, unnaturally bright, and shadowless.[6]

Some ethnographers, though by no means all, have expressed a degree of dissatisfaction with ethnographic realism (Marcus and Cushman 1982). Much of the initial discontent was generated by readers and critics from outside ethnographic circles who wondered just how personal experience could serve as the basis for a real, bonafide scientific study of culture. As a response to these self-appointed "real scientists," some ethnographers tried to make visible—more accurately, textualize—their discovery practices and procedures (Agar 1980). A degree of ironic embarrassment followed, for it seemed the more scientific ethnographers tried to be by writing about their methods, the less scientific those methods appeared. Such embarrassment accompanies many scientific fields these days, not just ethnography (Latour 1987). But one consequence of the ethnographic introspection of the 1960s and 1970s has been the spread of a methodological self-consciousness and a concern for reflexivity that has not gone away. Nor has guilt and anxiety expressed in some of the early inward-turning work gone away either. If anything, the moral ambiguity and political complicity associated with ethnography has grown ever more obvious and problematic in the shrinking and increasingly interconnected post-colonial world.[7]

In the wake of this heightened self-consciousness, alternatives to ethnographic realism have emerged. One, in particular, is now rather well developed. "Confessional ethnography" is a genre of fieldworker trials and tribulations that moves a reader's attention from the signified (the studied culture) to the one who, quite literally, signifies (the ethnographer).[8] The research process itself—fieldwork— becomes the focus of an ethnographic text. Its composition rests on moving the fieldworker to center stage and displaying how the writer came to know a given social world. Although often set apart from an ethnographer's realist accounts, confessional ethnography may nonetheless convey a good deal of the same sort of cultural information and speculation put forth in conventional realist works but in a more personalized and historically-situated fashion (e.g., Dumont 1978; Rabinow 1977). Thus what began as an attempt to shore up the ethnographic trade and make it safe for science turned out to have almost the opposite effect. It cracked open established representational practices and ushered in a period of increasing textual experimentation in ethnography.

Consider, for example, three other forms of ethnographic writing. Each of these forms, like the confessional, have isolated precedents to be found deep in the ethnographic archives but, as a genre, each contrasts sharply with ethnographic realism and have been taken up by more than a few contemporary writers for just that reason. "Dramatic ethnography" rests on the narration of a particular event of sequence of events of obvious significance to the cultural members studied. These ethnographies present unfolding stories and rely more on techniques drawn from literary fiction and personal essays than from plain-speaking, documentary techniques—the style of nonstyle—drawn from scientific reports (e.g., Erickson 1976; Shore 1982). "Critical ethnographies" provide another genre wherein the represented culture is located within a larger historical, political, economic, social, and symbolic context than is said to be recognized by cultural members. This pushes the writer to move beyond traditional ethnographic interests and frameworks when constructing the text (e.g., Willis 1977; Nash 1979; Traweek 1988; Foley 1990). As a final illustration, "self-" or "auto-ethnographies" have emerged in which the culture of the writer's own group is textualized. Such writings often offer a passionate, emotional voice of a positioned

and explicitly judgmental fieldworker and thus obliterate
the customary and, ordinarily, rather mannerly distinction
between the researcher and the researched (e.g., Hayano
1982; Young 1991).[9]

A good deal of the narrative variety now visible in ethnographic writing is also a consequence of the post-1960s
spread of the specialized and relatively insular disciplinary
aims of anthropology and, to a lesser extent, sociology.
Growing interest in the distinctly modern idea of culture—
as something held by all identifiable groups, organizations,
and societies—has put ethnography in play virtually everywhere. No longer is ethnography ordered and organized
principally by geographic region, society, community, or
social group. Adjectival ethnographies have become quite
common, and libraries are now well stocked with works in
medical ethnography, school ethnography, occupational
ethnography, organizational ethnography, family ethnography, and many more. One result of these intellectual and
territorial moves of both at-home and away ethnography
has been a noticeable increase in the novel and provisional
forms in which ethnography is cast. Purists may regard this
proliferation of styles as a dilution or, worse, a bastardiza-
tion of the trade, but others—myself included—take this
upswing in ethnographic styles as a welcome offering of
alternatives (some good, some not so good) to certain taken-
for-granted and seemingly calcified representational techniques of both realist and confessional writings.

This expansion of ethnographic interests, methods, and
styles is, of course, a product of the third moment of ethnography—the reading of ethnographic texts by particular
audiences and the kinds of responses these texts appear to
generate among those audiences. Of interest here are the
categories of readers an ethnographer recognizes and courts
through the topical choices, analytic positioning, and composition practices displayed in a text. Take, for illustrative

purposes, three loosely demarked audience categories. Collegial readers are those who follow specific ethnographic domains most avidly. They are surely the most careful and critical readers of one another's work and the most familiar with the past and present of ethnography. General social science readers provide a second category but operate outside ethnographic circles. These are readers attracted to a particular ethnographic work because the presumed facts (less often, the arguments) conveyed in the work helps further their own research agendas. Perhaps as a result of their exploitative aims, they are often the least tolerant of the breaching of narrative conventions in ethnography. Finally, there are some who read ethnography more for pleasure than professional enlightenment. Certain ethnographic works put forth in *mirable dictu*—lucid, straightforward language—attract a large, unspecialized lay audience for whom the storytelling and allegorical elements of an ethnography are salient. Such readers look for a familiar format—a traveler's tale, a romantic adventure, a personal journal, an investigative report, or, perhaps most frequently, a widely acclaimed ethnographic classic(s) of the past—when appraising the writing. Ironically, the ethnographer charged with being a novelist manqué by colleagues and other social scientists is quite likely to be the ethnographer with the largest number of readers.

For each reader segment, particular ethnographic styles are more or less attractive.[10] Collegial readers may take in stride what those outside the field find inelegant, pinched, and abstruse. Yet the growing segmentation across collegial readers may also suggest that many are puzzled as to what their nominal ethnographic colleagues are up to with their relatively odd topical choices, particularistic research techniques, peculiar theoretical concerns, and occasionally distinctive prose styles. This creates something of a dilemma because it suggests that not only is there considerable distance between the general reader and the ethnographic specialist but that the distance between differing segments of ethnographic specialists themselves is growing. Although ethnography is itself in little or no danger of vanishing, the ethnographic community is now a very splintered—however splendored—thing.

Still, the trade prospers—at least numerically in terms of those who identify with the qualitative fieldwork traditions of ethnography. Those eager to do backyard or far-away fieldwork, to put culture to print, and to read about it in some form or other are probably more numerous than ever. But, as I want this quick and quirky review to suggest, just how a culture is rendered intelligible in the first moment of ethnography and, in the second moment of ethnography, passed on in a fashion that persuades others of its value and truth when read in the third moment of ethnography are now matters of considerable concern and debate. New questions are being asked of ethnography. Experimental works are being composed. Many if not most of the representational techniques of realist (alternatively, classical) ethnography are now seen by many as dated, naive, and, in a certain light, both professionally and socially indefensible.

In short, one might say that the cat is out of the bag and it seems unlikely that the sort of "just do it" innocence (and spirit) that once characterized ethnography will ever return. The very partiality, self-limitations, paradigm conceits, and institutional constraints are now simply too well known to be ignored (or, for that matter, overcome). Moreover, an acute textual awareness has developed in some circles based on close literary readings of ethnographic work. From such readings comes the view that an ethnographic truth is, like any truth (including this one), a rhetorical category whose meaning and shape varies with the contingencies of history and circumstance.

This is not, as some traditionalists might argue, the beginning of an inevitable slide into solipsism, relativism, or (gasp) nihilism—an "anything goes" approach to contemporary ethnography. My reading of the current turn toward text and language in ethnography is governed by a belief that holds rhetoric, broadly defined, to be the medium through which all truths or certainties are established (and shaken). Thus, for example, to look closely at well-received or persuasive ethnographic texts, to their compositional practices rather than through them, to the worlds they portray is to examine how a culture becomes a substantial reality for a given set of readers and perhaps beyond. By looking at representational choices and their changes over time is to learn (among other things) just how ethnographers construct differences of various kinds. These surface differences may flatter or shatter the expectations held by readers but to move beyond a surface reading is to force an ethnography to tell a different story than it was intended to tell—a story about its makers and takers rather than its subjects. Not all texts will emerge with credit from such readings, but, depending on the text and reader, some will, and presumably by paying attention to the way those works are put together we will learn more about the art (and science) of our representational trade.

Deconstruction Reconstructed

To examine the compositional practices of ethnography requires setting some sort of limit about what counts as an ethnography in the first place. Because I have come to regard the breakdown of standard ethnographic topics, borders, and styles as something to celebrate, not mourn, I cannot take a very hard line on this matter. Suffice it to say that a text is axiomatically an ethnography if it is put forth by its author as a nonfiction work intended to represent, interpret, or (perhaps best) translate a culture or selected aspects of a culture for readers who are often but not always unfamiliar with that culture. Giving such works close textual attention will not alter their status as ethnographies. Elliot Liebow's (1967) *Talley's Corner* is an ethnography whether or not anyone likes it and would still be an ethnography even if no one liked it. But *Talley's Corner* can also be read for its own sake, thus directing attention to the text itself—to such features as authorial voice, topical choice and arrangement, the use of master and minor tropes, the eliding of time, narrative conventions, rhetorical thrusts, truth claims, and so forth.

As I suggested earlier, the increased interest in the second and third moments of ethnography reflects a relatively recent intellectual shift within ethnographic circles. This shift toward text is, of course, part of a much wider scholarly turn toward meaning and language wherein the relationship ordinarily held to obtain between a description and the object of such description is reversed. The ordinary or commonsensical view holds that the objects of the world are logically prior and thus limit and provide the measure of any description. Vocabulary, text, and representation of any intendedly nonfictional sort must be constrained by fact. But, as virtually all ethnographers now realize (however much they may complain), language has been promoted in the intellectual scheme of things. Language is now auditioning for an *a priori* role in the social and material world, a role that carries constitutional force—bringing facts into consciousness and therefore being. No longer then is something like culture or, for that matter, atoms and quarks thought to come first while our understandings, models, or representations of culture, atoms, or quarks come second. Rather, our representations may well come first, allowing us to selectively see what we have described.[11]

This reverse argument has gradually wormed its way into various ethnographic communities. It is quite common these days to state rather matter-of-factly that the language and models that ethnographers have available to them—the conceptual tools that precede the doing of ethnography— shape what will be seen in the field, written in a report, and read by those who purchase their texts. If, for example, the prominent linguistic categories available to urban ethnographers include various forms of social disorganization, it is likely that they will also look for events associated with city life in just these terms. Violence, drug taking, and crime thus become indicators of disorganization. The representational details and patterns of their work will follow from what writers feel fit a given category. If the representational language that typifies the research community is full of concepts like deviance, disintegration, and decline—all drawn, say, from textbook sociology—an ethnographic study of city life will produce events that fit these very features rather than events that fit features associated with different concepts such as displacement or destablization as drawn, respectively, from the vocabulary of postmodernism or critical theory.[12]

The point of consequence is that simply to describe this reversal— related perhaps to what Rabinow (1986) calls "the desire to anthropologize the West"—is also to display the problem that ethnographic representations currently face. Ideas about empirical evidence, objectivity, reason, truth, coherence, validity, measurement, and fact no longer provide great comfort or direction. If such concepts are relative, not absolute, they are always contestable in whatever form they appear—although this is not to say that such concepts are thereby rendered irrelevant or unthinkable.

Again, this reversal is not a terribly controversial issue these days—at least among most practicing ethnographers. The priority of the signifier over the signified, the placing of implicit quotation marks about terms such as "truth" and "reality" (hedges from which these words are unlikely to ever escape), and the now problematized foundations of some of our most sacred concepts (from "self" to "society") are all ideas that have been absorbed and, if not canonized, at least recognized by ethnographers as presenting troublesome epistemological issues with which we as writers must in some fashion deal. What remains to be seen, however, is just how this turn toward language alters—if at all—traditional ethnographic practices in the field, behind the desk, and in the library or easy chair.

At first glance, fieldwork traditions seem to be securely in place despite the in-house hammering they have taken in both anthropology and sociology. Ethnographers still claim a good deal of their authority on firsthand experience. While hardly the boastful and brash experiential positivism of an earlier era, fieldwork nonetheless continues to be held responsible—at least partially—for the written account of a studied group. Indeed, ethnographers remain inextricably linked to their people, their turf, and their culture. This tight connection between authors and authored is based on the continuing faith that what is learned in the field will somehow outweigh or counterbalance the anticipation of theory and other preconceptions carried by fieldworkers.

This has long been the case. Thus, in anthropology, Evans-Prichard (1940) remains tied to the Neur, Firth (1936) to the Tokopia, Geertz (1973) to the Balinese, and Rosaldo (1980) to the Ilongots. To a lesser degree, it is also true of sociology (in the United States), where Whyte (1943) is closely linked to the street corners of North Boston, Goffman (1961) to mental hospitals and inmates, Manning (1977, 1980) to the city police, and Becker (1982) to the producers, exhibitors, curators, and dealers (among others) who make up various cosmopolitan art worlds. Marcus (1994, 521) calls this the "one tribe, one ethnographer" rule

and considers it a domain or territorial rule remarkable for its apparent staying power. Certainly, there are
important disciplinary figures in ethnography not so directly linked to specific social domains, but their contributions to ethnography—although not to cultural theory—are
often regarded as fragile and speculative because they are
not embedded in an intense, lengthy, and hence presumably
rich field experience.[13]
    The tenacity of this position is strong—so strong that the
idea of something like an ethnographic revolution or break-
through is itself a rather improbable and odd notion. The
object of ethnography is seen as simply too much "out there."
Traditionally, fieldwork implies either discovery (going where
no one has gone before) or elaboration (building on and
extending the pioneering cultural portraits of others by
others). Overturning previous representations is not often
claimed and restudies of the same group of people by different ethnographers are rare indeed.[14] Cultural theory may
proceed disjunctively, contentiously, by lurches or so-called
paradigm shifts, but not ethnography. Advancement in an
ethnographic domain comes cumulatively through the
steady elaboration of a given culture itself subject to temporal shifts brought about by known (or, in principle, knowable) internal or external changes. Thus the ethnographic
writings of outmoded theorists can continue to instruct even
if the conceptual frameworks surrounding such accounts
are considered hopelessly behind the times.
    Yet little by little this unifying faith in the lasting value
of ethnographic representations—although not fieldwork—
is being questioned as ethnographic texts themselves are put
to close examination. A kind of ethnography of ethnography
is emerging through textual study, and new understandings
are gradually altering the way we think about cultural
representation practices both past and present. Yet having
new or transformed categories available to describe ethno-

graphic practices does not necessarily alter those practices. Reading, analyzing, and writing about an ethnographic work is not the same thing as creating one, and few if any recipes for improved performance are likely to follow directly from textual analysis. A good deal of the work to date has been to pick apart or deconstruct various texts, to search for the ways they fail to make the points they are trying or claiming to make. But the result of this work does not provide a better way to do ethnography. It does, however, remind us of the limits of representational possibilities and makes a strong argument to counter any faith in a simple or transparent world that can be known with any certainty.

By and large, these deconstructive efforts have been aimed at the most persuasive and respected ethnographic writings of the past (Clifford and Marcus 1986; Geertz 1988). The result is not itself an ethnography but a critique of one (or more). Occasionally, however, ethnography itself starts from an analysis or deconstruction of previous representations of a given culture (including but not limited to ethnographic ones). This textual orientation is relatively new and provides something of an ironic twist to the fashionable idea that culture can be studied "as if" it were a text by suggesting that culture might not amount to much more than a text in the first place. There is perhaps poetic justice here, for the ethnographers of one generation find themselves treated by those of the next generation as "others" and subjected to something of the same rough and tumble exigencies of cultural representation that they put their own people through. Students of culture these days may be less likely to call for a Festschrift for their mentor than to call into question their mentor's work.

Cultural anthropology provides a number of splendid examples of this re-reading of the ethnographic past. Classical ethnographies of remote, invisible, or otherwise "out of the way" people have become increasingly unpersuasive, in part because the presumption of the great divide between modern and traditional communities has broken down and in part because the idea of a bounded, independent, undisturbed, and self-contained society is today suspect (Geertz 1994). Thus descriptions of the "People of the Plains" or the "Ashanti Character" are repositioned as representations of a relatively powerless, displaced, and sometimes despised people who are nonetheless altogether agile and adaptive out of necessity. The point driven home in these re-presentations is that the group portrayed is anything but isolated, timeless, or beyond the reach of contemporary society. The wistful assumption of "one place, one people, one culture" no longer holds the ethnographic imagination in check. This is made quite clear in what Marcus (1994) calls the "messy texts" of a deterritorialized, open-ended, and "new" ethnography that attempts to foster an idea of how lives around the globe may be contrasted yet still interconnected.

Important messy texts do not lament the loss of the anthropological object but, in fact, invent a more complex object whose study can be as revelatory and as realistic as the old. Consider, as an exemplar, Kondo's (1990) subtle portrait of everyday life on the shop floor of a small, family-owned factory in Tokyo and the multiple, gendered, and crafted "selves" that seem to emerge in such a context. Consider also Tsing's (1994) dense, occasionally hesitant but always moving treatment of a much abused and marginalized Indonesian group she calls "The Meratus." Both authors are explicitly critical of previous "holistic" representations that have settled on those of whom they write and the encrusted fiction that these people reside in a pristine, encapsulated "natural" community—a cultural island—whose traditions persist outside the contemporary world.

Back home in North America, anthropologists are also at work on new objects of study. Consider here Fjellman's (1992) collage-like and code-cracking *Vinyl Leaves*, a representation of DisneyWorld cast off in a slapdash and breathless postmodern style, or Moffatt's (1989) embracing of Margaret Mead's imagery in *The Coming of Age in New Jersey*, a vivid, emotionally charged representation of what Moffatt saw and heard during his stay in the dormitories of Rutgers University in the mid-1980s. These works violate the image of the ethnographer as the intrepid traveler who journeys to exotic locales to bring back the news of the native while at the same time they challenge realist codes of representation reflecting prevailing ideas of the "other" because the other is none other than ourselves.

Defamiliarization is something of an emerging strategy for ethnographic representation. Nowhere is this more apparent than in recent work that examines reader responses to a variety of cultural products including, centrally, texts. Take, for instance, Lutz and Collins's (1992) close reading of the *National Geographic* and its romantic, upbeat, glossy, and unabashed see-for-yourself style so popular in the United States where the color photograph is taken as a particularly sound measure of reality. Lutz and Collins manage to make the magazine tell a different story than the one to which we are accustomed—a story about the makers and readers of the *National Geographic* rather than the subjects of its photographic gaze. Similar tales are constructed by Radway (1984) and Liebes and Katz (1990) about, in turn, the readers of formula romance novels and the culturally diverse viewers of the epic television series *Dallas*. These writings produce what I think are profoundly ambiguous images of all-too-familiar cultural objects and thus push ethnography into the rather novel but altogether useful role of making the familiar strange rather than the strange familiar.

The reception to topical and narrative innovations in ethnography varies no doubt across audience segments, but many of us are reading experimental texts and wondering about their possibilities and relevance to what we are currently doing. Yet we also know that if the experimental turns paradigmatic, the future of our trade may be in grave jeopardy for we would be left with nowhere in particular to go and with no visible models for our craft. This is, I think, unlikely because style, not genre, is immediately at issue, and, in point of fact, few ethnographers are writing experimental—or even messy—texts.

Nor is it the case that all ethnographic conventions are currently up for grabs. What would it mean, for example, if we were not to accept certain settled ethnographic practices? Would it mean that we would not go to the field to conduct our studies? Would it mean that we would not take notes when in the field? Would it mean that we would not try to publish our work in scholarly outlets and be responsive to colleagues and professional peers? Or, sin of sins, would it mean that we would not read and acknowledge the previous work done in a given ethnographic domain?

Questions of this sort are almost (but not quite) purely imaginary for they suggest lines of action that are more or less unthinkable for anyone self-identified as an ethnographer. The issue at hand is not to evaluate the options for there are none (at least now). These are practices an ethnographer follows because they constitute membership in a community of ethnographers. They are not practices offered up for approval or disapproval. No one says to the would-be ethnographer, "Hey, listen up now, we usually go to the field for a year or so and then write up what we learn. Do you think you can live with that?" To the contrary, the would-be ethnographer becomes an ethnographer by doing the same sort of things others in the trade have done before and so discovers the obligatory ways through which writings we call ethnographies are produced. The normative aspects of ethnography are not piled on top of a set of everyday practices but come—kit and caboodle—with them. Ask ethnographers to justify their reliance on fieldwork and they will be as befuddled by the question as plumbers are when asked to justify their use of a plunger or wrench. This is not to say that the conventions associated with either the first, second, or third moment of ethnography are unshakable or cast in stone. Both Stocking (1983) and Clifford (1983) track several highly significant changes in ethnographic practices. Most of us would now agree that all ethnographies owe whatever persuasive power they can muster to contingent social, historical, and institutional forces and no meta-argument can question this contingency. But when it comes to constructing a particular ethnography, this sublime contingency offers very little aid because any particular ethnography offered up to readers must make its points by the same means that were present before the contingency was recognized—through the hard work of presenting evidence, providing interpretations, elaborating analogies, invoking authorities, working through examples, marshalling the tropes, and so on. The nature of ethnographic evidence, interpretation, and authority may, of course, all change modestly or radically over time, but the appeal of any single ethnography will remain tied to specific arguments made within the text and referenced to a particular, not general, substantive and methodological situation.

What I am claiming, of course, is the possibility that we can assert both the textuality of ethnographic facts and the factuality of ethnographic texts. We can do so because the two claims lie in quite different domains. To say, for instance, that ethnographic facts are socially constructed (yawn) is a general claim and not one that can be applied willy-nilly to particular facts. A certain fact is flimsy or firm on the basis of the arguments presented (and received) on its behalf. When such facts are recognized as questionable, the arguments and views based on them are discredited also. Textuality replaces factuality but only after previous views have been dislodged and new facts move into place. These new facts are as firm as the old but are supported by a new and different perspective. It is a little like recognizing that the explanation of a joke is not itself funny but at the same time realizing that knowing so does not help one construct hilarious one-liners.

The work at the coal face of ethnography goes on therefore in much the same way as it did before textuality came into vogue. Evidence must be offered up to support arguments whose pedigree must be established in a way that will convince at least a few readers that the author has something credible to say. Changes in attitude are always possible, and what is persuasive to one generation may look ludicrous to another. To some perhaps, the textuality and factuality of ethnography is paradoxical. But, following Fish (1989), I think the paradox vanishes with the realization that ethnography—like literary theory, law, molecular biology, astronomy, or astrology—does not remain the same because its facts, methods, genres, theories, and so forth all survive the passage of time but because in the midst of change an audience still looks to it for the performance of a given task. In the case of ethnography, what we continue to look for is the close study of culture as lived by particular people, in particular places, doing particular things at particular times.[15]

Chapter and Verse

The following eight chapters provide close looks at— rather than through—a variety of contemporary ethnographic writings. My aim in putting the collection together is to link the newly emergent textual awareness of ethnographic work to readers worried about what such an awareness might mean for them and their work. This collection goes some distance, I think, in opening up new topics, contributing to the ongoing and lively conversation on old ones, and providing some sound advice for the faithful who practice the ethnographic trade. The analysis of text constitutes in good measure what the ethnography of ethnography is currently about, and the work put forward here can be located squarely within this domain. Clearly, these writings —while quite often critical of current practices—are meant to be constructive, to provide a sort of therapy to help nudge ethnography along and allow ethnographers—veteran or wannabe—to be better able to cope with the none too clear representational demands placed on them in today's world.

The chapters are loosely organized around various forms of ethnographic writing. In the next chapter, Jean Jackson tells us what anthropologists think of their fieldnotes. Not much, it seems, even though most of her informants admit— with occasional misgivings and regrets—to treating their own notes as both secret and sacred. Yet judging from the many stories she gathered about these classified Saint's Bones of Ethnography, there is no unified version of what fieldnotes stand for nor how they are used to build an ethnographic report. Harry Wolcott also considers fieldnotes in Chapter 3, where he takes up the primal question "From whence ethnography?" Brushing past text-centered views, he locates its origins in the materials gathered in the field (written or remembered) and reminds fieldworkers that ethnography is more than a slogan or label. It is, in his view, a commitment to provide a "cultural account" for the actions of an individual or group. What constitutes such an account is the object of his affection in the chapter. This is a theme picked up by Michael Agar in Chapter 4. He looks closely at the working ways and representational styles of writers associated with literary or new (now old) journalism and finds them wanting. Questionable facts are covered by elegant prose. Creative nonfiction, in Agar's opinion, does not adequately link the investigatory process to the written product. That many of the same issues apply to past and present ethnography is a point underplayed but not missed in this chapter.

Moving back to examine some of our own compositional practices, Eyal Ben-Ari provides a close look at the way acknowledgments are composed in ethnographies. Such intimate "extratextual" passages are treated not only as opportunities to enhance the authenticity and credibility of the ethnography but also as opportunities to booster the status, career, and character of the ethnographer. The work can be read both as a delightful send-up of some of our indirect pretentions and as a serious analysis of ethnographic reflexivity on pages nominally reserved for the less serious. Gary Alan Fine and Daniel Martin in Chapter 6 take us inside the domain of the published work. It is a quite famous domain at that for they take up the literary practices of Erving Goffman as illustrated in *Asylums,* his only ethnographic work. Their reading of this work points to Goffman's skilled use of sarcasm, satire, and irony in the making of his savage and memorable tale. Laurel Richardson follows with a plea in Chapter 7 to dramatically alter conventional ethnographic reporting practices. She argues for the critical importance of narrative in research reports and develops the notion of a "collective story" as a way of both studying and structuring ethnographies in a fashion that is personalized, evocative, and open to reader interpretations.

The late Marianne Paget provides a reading of a most experimental ethnographic moment in Chapter 8. The account she offers is of her own research as presented on stage in a dramatization of her studies of doctor-patient conversations. The chapter points to some of the ways written texts fail to communicate or persuade because of their bloodless form. Although the words remain the same, surrounding them with stagecraft gives them life and new meaning. Peter Manning closes the volume in Chapter 9 by taking up the "requirements" of postmodern ethnography. He does so through a careful assessment of the claims put forth in three well-received experimental ethnographies, concluding that postmodernism provides an opportunity to reinvigorate ethnographic research. It can do so primarily by welcoming topical, methodological, and stylistic diversity and thus serves to subvert authoritative definitions of culture and technique-driven research. A move toward postmodernism in Manning's view means more subject matter, more attention to neglected or marginalized areas of social life at home or away, more opportunities to cross traditional disciplinary and topical borders, and more ways to frame research questions than is now the case. Such a move offers, in short, fewer rules but more work for ethnographers.

From fieldnotes to performance, from literary criticism to textual practice, from sign to signified, from anthropology to sociology, from modernism to postmodernism, there is much variety to follow. Each chapter offers some good suggestions as to the work that lies ahead if we are to broaden our ethnographic interests and alter the ways we promote these interests. But reader beware! There are many ways to read a book. Good readers are perhaps as rare as good writers, and, authorial intentions aside, there is only so much a writer can tell. Reading is also a creative act and perhaps a far more creative act than we have to date recognized. Reading is the third moment of ethnography, and it may be, dear reader, the determining one. Read on.

Notes

1. This much procrastinated chapter began as a brief introduction to the articles that made up a special issue of the *Journal of Contemporary Ethnography* published in 1990 (vol. 22, no. 1) on "The Representation of Ethnographic Research." It ran five pages and was titled "Great Moments in Ethnography." The introduction has grown and its name has changed, but its intent remains the same: to set up and off the same articles—plus two—that comprised the special issue. I must thank Peter Manning and Mitch Allen for pushing this project forward and encouraging me to rework my skimpy introduction into something that resembles—in length if not in quality—the other chapters in this book.

2. This, of course, raises the question of how any single scholar can possibly keep up with such a large and ever expanding literature. The answer in principle and in practice is that he or she can't, for the potentially relevant ethnographic materials (on a society, region, or people) are overwhelming and new journals, new theories, new problems, new topics, new concepts, and new critiques of older works multiply with each passing year. Moreover, scholars must now know not only their Marx, Weber, and Durkheim but also be familiar with the works of Gramsci, Baktin, Habermas, and Rorty and *au courant* with the fashionable French such as Bourdieu, Derrida, and Foucault. Even fieldwork itself has grown increasingly textual as materials that were once routinely ignored, such as government records, novels, biographies, popular magazine articles, and news reports, are now treated by many ethnographers as important source materials. It seems the best we can do these days is to selectively pursue and cultivate an ever diminishing proportion of the relevant literature that comes our way and assume an attitude of benign neglect toward the rest. Stocking (1992, 362-65) has some sharp but discouraging observations to make on the difficulties of keeping up with the field in cultural anthropology as do many of the authors represented in Faradon's (1990) collection of essays on localizing strategies in ethnography.

3. Much of the debate turns on what to make of the sacred heart of ethnography, the culture concept. Some critics, notably those with intellectual roots in deconstructive literary criticism, regard the idea of a distinct, bounded, and unifying culture in today's world as little more than a superstition carried over from nineteenth-century discourse and argue that an "incrudulity toward metanarratives" should characterize all social study (Lyotard 1984). Other critics within the many folds of ethnography also regard the culture concept as something of an embarrassing colonial artifact in serious need of repair (Fabian 1983;

Marcus and Fischer 1986). Nonetheless, despite the critical fire, there is still an insistence in almost all camps that any serious study of social life must be grounded ethnographically. The debate is then not so much about the doing of ethnography as it is about the conceptual positioning of such work. Hannerz (1992) provides one of the more useful anthropological reworkings of the culture concept in the context of a postmodern, information-intensive world. See also Griswold's (1994) sociological treatment of culture in a rapidly changing age. Both authors jettison unicultural perspectives in favor of multicultural ones emphasizing polycentrism, local innovation, and widespread cultural diffusion.

4. The term "moments" may be confusing. Denzin and Lincoln (1994, 7-11), for example, uses the term to denote particular historical periods in the development of an intellectual field—in their subject case, the emergence of qualitative research techniques in the social sciences. My use of the term refers to the stages through which a particular ethnography must pass—fieldwork, publication, and consumption. The latter stage is justified on the grounds that an unread ethnography is not, properly speaking, an ethnography at all. For a more elaborate treatment of these stages, see Van Maanen (forthcoming).

5. These pen pal arrangements were aided by the guidebook *Notes and Queries in Anthropology* first published in 1874 with the subtitle *"for use of travellers and residents in uncivilized lands"* and revised regularly, without the subtitle, into the mid-twentieth century. The idea was to provide the armchair ethnographer's pen pal, the so-called man on the spot, with a set of questions to pose to local informants (Stocking 1983). The goal was to standardize the slabs of information gathered by the men on the spot. These slabs were sent home to be pondered, interpreted, and eventually written up by a "real" ethnographer.

6. I have in mind as Studio Portraiture work some of the more scientifically oriented or formal ethnographies written, it seems, to track, illustrate, and document a particular theory of the social world. Baumgartner's (1988) *The Moral Order of a Suburb* provides, for example, an intriguing portrait of the "cordial detachment" that marks contemporary American life. The work is, however, one that allows few interpretive doubts to slip into view. All people, events, and circumstances represented by the author neatly fit her analytic categories. Halle's (1993) *Inside Culture* is another example of ethnographic scholarship that is tied closely to a given culture theory. I hasten to add that I find considerable value in both works, but both are also remarkable for their unblinking use of realist conventions.

7. The rise and fall of Project Camelot and the Thailand Controversy forced ethical and political issues out in the open and injected an important self-consciousness into fieldworkers operating far from home

(Horowitz 1967; Wakin 1992). In the postcolonial world, the observer is perhaps as destabilized as the observed. No longer comforted and protected by colonial power, ethnographers face radically different problems entering, staying, and leaving the field (let alone learning in the field). Reflexive, self-critical, dialogic approaches to ethnography seem a contemporary necessity. For some recent and highly personalized perspectives on many of the changes that cultural anthropology has undergone in the postcolonial period, see the autobiographic essays collected by Fowler and Hardesty (1994).

8. A joke by Marshall Salhins and reported by Marcus (1994, 569) is worthy of inclusion here: "But as the Fijian said to the New Ethnographer, 'That's enough talking about you, let's talk about me!' " Self-discovery and personal quest are to be sure a part of ethnography but, as the joke suggests, such matters are not to be pushed too far—at least in writing. Where exactly the limits of ethnographic reflexivity are to be found remains a most open question.

9. The text only hints at the kinds of ethnogaphic experimentation now occurring. Nigel Barley (1983, 1986), for example, develops a kind of "comedy ethnography" based on some of his fieldwork misadventures. Hebdige (1979, 1987) works out a version of "hip-hop ethnography" put forth in the very pop culture idiom that is the subject of his study. Frolick (1990) uses the voice of an invented character "Luke" to shape a "fictional ethnography" about spiritual healing in the United States. These works are hardly conventional, but they all carry strong ethnographic sensibilities and contribute to the genre bending now taking place. What most experimental works display is a resistance to received analytic categories and concepts; thus the subject and lines of study are kept open and unsettled (see Manning, this volume). Objectivity, if it is claimed at all, is of a highly situated sort and the writing is impressionistic rather than interpretive (Van Maanen 1988, 101-24).

10. Taste in ethnography results from what is no doubt a complex interaction involving ethnographers, their mentors, their students, their subjects, their critics, and their readers (increasingly their subjects as well). The process is rather decentered and beyond the grasp of any one group to fully control or monitor—although, until recently, ethnographers themselves probably held the upper hand. Most of us, it seems, follow the traditions in which we were trained and are thus committed generationally and institutionally to a particular perspective, objectivity, research etiquette, and topical, if not stylistic, preference. For instance, sociological fieldworkers operating in the Chicago School traditions often define within a complex society the equivalent of a bounded little island society and go about studying and writing about it in quite similar (and traditional) ways whether it is a street gang, a fitness center, a police

agency, a first-year medical school class, or an engineering division of a *Fortune* 500 company. Appreciation of ethnographic work created in the Chicago School shadow depends on how much one has already accepted and absorbed Chicago School ideas and approaches and just how directly one can trace one's own intellectual roots back to the founders and other legendary Chicago figures (e.g., from Becker to Hughes to Parks). On the Chicago School of sociology and its distinctive ethnographic tastes, see Bulmer (1984) and Fine, ed. (forthcoming).

11. This language-first switch produces a most culturally relative version of reality and suggests that perception is as much a product of imagination as imagination is a product of perception. Reality, then, emerges from the interplay of imaginative perception and perceptive imagination. Language and text provide the symbolic representations required for both the construction and communication of conceptions of reality and thus make the notions of thought and culture inseparable. Because culture comes to us in large measure through ink on a page, the careful examination of previous cultural representations is a necessary analytic step. The textual turn in ethnography comes from the perhaps belated recognition that any cultural portrait exists within a context of already existing portraits. New writings are to varying degrees parasitic on old writings and few, if any, contemporary ethnographic subjects are completely unknown. This leads some writers such as Marcus (1994) and Clifford (1988) to argue that ethnographers should abandon the idea that there are new worlds to discover and concentrate instead on the deconstruction and reconstruction of social worlds already—in different ways —represented. An engaging example of some textually focused ethnography is found in Dorst's (1989) *The Written Suburb.*

12. This is not to say that the assumptions that undergird postmodernism or critical theory are themselves beyond suspicion. They too rest on unexamined assumptions. At any level, the tools of revisionist analysis are vulnerable to the same kind of deconstruction they claim to perform on a targeted writing. This can produce something of an intellectual funhouse where authors, texts, concepts, riddles, labels, theories, and phrases (both catchy and stilted) bounce off one another. To wit, following Dumont's (1986) example, a reader can track Rabinow's (1986) deconstruction of Clifford's (1982) deconstruction of Leenhardt's (1937) ethnography (in French) of the New Caledonians. Where the New Caledonians themselves come out in this intertextual blender is anyone's guess, for, as deconstructionists are only too happy to point out, there are no ultimate standards on which to test the validity of any given reading. No matter how deep a writer may go in questioning the arguments of previous work, there will remain in the offered work arguments whose clarity and strength depend on the same kind of historical, institutional,

and personal factors shown to influence and hence undermine the work of others. Although reading what Derrida (1976) calls the "text in the text" certainly raises problems for ethnographers, it does not solve them. Ironically, as Fish (1993) forcefully suggests, the more one is persuaded by deconstructive arguments, the less one can do with them. At most, deconstruction can be used to refute the truth claims of others, but it cannot be used to make new truths. Such is the state—and point—of deconstruction.

13. To date, the "one tribe, one ethnographer" rule fits anthropologists more closely than sociologists. Although Sahlins's classic *bon mot* "sociologists study the West and anthropologists get the rest" still holds, its sweep is perhaps less encompassing today than yesterday as anthropologists become repatriated and sociologists earn frequent flier miles. Yet it is still the case that anthropologists more so than sociologists are likely to visit and revisit a field site over a full career, thus developing not only deep and lasting personal ties to a community but also a relatively keen appreciation for the various kinds of social changes that mark "their" community over time. On some of the distinctive features of extensive, long-term, single-site fieldwork, see Foster et al. (1979) and Fowler and Hardesty (1994).

14. This is not to say that representational disagreements are non-existent in ethnography. Certainly, there have been some quite spectacular disputes on just whose representation of a people is most trustworthy (e.g., Redfield vs. Lewis 1964; Mead vs. Freeman 1983; Whyte vs. Boelen 1992). Yet these debates are rare and work largely as exceptions that prove the "one ethnographer, one tribe" rule.

15. By concluding on such a note, I am asserting that ethnographers are at their best when mucking around the empirical base camps of social science than when perched (always precariously) on some theoretical mountain top. This has, I think, always been the case. What may have changed in the past ten or so years is that the mists surrounding the base camps are gradually clearing. Gone perhaps are the illusions of progress by theory, by formal models, by positivism (or antipositivism), by methodological purity, and so on. With no fixed, natural, objective, or universal criteria to guide ethnography up to the mountain top, there is no alternative but to get down to the specific studies that make up the field(s) and acknowledge that ethnographic values, criteria, and perspectives spring from the specific interests and histories of ethnographic writers. These can never be placed above criticism, of course, as ethnographic writers are beings—human beings—who are everywhere and always socially situated and purposive. For some far more eloquent versions of this zero-point argument, see Bruyn (1966), Gans (1982), Rosaldo (1989), and Whyte (1994).

References

Agar, M. 1980. *The professional stranger.* New York: Academic Press.

Barley, N. 1983. *The innocent anthropologist.* New York: Holt.

———. 1986. *Ceremony.* New York: Holt.

Baumgartner, M. P. 1988. *The moral order of a suburb.* New York: Oxford University Press.

Becker, H. S. 1982. *Art worlds.* Berkeley: University of California Press.

Boelen, M. A. M. 1992. Street Corner Society: Cornerville revisited. *Journal of Contemporary Ethnography* 21:13-42.

Boon, S. A. 1982. *Other tribes, other scribes.* Cambridge: Cambridge University Press.

Bruyn, S. T. 1966. *The human perspective in sociology.* Englewood Cliffs, NJ: Prentice Hall.

Bulmer, M. 1984. *The Chicago School of sociology.* Chicago: University of Chicago Press.

Clifford, J. 1982. *Person and myth: Maurice Leenhardt in the Melanesian world.* Berkeley: University of California Press.

———. 1983. On ethnographic authority. *Representations* 1:118-46.

———. 1988. *The predicament of culture.* Cambridge, MA: Harvard University Press.

Clifford, J., and G. E. Marcus, eds. 1986. *Writing culture.* Berkeley: University of California Press.

Clough, P. 1992. *The ends of ethnography.* Newbury Park, CA: Sage.

Denzin, N. 1988. *Interpretive interactionism.* Newbury Park, CA: Sage.

Denzin, N. and Y. Lincoln. 1994. Introduction. In *The handbook of qualitative research,* edited by N. Denzin and Y. Lincoln, 1-17. Thousand Oaks, CA: Sage.

Derrida, J. 1976. *On grammatology.* Translated by G. C. Spivak. Baltimore: Johns Hopkins University Press.

Dorst, J. 1989. *The written suburb.* Philadelphia: University of Pennsylvania Press.

Dumont, J. P. 1978. *The headman and I.* Austin: University of Texas Press.

———. 1986. Prologue to ethnography or prolegomena to anthropology. *Ethos* 14:344-67.

Erickson, K. 1976. *Everything in its path.* New York: Simon & Schuster.

Evans-Prichard, E. E. 1940. *The Nuer.* Oxford: Oxford University Press.

Fabian, J. 1983. *Time and the other.* New York: Columbia University Press.

Faradon, R., ed. 1990. *Localizing strategies.* Edinburgh: Scottish Academic Press.

Fine, G. A., ed. Forthcoming. *The Second Chicago School?* Chicago: University of Chicago Press.

Firth, R. 1936. *We, the Tikopia.* London: Allen & Unwin.

Fish, S. 1989. *Doing what comes naturally: Change, rhetoric and the practice of theory in literary and legal studies.* New York: Oxford University Press.

————. 1993. *There's no such thing as free speech . . . and it's a good thing too.* New York: Oxford University Press.

Fjellman, S. 1992. *Vinyl leaves.* Boulder, CO: Westview.

Foley, D. E. 1990. *Learning capitalist culture.* Austin: University of Texas Press.

Foster, G. M., T. Scudder, E. Colson, and R. Kemper, eds. 1979. *Long-term field research in social anthropology.* New York: Academic Press.

Fowler, D. D., and D. L. Hardesty, eds. 1994. *Others knowing others.* Washington, DC: Smithsonian Institution Press.

Freeman, D. 1983. *Margaret Mead and Samoa.* Cambridge, MA: Harvard University Press.

Freilich, M. 1970. *Marginal natives.* New York: Harper & Row.

Frolick, F. 1990. *Healing powers.* Chicago: University of Chicago Press.

Gans, H. J. 1982. The participant-observer as a human being. In *Field research,* edited by R. G. Burgess, 221-33. London: Allen & Unwin.

Geertz, C. 1973. *The interpretation of cultures.* New York: Basic Books.

————. 1988. *Works and lives.* Stanford, CA: Stanford University Press.

————. 1994. Life on the edge. *New York Review of Books,* 7 April, 3-4.

Goffman, E. 1961. *Asylums.* Garden City, NY: Anchor.

Griswold, W. 1994. *Cultures and societies in a changing world.* Thousand Oaks, CA: Pine Forge Press.

Halle, D. 1993. *Inside culture.* Chicago: University of Chicago Press.

Hammersley, M., and P. Atkinson. 1983. *Ethnography.* London: Tavistock.

Hannerz, U. 1992. *Cultural complexity.* New York: Columbia University Press.

Hayano, D. M. 1982. *Poker faces.* Berkeley: University of California Press.

Hebdige, D. 1979. *Subcultures.* London: Methuen.

————. 1987. *Cut'n' mix.* London: Methuen.

Horowitz, I. L. 1967. Project Camelot. In *Ethics, politics and social research,* edited by G. L. Sjoberg. London: Routledge & Kegan Paul.

Jacobson, D. 1991. *Reading ethnography.* Albany: State University of New York.

Kuper, A. 1977. *Anthropology and anthropologists.* London: Routledge & Kegan Paul.

Kondo, D. 1990. *Crafting selves.* Chicago: University of Chicago Press.

Latour, B. 1987. *Science in action*. Cambridge, MA: Harvard University Press.

Leenhardt, M. 1937. *Do Kamo: La personne et la mythe dans la monde mélanésien*. Paris: Gallimard. (Trans. by B. Gulati as *Do Kamo: Person and myth in the Melanesian world,* University of Chicago Press, 1979)

Leibes, T., and E. Katz. 1990. *The export of meaning*. New York: Oxford University Press.

Lewis, O. 1964. *Life in a Mexican village: Tepoztlan revisited*. Urbana: University of Illinois Press.

Liebow, E. 1967. *Talley's corner*. Boston: Little, Brown.

Lofland, J. 1974. Styles of reporting qualitative field research. *American Sociologist* 9:101-11.

Lutz, C., and J. Collier. 1992. *Reading National Geographic*. Chicago: University of Chicago Press.

Lyotard, J. 1984. *The postmodern condition*. Minneapolis: University of Minnesota Press.

Malinowski, B. [1922] 1961. *Argonauts of the Western Pacific*. New York: E. P. Dutton

Manning, P. K. 1977. *Police work*. Cambridge: MIT Press.

————. 1980. *The narc's game*. Cambridge: MIT Press.

Marcus, G. E. 1994. What comes (just) after "post"? The case of ethnography. In *The handbook of qualitative research,* edited by N. Denzin and Y. Lincoln, 565-82. Newbury Park, CA: Sage.

Marcus, G. E., and D. Cushman. 1982. Ethnographies as text. *Annual Review of Anthropology* 11:25-69.

Marcus, G. E., and M. Fisher. 1986. *Anthropology as cultural critique*. Chicago: University of Chicago Press.

Moffatt, M. 1989. *Coming of age in New Jersey*. New Brunswick, NJ: Rutgers University Press.

Nash, J. 1979. *We eat the mines and the mines eat us*. New York: Columbia University Press.

Rabinow, P. 1977. *Reflections on fieldwork in Morocco*. Berkeley: University of California Press.

————. 1986. Representations are social facts. In *Writing culture,* edited by J. Clifford and G. E. Marcus, 234-61. Berkeley: University of California Press.

Radway, J. A. 1984. *Reading the romance*. Chapel Hill: University of North Carolina Press.

Rosaldo, R. 1980. *Ilongot headhunting, 1883-1974*. Stanford, CA: Stanford University Press.

————. 1989. *Culture and truth*. Boston: Beacon.

Said, E. W. 1989. Representing the colonized. *Critical Inquiry* 15:205-25.

Sanjek, R., ed. 1990. *Fieldnotes*. Ithaca, NY: Cornell University Press.

Shore, B. 1982. *Sala'ilua: A Samoan mystery.* New York: Columbia University Press.

Spradley, J. P. 1979. *The ethnographic interview.* New York: Holt, Rinehart & Winston.

Stocking, G. W., ed. 1983. *Observers observed.* Madison: University of Wisconsin Press.

———. 1987. *Victorian anthropology.* New York: Free Press.

———. 1992. *The ethnographer's magic.* Madison: University of Wisconsin Press.

Traweek, S. 1988. *Beamtimes and lifetimes.* Cambridge, MA: Harvard University Press.

Tsing, A. L. 1994. *In the realm of the diamond queen.* Princeton, NJ: Princeton University Press.

Van Maanen, J. 1988. *Tales of the field: On writing ethnography.* Chicago: University of Chicago Press.

———. Forthcoming. Ethnography. In *Encyclopedia of the social sciences,* vol. 2, edited by A. Kuper and J. Kuper. London: Routledge.

Wakin, E. 1992. *Anthropology goes to war.* Madison: University of Wisconsin Center for Southeast Asia Studies.

Werner, O., and G. M. Schoepfle. 1986. *Systematic fieldwork.* 2 vols. Newbury Park, CA: Sage.

Whyte, W. F. 1943. *Street corner society.* Chicago: University of Chicago Press. Republished in 1955 with method appendix.

———. 1994. *Participant observer.* Ithaca, NY: Cornell University Press.

Willis, P. 1977. *Learning to labour.* London: Routledge & Kegan Paul. (U.S. edition, 1981, Columbia University Press)

Young, J. 1991. *An inside job.* Oxford: Oxford University Press.

2

"Déjà Entendu"

The Liminal Qualities
of Anthropological Fieldnotes

JEAN E. JACKSON

During the past three years I have been interviewing fieldworkers, almost all of them anthropologists, about their fieldnotes. I became interested in this topic while exploring my own relationship to my fieldnotes for a symposium on the topic (see Jackson 1990). However, chats with fellow anthropologists proved so fascinating that I decided on an interview format and began looking for "natives" in a more systematic fashion. The rather nonrandom sample of seventy that has resulted is mostly from the East Coast, with a bias toward the Boston area. With the exceptions of one archaeologist, one psychologist, two sociologists, two political scientists, and one linguist (all of whom do research "in the field"), all are card-carrying anthropologists in terms of training and employment.[1] The only representativeness I have attempted to maintain is a reasonably balanced sex ratio and a range of ages.[2] Although the data come from anthropologists,[3] I suspect that any fieldworker will respond to and identify with most of the themes this chapter addresses.

Virtually all respondents expressed strong and ambivalent feelings about their notes. The subject of fieldnotes is clearly complex, touchy, and disturbing for most of us. Probing into why this is so tells us some things about social science—particularly anthropology—and its discontents.

A productive approach for understanding these unruly feelings is to analyze all the ways in which fieldnotes are liminal—possessing the characteristic of being betwixt and between, "neither fish nor fowl." Twilight is a temporal liminality, swamps a geographical one, lungfish a zoological example, hermaphrodites a sexual liminality. Liminality necessarily occurs when we impose classification systems upon the natural world; what is interesting is that it is a conspicuous feature in the symbol system of every culture, often accompanied by marked affect.

Why liminality is highlighted in ritual and symbol and associated with high affect is debated in the literature. A functionalist social-structural explanation would suggest that since liminality reveals gaps and confusions in rules and classifications, to highlight liminality in symbol and ritual is to appropriate threatening ambiguity to illustrate just how important clarity and unambiguity are.[4] A functionalist psychological explanation would deal with the ways in which "betwixt and between" phenomena disturb one's sense of order and purpose and are hence emphasized and paid attention to because the resulting sense of order and control relieves anxiety.[5] This chapter suggests that a clue to the source of the strong feelings that interviewees revealed about the topic of fieldnotes lies in their striking liminality.

How are anthropological fieldwork and fieldnote-taking liminal? To give a sense of my argument, let's imagine me watching a ritual during my field research in the Northwest Amazon. The ritual itself, a male initiation rite, has all of the features associated with ritual liminality: ambiguity, a dissolution of most or all categories and classifications, role reversals, a suspension of numerous rules, periods of seclusion, and a stress on the absolute authority of the elders (Turner 1967, also 1974). The other ritual I am engaged in, fieldwork and fieldnote-taking, involves similar liminalities. To begin with, I am only marginally participating in the Tukanoan ritual: for one thing, I am not a native, and furthermore, the work I am engaged in requires that I not participate fully. My continual movement back and forth between participant and observer roles, between incorporation into the community and dissociation from it[6] is a quintessentially betwixt and between status. My behavior, especially my fieldnote-taking, serves to remind me, and them, that I am in the field but not of the field.

I am also betwixt and between in that in this particular fieldwork I am in between student and professional status. I am also geographically and culturally floating in a kind of limbo,[7] because although I am indeed far from home in any number of respects I will not remain with the Tukanoans I now live with.[8] Like the male initiands, I am also, in a sense, in a period of seclusion, during which many familiar categories and classifications are dissolved. Moreover, role reversals have occurred insofar as I have gone from being a graduate student to an ignorant, rude, snooping child (see Jackson 1986). And although I have the status of relatively wealthy, authoritative, and high-prestige outsider, I am also extremely dependent on the people I live with for "emotional gratification, food, information, shelter" (Kondo 1982, 4). Fieldwork is clearly liminal in many respects; in the following section I systematically outline how fieldnotes reflect and contribute to this state.

Types of Liminality in Fieldnotes

I have organized the kinds of liminality revealed in the interview material into three overarching categories: (1) betwixt and between worlds, (2) betwixt and between selves, and (3) betwixt and between words. The first discusses the kinds of liminality found in the generic fieldwork enterprise. The second refers to the ways in which fieldnotes mediate between the fieldworker's different roles, stressing his or her personal relationship to fieldnotes. And the third refers to the liminalities found in the relationship between fieldnotes and other genres of writing. It should be noted that these categorizations are somewhat arbitrary and hence some topics are inevitably mentioned in more than one section of the article—for example, the issue of privacy.

BETWEEN WORLDS

Between Home and Field. While in the field, fieldnotes connect the anthropologist to home, to the anthropological profession, and, upon return to base, to the field. For example, several interviewees noted that fieldnotes served to remind them (and the natives) that they were doing a project, not just "sitting on a mountain in Pakistan drinking tea." One interviewee said, "My field notebook was always a small notebook that would fit into my pocket. As a result it was a kind of badge." Several also mentioned that, at first, they generated fieldnotes to reassure themselves and their advisors that they were "doing their job."

For many respondents, fieldnote-taking often seems to reflect a more general tension, both geographical and temporal, between being there, immersed, trying to "go native" to some extent, and simultaneously thinking about the subsequent analysis and write-up. One respondent stated, "As Lévi-Strauss says about the Nambicuara, with me in Paris and them in Brazil, then it works. From a distance. While there, you and they are one, and it doesn't work."

Upon return, except for a few artifacts, the fieldnotes are the only physical link between the anthropologist and this powerful experience. Fieldnotes are the means through which the significance of this experience becomes transformed from an engrossing period, in which everything in one's life is radically altered, to a period of being engrossed in a writing project, one that will establish or maintain one's professional career:

> Looking at them, when I see this dirt,[9] blood, and spit, it's an external tangible sign of my legitimacy as an anthropologist.[10]

> Yes, the only physical stuff you have from fieldwork. It made you an anthropologist . . . and the only evidence was the stuff you brought back.

One might want to claim that, in a certain sense, anthropologists are always in a liminal state between the two cultures, regardless of which one they're in at a given point in time, and that fieldnotes continually remind them of this. The links that fieldnotes create to both cultures sometimes seem alienating and wrong; as we shall see, interviewees express this with comments about resenting their fieldnotes.

The field is also a liminal state between two very different stages in graduate training. It is commonplace that fieldwork is a coming-of-age process. Several interviewees offered pithy and often sophisticated remarks:

> Fieldnotes is an extension of that rite of passage called fieldwork. That says it. One of the Palladiums of fieldwork as a kind of holy ritual process . . . fieldnotes becomes one of those objects that bring good out of this rite of passage.

> When I was a student, the fact that you had come back from the field . . . you could call full professors by their first name. The more esoteric, exotic [your fieldwork site was], the more you had passed your serious rite of passage.

Doing fieldnotes a certain way (or, for some, doing them at all) is often associated with one's mentor and graduate department philosophy. As graduate students mature and increasingly choose to "do it my way," changes in their approach to fieldnotes can be a part of this maturing (see Jackson 1990). For some anthropologists, fieldnotes are a diploma, and the continued production of fieldnotes is a sign that one is a member in good standing in the anthropological club. However, for a few interviewees fieldnotes are less tools of the trade and more crutches of the apprentice. In either case, how one writes and uses fieldnotes can represent one's training, graduate school persona, *and* one's liberation from graduate school and dependent, cadet status.

Traditionally, anthropological fieldwork has implied research involving isolation, a lengthy stay, and layers of difficulty in obtaining information.[11] Overcoming these difficulties is seen as demanding a near-total marshalling of one's talents and resources. Fieldnotes are precious for many reasons: because of the labor of getting them, because they are one's ticket to a dissertation, subsequent publishing and a job, because the information is unique, and so forth. While hard work in any research creates value for the resulting documents, the irreplaceability of many sets of fieldnotes and the special circumstances under which they are obtained make their value unique, different from notes taken in a library, for instance, or during a laboratory experiment. As respondents affirm, you "sweat blood" for them. Yet many interviewees also commented on how worthless their fieldnotes were in some ways—because they were indecipherable, incomplete, disordered, and so on. The very factors that make them valuable upon return home (they were gathered in an exotic, isolated, "primitive" setting) make them deficient in terms of other "home" criteria (one does not have time to order fieldnotes, one writes them by hand—sometimes clandestinely—and so they are messy, etc.). Once again we see contradictory and ambivalent opinions expressed about fieldnotes.

The boundaries of the field can be fuzzy or can shift over time. Many fieldworkers enter and leave the field several times, and if one takes one's fieldnotes to a hotel room in a city, for example, for interim analysis, both the anthropologist and fieldnotes will occupy a geographically liminal state. One interviewee stated, "You should get away and go over them, talk to them."

Or the boundaries of "the field" can shift in other ways. One respondent said, "For example, in Nicaragua, it's such an ongoing event, and I can't say, 'Something's happening but it's not of relevance.' "

Fieldnote-taking can be a crucial defining feature of just what the field is. An anthropologist who studies recombinant DNA laboratories commented, "Sometimes I don't take notes on purpose. . . . I use it as a protective device. My way of turning off."

Between Fieldworker and Native. Anthropologists often claim that a special relationship occurs between themselves and the native. This idea was present in some interviewees' definitions of fieldnotes:

I don't think the *fact* of notes is unique, but the type of notes is . . . special. We try so hard to get close to the people we're working on. Most anthropologists are not really satisfied until they've seen them, seen the country, smelt them. So there's a somewhat immediate quality to our notes.

It is commonplace that anthropology depends on this "going native" aspect of information gathering far more than sociology or, even more so, psychology. A clinical psychologist wants to acquire understanding and empathy but hardly feels pulled to "go native." Anthropologists say that "your measure of success is how comfortable you feel . . . and to what degree you become socialized to the culture." But a conflict exists in any fieldwork situation, first, because as we have seen, the natives do not ever permit one to "go native" entirely and, second, the anthropological enterprise depends on a precarious, liminal balance between being an insider and an outsider:

> Anthropology is a combination of this interaction with people and writing. Fieldnotes is an intermediate step between the immediate experience of interaction and the written outcome . . . no matter how much one may understand the other, it doesn't have a certain kind of reality until it's put into fieldnotes.[12]

Fieldnotes can thus be seen to mediate between anthropologist and native. In the following quote, a certain sense, *both* anthropologist and fieldnotes play this role: "Oneself is the instrument. In relationship with the other. And fieldnotes is a record of that."

One respondent answered the question about anthropologists creating their documents thus: "But the 'create' part is somewhat accurate because it is being filtered through the person one is talking to, who's creating the document." Often, the anthropologist's nonnative status, his or her being neither fish nor fowl, can aid the research. The element of geographical liminality was noted by one respondent: "Most people had confidence that I wasn't a witch, for instance, and they could tell me things that wouldn't have consequences down the road because I'd just take it away with me." Many interviewees felt that fieldnotes set up barriers between themselves and the natives. One must gain confidence and intimacy to get good fieldnotes, and this can be aided by the natives' "not knowing" or "forgetting." One interviewee stated, "The main thing is that they didn't realize I was taking notes." Another interviewee said, "The people being observed forget you're there. There is something unethical about that, they go on about their business, and you're still observing." The moral unease this engenders comes out in statements such as "I always feel as though I have a dual identity, it makes me feel sneaky and dishonest" and "Oftentimes a conversation the other person thinks is spontaneous, I begin to turn it into an interview, and I think that's highly questionable." This ambivalence about the anthropologist/native relationship often comes out in concern about ownership of fieldnotes. One anthropologist agonized over this issue for a long time:

> My issue has always been, what right do I have to divulge this information that's been given to me? The Bakaga are very jealous of their songs. So it's an issue of confidentiality, but within the local context. I eventually decided, resolved it. Yes, I do, and, furthermore, I have an obligation.

He made his decision in part by considering these fieldnotes as *not* his. He said, "Several older Bakaga decided to turn their knowledge over to me. So I'm a caretaker. It's not mine. I feel I can't make decisions about it." This individual first speaks of making a decision and then says he feels he cannot make decisions.

Anthropologists and their fieldnotes are in a liminal situation insofar as many speak of the notes being neither entirely the private property of the anthropologist nor of anyone else. In some cases, others' use of fieldnotes can potentially harm the native community; an example given below of fieldnotes being subpoenaed illustrates this quite well. Many interviewees mused about whether their notes were strictly private property or somehow belonged to the native community. One interviewee stated, "It is an issue with the Jakanda, but I feel I sweat blood for them so when a young Jakanda anthropologist who hasn't done anything says the notes belong to them I don't feel too conflicted." But he later said,

> After I die they ought to be available to others, although I don't want to think about it—then my paranoia comes back. But enough scarce resources have been spent on me by funding agencies, and the Jakanda gave me so much, and so they should be available.

A further complicating factor is natives' claims to fieldnotes because of confidentiality. One respondent said, "On the other hand, my question is that taking fieldnotes . . . we're reporting on the public and private lives of the natives. To what extent are the documents our own? And for either side, the observer and observed. I don't think there's an easy solution."

Fieldnotes' mediating between anthropologist and native can be further complicated by natives' feelings about notebooks, cameras, and tape recorders. Suspicion, dislike, and misunderstanding abound in the interview materials. Geographical, temporal, occupational, and perhaps motivational liminality infuse the following example of interaction between anthropologist and informant. An interviewee stated,

I couldn't take out the notebook, it was disruptive. She knew I was writing it down, but it changed her storytelling. The next day she'd clarify. So the first chance I got, I'd go into the next room and type it up. She wasn't resentful [of my note-taking], but it interrupted the flow. At some level she'd forget she was telling things to [me] who was "working," and the next day she'd remember.[13]

Fieldnotes figure in interviewees' attempts to deal with negative feelings about informants. Many anthropologists use fieldnotes, especially a diary,[14] for what we can call the "garbage-can function"—a private place to vent spleen, to have control, to speak in a civilized language for a while:

Fieldnotes allow you to keep a grip on your sanity.

I learned that an anthropologist never becomes a member of the society one is studying, and one has to accept it. This journal gave me a release, I could express this, if only to myself.

Finally, fieldnotes' role as a link between anthropologist and native conflicts with the notion of fieldnotes as emotionally detached, scientific materials:

After he died I couldn't play the tapes. . . . I couldn't even look at them. It has a lot, I suppose, to do with your relationship to the people. They never were "subjects" of my research. So I've always had a hard time seeing this as "data."

The question of whether anthropology is humanities or science is the focus of a great deal of debate in the literature. Grappling with this issue led interviewees to disclose contradictory feelings about their fieldnotes because the notes themselves possess this "neither fish nor fowl" epistemological status:

I know a lot of people will be antagonistic, but the more the anthropologist can stand outside the fieldwork process emotionally, the better off the document will be. This is always a problem because on the one hand to get the data you have to be emotionally involved, but to write the document you have to be emotionally distant.

I'm a Boasian and fully believe in asking people what's on their minds, but I try to write down what they say as literally as possible . . . and what they say is the fieldnotes.

How I listen to an interview . . . what I have to do to be able to hear . . . trying to enter their consciousness and their reality.[15]

Between Experience and Representation: Fieldwork versus Fieldnotes. Despite the fact that fieldnote-taking is ostensibly a part of fieldwork, many anthropologists say they feel a tension between doing fieldwork and writing fieldnotes. As Thoreau noted, we cannot both live our lives and write them, and many interviewees commented on how frustrating it is to try to live the life of the natives as fully as possible and yet find time to write up the information gathered:

I had the same obsession with completeness everyone else does. Except . . . you end up not doing fieldwork. Ten minutes can take 4 hours' write-up . . . an anthropological dilemma.

Many interviewees described how fieldnotes can disrupt the flow of fieldwork:

I slowed down. More concerned with the hour to hour. You forget to take notes because you feel this is your life.

Many fieldworkers clearly feel that writing and processing fieldnotes is a lonely activity, a burden, and sometimes an ordeal. Simple exhaustion and time crunches account for some of this, as well as other material difficulties such as lack of light or space. A few interviewees spoke of longing to be liberated from the fieldnotes and what they represent, and a very few actually took this step, justifying it in terms of time constraints. One respondent stated, "Fieldnotes get in the way. They interfere with what fieldwork is all about." Yet for many the two are inextricably linked:

> So I think there was something about the typing of the notes that was very important . . . a ritual. That part of the day when you felt you were accomplishing something.

> [I had] to write something down every day. To not accept everything as normal.

Several anthropologists spoke of a need to be concerned about being too much "in the field." One respondent said, "So I feel better taking notes . . . because it's clear that we're interviewing." Some commented that fieldnotes help preserve a necessary, although at times painful and disturbing, marginal status with regard to going native.[16] One interviewee said that "your wife and kids will probably go more native than you" because the fieldwork enterprise *requires* that you not live like the natives.

Fieldnotes are thus in several respects both an aid and a hindrance to fieldwork—another ambiguous, liminal status.

BETWEEN SELVES

This section explores the anthropologist's personal relationship to his or her notes. It could also be titled "between roles." As we have already seen, fieldnotes both mediate between and serve as symbols of the roles the anthropologist plays, at times highlighting the contradictions between them. Furthermore, many anthropologists identify with, yet also feel alienated from their notes. I term this the "me/not me" liminality.

Fieldnotes and Self. Quite a number of interviewees' definitions of fieldnotes involved the self in some fashion.

To one respondent, fieldnotes are "the description of the situation that the anthropologist is in with respect to the intellectual problem—the reason for being there in the first place. Archival stuff is field *data*. Notes are the documents *you* create."

For some anthropologists, fieldnotes are an assistant, an aide-memoir, in a fairly uncomplicated, straightforward manner. In these instances the boundaries between fieldnotes and self are fairly clear-cut. A respondent said that fieldnotes "fix in my memory the incident I'm describing so that when I later read them, a flood of detail comes back into conscious memory, and the subsequent analysis I do is not of the fieldnotes but of the memory."

For some interviewees, fieldnotes fall far short of memory. For these anthropologists, memories contain graphic or aural qualities that conventional fieldnotes cannot compete with.

> I was disappointed that they weren't as magical as my memory. My memory is a recreated memory, and there are a lot of visual features to my memory, whereas fieldnotes were much more sort of mere rendering. They jog my much more real memories of the events.

For some interviewees, fieldnotes are "not me" in an almost competitive way. While fieldnotes' superior recall is acknowledged as an aid, they are nonetheless resented and sometimes envied for being more accurate. They remind one of one's faulty memory, or they cramp one's style:

In a way when doing my thesis I in a certain sense wanted to
lose them because then I would write it up out of whole cloth,
my understanding of them and my knowledge of other low-
land South American societies. My fieldnotes were constantly
contradicting this. Challenging my constructions of Bamipa
culture and social life, so in that sense I wanted to just be rid
of them. So they've always been a good corrective to oversim-
plification. They've been a constant critic, a critic who knows
the Bamipa better than I do in certain regards.

[It's like] saying Leach's book is brilliant *because* he lost his
fieldnotes. . . . He could sort of invent, or create, embroider,
rather than be tied down to the messiness of daily data.

Anxiety about loss of fieldnotes has come up so many
times and so dramatically—images of burning appear quite
often—that I have concluded that for some interviewees fear
about loss is accompanied by an unexamined attraction to
the idea. The many legends, apocryphal or not, about lost
fieldnotes probably fits into this category of horrorific and
yet delicious, forbidden fantasy. One interviewee said, "So
maybe the people who lost their notes are better off."

Other interviewees spoke of an unclear relationship between memory—"headnotes" (Ottenberg 1990)—and written notes. Here the boundary between self and fieldnotes
becomes fuzzier:

So they [other people] think I'm not using them. I *am,* though.
But people look at that [unopened packages of fieldnotes] as
a kind of laziness. [But] *I* am the best field notebook I have.
I know the information.

Various quotes revealed a fear of fieldnotes dominating or
at least having too much power or too much presence, such
as "They can be a kind of albatross around your neck" and

"They seem like they take up a lot of room. . . . They take up too much room."

Fieldnotes can represent a requirement to justify or judge oneself, as they did for the interviewee who stated, "Only when doing this are you constantly asked to evaluate yourself, are you asking yourself, you're asking, 'What am I doing?' " And the evaluation might not be favorable, as in the following responses:

> It's partially a fear. Part is that it's your personal property, people can see you in a state of intellectual undress. People don't like to have to defend themselves. Why don't I have quantitative data for sheep? I don't *know* why!

> Rereading them, some of them look pretty lame. How could you be so stupid or puerile?

Or they can be an affirmation:

> [There's] a feeling of confidence that if one could manage this one could manage almost anything.

> I do get pleasure in working with them again, particularly my notes from my first work. A feeling of sort of, that is where I came in, and I can sometimes recapture some of the intellectual and physical excitement of being there.

Many interviewees spoke of how fieldnotes reveal what kind of person one is: messy, responsible, procrastinating, exploitative, tidy, compulsive, generous. Because of all the ways in which fieldnotes are linked to important issues in interviewees' life and work, fieldnotes themselves become a sign and symbol of who the individual is, as a professional and, to some degree, in a comprehensive sense:

When I think of activities I do, that's a lot closer to the core
of my identity than most things.

I have a lot of affection for my notes in a funny way . . . their
role here—in the U.S., my study, in terms of my professional
self. Something about my academic identity. I'm not proud of
everything about them but I am proud of some things about
them . . . that they represent. Probably in a less conscious
way some motive for my not wanting to make them too public.

My primary identity is someone who writes things down and
writes about them. Not just hanging out.

Thus fieldnotes provide an ongoing opportunity to examine
oneself, at times are seen as an extension of self, and, for
many, they can be a validation or betrayal of self. An
interviewee said, "Fieldnotes can reveal how worthless your
work was, the lacunae, your linguistic incompetence, your
not being made a blood brother, your childish temper." An
interesting illustration of this is one anthropologist's account of how her subpoenaed fieldnotes were discredited, as
a way of discrediting her expertise and authority:

"They're dog's breakfast!" they [the opposition lawyers] would
say. "How can you expect anything from this?" . . . It had been
written on a [piece of paper on] the back of a Toyota and [was]
totally incomprehensible to anyone but me. But it was an
attack on my credibility. . . . I said, "This is a genealogy."
"*This* is a genealogy?" Our lawyer would jump in, "Yes, of
course."

Malinowski's (1967) diary was mentioned by many interviewees regarding this issue. With regard to whether they
will validate or discredit the self, fieldnotes are most defi-
nitely betwixt and between.

For many interviewees, the unique qualities of the field
make fieldnotes a far more unique and personal document

than other kinds of note-taking. As already noted, creating fieldnotes—and subsequently working with one's creation —evokes powerful feelings for many anthropologists. While the strength and nature of such feelings vary with the anthropologist, the project, and the actual field situation, fieldnotes' ability to elicit strong feelings is due, in part, because one is disoriented, challenged, confused, or over-stressed *and* euphoric, energized, and engaged when creating them. This results in their creators feeling attached to them and identifying with them apparently far more than how most lawyers, journalists, or psychologists feel about their notes—which is not to say that these professionals do not have strong feelings about some of their notes; it is a question of degree. An interviewee stated, "One feels possessive towards fieldnotes because they are so linked to oneself. . . . It's like they're part of me. To turn them over to a university archive is one of the most difficult things to do." Another interviewee commented on the link between field-notes and self, with reference to Boas's diary: "[They] reveal a lot and for that reason they are valuable documents. Does the anthropologist see the culture, or see himself in the culture . . . see the social context from which he comes as somehow replicated in the culture?" Interestingly, this interviewee thinks she will destroy her fieldnotes before she dies.

The existence of a set of fieldnotes can, as we have seen, be an affirmation or represent accomplishment or the meeting and overcoming of a stiff challenge. But fieldnotes, once created, can represent potential alienation and unintentional hurt to oneself and the natives. Of course, this issue of potential alienation is a major difference between field-notes and headnotes. The written notes become far more separated from one's control, even taking into consideration the lack of control associated with memory's tendency to fade and distort. For most anthropologists, fieldnotes demand serious attention with regard to confidentiality, privacy versus sharing, and obligations to the profession and posterity. For example, one anthropologist felt torn by his obligations to the pro-Indian organization that facilitated his gaining access to his fieldwork community. He stated, "They applied considerable moral pressure [to have access to his fieldnotes]. The danger is that when I'm speaking I can be polite, but the fieldnotes are in black and white." Whereas memory and cognition are eternally changing, or at least are potentially doing so, fieldnotes, once written, become fixed— although, of course, the mind can work with them at different times and reinterpret them. As we have seen, memories are not fixed and can paradoxically appear to be more useful for this reason. An interviewee said that "it reifies certain things, to get it into boxes. For me . . . a lot gets lost when they're translated onto these cards." Hence headnotes can appear to be both truer to and more congruent with one's sense of self. But since memories can fade and become distorted, we have some compelling reasons why the anthropologist's relationship to fieldnotes typifies a liminal, ambiguous state. Fieldnotes are both better and worse than headnotes; they evoke a high degree of both negative and positive affect, and the rules for how to think about and write them are confused, leading one to doubt oneself.

One interviewee differentiated fieldnotes from other written materials connected with fieldwork precisely in terms of the connections between written record, mind, and memory:

> That might be closer to a definition of a fieldnote: something that can't be readily comprehended by another person. . . . A newspaper clipping can be a fieldnote if it needs to be read by me. . . . It's what I remember; the notes mediate the memory and the interaction.

For many anthropologists, fieldnotes' ability to trigger memory and occasion new analysis greatly increases their value. However, this is complicated because of the issue of reliability of one's memory, as illustrated by the following:

> I don't mean to sound too Proustian about it, but suddenly an event years later causes you to rethink, reconceptualize your field experience, but also will trigger off memories you may not have recorded. What is the status of that material?
>
> So I didn't take notes, I would rely on my memory. . . . I didn't realize before fieldwork the incredible selectivity of one's mind. A source of great anxiety. I felt I shouldn't be filtering as I was. I eventually concluded that I couldn't do anything about it, and so became reconciled.
>
> Are memories fieldnotes? I use them that way, even though they aren't the same kind of evidence. It took a while for me to be able to rely on my memory. But I had to, since the idea of what I was doing had changed, and I had memories but no notes. I had to say, "Well, I *saw* that happen." I am a fieldnote.

An interviewee commented on other consequences of the close link between fieldnotes, mind, and self by stating, "Unlike the historian, or literary scholar, where the text is independent to some extent, he approaches it with a kind of freshness. The anthropologist spends so much time going over the same material, there's a quality of *déjà entendu.*" Another interviewee spoke of the act of creating fieldnotes as depleting self: "I'd get only one chance to write it down, because every time you do you use up your quota of freshness of insight. You run out your string on that." For some, mind and fieldnotes are completely interdependent; as one interviewee stated, "It's not a random sample, it's much better designed. But because the design and values are in my head, it's dead data without me." Another noted that as understanding increases, fieldnotes decrease—the notion that comprehensive fieldnotes are produced only at the apprentice stage:

> He [my advisor] said he could make sense of early notes but less sense of them later, even though I understood more. I was making telegraphed notes by then . . . a dramatic dropoff. . . . So I wrote less and less as I was learning more and more.

For some, fieldnotes interferes with the dynamic interaction between mind and fieldwork. An interviewee stated, "The record is in my head, not on paper. The record on paper, it, because it's static, interferes with fieldwork. . . . Keeping fieldnotes interferes with what's really important." A complex interdependence involving mutual support and mutual impediment clearly exists between fieldnotes and mind. This mutual dependence involves order, comprehensiveness, and veracity and both negative and positive value— potential benefit to the fieldworker and his or her intended audience[17] and potential danger to the fieldworker and the native.

Sometimes, the interviewee, working with the fieldnotes, feels different in some way from the person he or she was when creating the fieldnotes, as shown by the following quotes:

> Later I can see people's intentions more clearly. So there is more value in the notes, in hindsight. In some ways, it's like looking at another me.

> They're useful as a document for what happened and as a device for triggering new analysis, to go back as a different person or with different theoretical interpretations, at a different stage in life.

Sometimes, anthropologists work with these earlier selves as well as the information fieldnotes contain. One anthropologist stated,

> Especially after time has passed, and you go back and it's as if they're written by someone else. I find myself interpreting and scrutinizing them. Wouldn't change them. I write commentaries and date the commentary. Poking fun at myself, usually, I guess, with posterity in mind.

Many interviewees speak of the consequences of fieldnotes' separation from self. For example, one interviewee said, "A separate body of work, now, and sometimes I don't recognize what I've written, so now reviewing my fieldnotes is sometimes like doing fieldwork all over again."

Even though fieldnotes have a separate existence, for many interviewees their notes and their selves are spliced in a kind of organic, mystical way. Other factors contribute to respondents' confusion about this matter, of course, such as worries about compromising informants, the possibility of misinterpretation, or the possibility of personal material being read or even published without permission. As noted above, the specter of Malinowski's diary made an appearance in many of the interviews, as it did when an interviewee said, "What fieldnotes are good for is revealing something about the fieldworker. We now see Malinowski as a colonialist, racist, male chauvinist pig."

Many commented on the problematic status of their fieldnotes being used without them there to interpret:

> Whereas my notes are a mnemonic for me . . . and therefore more information will come out of the notes than is there, but I have to be there. I don't know how to deal with this. For example, I have a number of different genealogies. I make a

comment in the notes that it's wrong. But I don't explain why
this guy would say he was this kind of cousin. I know it,
though.

All my notes are mine. In some ways because I'm the only one
to decipher them. It is a certain amount of protection.

In sum, it is clear that fieldnotes are both "me" and "not me"
in many ways, and this quality poses problems for many
ethnographers.

The link between the potential value of fieldnotes for
others and the me/not-me theme comes up again and again
in the interviews: "Fieldnotes are rubbish, garbage, and will
be even more so upon my death"; "They are incredibly
important documents and I have to organize them, send
them to an archive"; "They are valuable, yes, but only so
long as I am alive to give them life and meaning." Clearly,
the complex and ambivalent attachment many anthropologists feel toward their fieldnotes confers an equally ambivalent value on them; in some ways, how anthropologists talk
about the value of their fieldnotes best conveys the quintessential me/not-me essence of fieldnotes. For some interviewees, the attachment is connected to the amount of time
invested in them:

I'm sure the attitude towards the notes themselves has a sort
of fetishistic quality—I don't go stroke them, but I spent so
much time getting, guarding and protecting them . . . if the
house were burning down I'd go to the notes first.

I busted my ass to get them. . . . I packed that [tape recorder]
all over. It linked me to the product, a real sacrifice to get it.

Other interviewees are attached because fieldnotes are connected to important experiences in their lives:

I do have that protectionist feeling. The first batch—it's like
the first child is different from the second. You love them both,
but the first is special. I wouldn't want them saved for posterity, yet I feel personally invested, too close.

I do have a feeling that they're an important part of my self
there. . . . In some ways they are associated with the experiences I had in Afghanistan, in particular the relatively powerful experiences, those incredible religious ceremonies.

For some, this attachment, along with other negative or
positive emotions, is triggered by the physical manifestation
of the notes. One interviewee stated, "I don't have the
physical associations with the tapes I once had . . . feeling
a kind of connection, an inability to separate from them. I
experience this still when I listen to them: a horror, shock,
disorientation." This quote reflects, somewhat extremely,
the complex feelings of connection and separation many
interviewees remarked on. Attachment, in all of its meanings, was expressed by one interviewee who said, "I read
through a chunk of them and then put them away. I write
and I can't bear to look at them." For some, the attachment
to the physical notes takes on an almost fetishistic quality.
Although the speaker's comments might be full of irony or
sarcasm, the feelings expressed are nonetheless fervently
felt, perhaps enhanced, because of this self-awareness:

It's like they're part of me. To put them in a box and mail them
Federal Express . . . I want to travel out there and put them
on the shelf myself, at least. Yes, they'll make copies. But it's
not copies, it's the originals that have the power.

One can make the argument that if fieldnotes are liminal,
secret, sacred, or somehow associated with these qualities,
powerful feelings will arise because of this alone:

It's—there's some power, it's like shutting it out, not repression, the equivalent of that in physical things. I haven't thought about this before but, yes, I have strong feelings. If I look in them, all this emotion comes out, so it's like hiding something away so it won't remind you, it won't be so powerful.

Looking back at the notes . . . I relive the emotions and have to process it all over again. . . . I wrote this piece about bureaucracies and every time I reread about the incidents I had to reprocess it, and I think I exorcised some of that negative affect, so that this time when I had to face a bureaucrat I didn't feel the anxiety and apprehension I had felt earlier . . . paranoia, uncertainty.

The typed notes, also, a sense of, often, aversion. I can sympathize with that feeling of not wanting to go too close to that part of the room.

Self and Other. The many expressions of anxiety and guilt in my interviews stem, in part, from the me/not-me liminality because of fieldnotes' ability to become separated from oneself and what one stands for. Doing fieldnotes, in some situations at least, creates the proverbial double bind. Writing fieldnotes constantly reminds many anthropologists that they are, in fact, not in the field just to be friends or just to help the natives, but to do research; as a consequence, interviewees reported experiencing feelings of being exploitative, of being a colonialist, and so forth. Hence their overall feelings, especially their ambivalence toward their fieldnotes, are heightened. We are reminded that a prime characteristic of liminal situations is high affect.

According to some interviewees, whether one is or is not creating documents—and what "documents" *means*—is problematic because of the role of the (native) other:

Maybe I just view my task not so much as creating but transmitting, being a broker, an intermediary, a partner. It's their words.

Well, it's not *we* who create our documents. It's funny, since I'm into the interpretive side of anthropology. But I really do believe that the events, the relationships, etc., are the primary documents that are comparable to the documents that historians deal with, and our fieldnotes are reflections, just like historians reflect.

I never think of my fieldnotes as a document. I feel the people are sort of a document. I did not create these people.

Anthropologists create documents not *ex nihilo*. My people's behavior is the document. I see them lived as documents, and as second order I write them as documents, and as third order publish them. The historian is cut off, the documents are bloodless. But I am not free, I'm also constrained. I can be corrected by my people as a historian cannot be. They're [historians] actually freer with the document. I can be corrected. . . . They [the natives] won't laugh at a joke. Or [I can be] physically stood up.

Because fieldnotes are a preparatory phase to writing ethnography, in this function they can be seen as helping to distance the anthropologist from an identification with the (native) other—the fieldworker moves away from the doing toward the writing part of the research. Yet many interviewees comment on how fieldnotes keep the connection to the field, thus helping continue the dialogue and identification with the other and the "collapse of identity" (Kondo 1982) felt by some anthropologists as necessary to successful fieldwork.

Quite a number of fieldworkers carry around with them images of additional others who are involved in their fieldnote-making. One anthropologist said, "My notes always assumed someone was looking over my shoulder, asking me to validate."

As noted above, many interviewees commented on how one's fieldnotes can be used to make *others'* points and test *others'* hypotheses. Hence there are two kinds of others interacting with self: the native other and the other who might read or otherwise use one's fieldnotes—once again, an example of fieldnotes' liminal status.

Thus fieldnotes are liminal because interviewees see them in terms of identification with and alienation from the self and in terms of both increasing and decreasing mutual understanding between self and other.

Between Words

This section continues the discussion of fieldnotes as an object that exists apart from their creator. Fieldnotes are separate objects that exhibit certain characteristics: they are written or taped words, ciphers, or other symbols that are recorded under certain conditions. They are a kind of literary genre, capable of being compared to other kinds of writing. These characteristics influence and constrain the relationship between fieldnotes and the fieldworker. Whether fieldnotes are understood or misunderstood, used productively or misused, depends in part on these characteristics. In short, this section asks, what *kinds* of words comprise a set of fieldnotes? Expectably, the answer is not at all clear.

Although all kinds of writing are the authors' creations, fieldnotes differ from other kinds of writings in that they are not for public consumption. Furthermore, the literary canon (if we can speak thus) defining their form and content is extremely vague. Furthermore, they are way stations rather than the end point.

Quite a number of interviewees commented on how field-notes occupy an interstitial place between observed "reality" and a finished piece of writing:[18]

When you're writing for a book you are writing for an outside audience. The fieldnotes are an intermediate stage. One fear is that they're subject to a lot of misinterpretation, a fear, one, that they are wrong and someone will use them, or, two, they're subject to manipulation the author doesn't want. In that sense they're a text, cut off from their roots, different from social reality.

Fieldnotes are betwixt and between in that they are midway between reality and a published document *and* midway between the anthropologist and the reader of any resulting publication.[19] "Raw" fieldnotes may make no sense to either the native or the Western reading public; most often they need the anthropologist as mediator, to explain and further transform them. One anthropologist stated, "They come in chronological order for most people, not neatly classified the moment you get it. . . . Half the work is sifting through those notes and creating something out of it." For this reason, one anthropologist located the personal, invio-lable aspect of fieldwork in the creative process *after* field-notes were taken:

I wouldn't mind sharing or reading someone else's, because what I'm doing with my fieldnotes no one else is going to do. You could write a paper that I wouldn't write on my fieldnotes.

Another noted the incongruence between the public na-ture of the final product and the private nature of this stage of the process of getting there: "It's curious that we make highly public published statements based on highly private materials."[20]

Questions about who has a claim to these words, who can do what things with them, came up in the interviews again and again:

> I gave 100 myths to a Yugoslavian who published them without citation. He sent me the book. I don't think he felt to blame. It was unethical, but it was descriptions, he didn't distinguish between his work and mine. But if it had been done in English I would have been extremely angry. . . . I felt it was appropriate to give them to him. He probably felt the myths didn't belong to me and they don't. But it's a lot of work.

One interviewee spoke of rights that changed over time: "I want first crack, I haven't even written my thesis. But there's a time limit as to how long I could sit on them without working on them." Another spoke longingly of the possibility of sharing: "It would be such an advantage . . . to enter a place with some of that background." Reluctance to share derives in part from the above-discussed link between field-notes and self:

> I haven't, and I'd be of two minds . . . who they are and what they'd want it for. Fieldnotes are—it's strange how intimate they become and how possessive we are.

For many interviewees, fieldnotes are betwixt and between a personal diary and a scientific document. One area of disagreement among interviewees with respect to defining fieldnotes is the degree to which they are seen as objective or subjective. Of course, a lot of this has to do with the individual's notions of how anthropology contrasts with other social sciences, anthropology's weaknesses and strengths, and how they, as individuals, fit with or rebel against the profession's canons and epistemological position:

A peculiar mixture of personal and hard data, and you always have to contend with this.

Because we do fall in between, we allow the personal . . . not sociologists, who can pull out 20,000 questionnaires. I don't think this is the way to get insight, but we do have a problem with our methods of being able to judge the competence.

But the highly personal, uncategorizable ones, they are much more meaningful.

Fieldnotes can represent the tension between controlled, "scientific" research and the osmotic, spontaneous, flexible kind. One interviewee reported on feeling disturbed at another anthropologist's highly systemized ways of acquiring and processing data: "It fits his compulsiveness. . . . I don't think he had room in that system for a fascinating spontaneous conversation with someone." The difference and distance between "objective" reality and subjective experience can change during the research; in the following case, fieldnotes were allied with the objective side:

What happened was the more I got into fieldwork the less I did [the fewer fieldnotes I took] . . . partly because my personal private experience or reaction to things and what was the more objective reality out there got less—the difference between them.

The ambiguous status of fieldnotes as a written record of both objective and subjective experience became apparent in anthropologists' critiques of other anthropologists:

Anthropologists have tended to fetishize their notes, they quote their notes as text.

Some anthropologists have never had a hunch and if they did, they'd be scared by it. The category "hunch" is something anthropologists don't bring to the field. This is why you should take a journal. I get tired of reflexive anthropology: "me, me, me." But hunches do come out in a journal.

A nice example of how subjective experience interconnects with "data" is the following: "That journal, of course, is also a kind of data, because it indicates how to learn about, yes, myself, but also how to be a person in this environment. Subsequently I see it as part of the fieldnotes." Many interviewees mention a trade-off between fieldnotes functioning as scientific documents that should be accessible to others and as a private journal. One interviewee said, "A bit of contradiction—the sort of private diary aspect is very important, but to the degree you censor them because someone else may have access, you inhibit this function."

However, the vast majority of anthropologists contrast fieldnotes with harder data; that is, however these interviewees defined fieldnotes, they managed to indicate in some form that a crucial component of fieldwork and note-taking involves attention to subjectivity:

> Something about the identity of anthropology, first of all, concerns the subjectivity of the observer . . . and . . . the definition of fieldnotes is a personally bounded—in the field—and personally referential thing.

The majority not only consider this unique to anthropology but also see it as a strength. One anthropologist said, "In anthropology we don't see it only as an extension of someone's self, but also a methodology of the discipline." A political scientist noted, "Anthropologists are self-conscious about this process called the creation and use of personal fieldnotes. I think it's dangerous that political scientists aren't." However, unease, ambivalence, and defensiveness on this subject also came across in many of the interviews:

If I felt that ethnography just reflected internal states I wouldn't be in this game.

I tend to believe my notes reflect reality as closely as possible.

Because, regardless of one's stance with respect to positivism or phenomenology, one worries about the effect of what is "in here" on what one observes "out there":

> [Fieldnotes are about] everything I saw and observed that I thought was relevant to what I saw as interesting. I realized I was imposing a structure that might be losing me things, but one has to do that.

Many anthropologists expressed the tension between the advantage of having a receptive, tabula rasa mind versus being informed, systematic, and selective. This emerged in discussions of the value and/or worthlessness of their initial note-taking as compared to later periods of fieldwork:

> Well, [the beginning of fieldwork is] a very useful and significant time. They [fieldnotes] are harder, because you feel you have to write everything down and you don't know what "everything" is.

One interviewee commented on a possible covert reason behind his department's not providing adequate training for fieldwork:

> I had to ask obliquely for fear of revealing my inadequacy. [The reply was] "Well, you know, just do it . . . and don't do anything stupid, but work it out." It was like parents telling their children about sex. When pushed past this they'd say, "Well, we don't want to constrain you, anthropology is changing, the boundaries are being constantly defined." It was deliberate that we were not inducted into the methods.

Finally, many anthropologists, predictably, expressed
conflicting, ambivalent feelings about future value:

> I don't know, I have moods of thinking I'd burn the whole lot
> before I die, and then moods of thinking that that would be
> quite irresponsible, and then moods of thinking "What makes
> you think they're so important, anyway?"

We have seen that the question about disposition of fieldnotes at death elicited many statements showing the ambiguous nature of fieldnotes as something intimately linked
to the anthropologist and yet having an existence apart.
Interviewees differed; for some, fieldnotes totally depend on
the fieldworker to give them meaning, while for others,
what changes after death is that the anthropologist, as well
as the natives, becomes an object of study via the fieldnotes.
One anthropologist stated, "After you die, your fieldnotes
become someone's historical documents." Here the creation
becomes the vehicle for a new creation about the creator.
Despite most interviewees joking about the unlikely event
of someone considering their work so important that they
would merit such attention, the ambiguous relationship of
fieldnotes to their creator came out clearly.

Fieldnotes are created documents[21] that share some features with novels, paintings, and musical compositions: they
are new, and yet they affirm already existing truths, sometimes extremely powerfully. Yet fieldnotes *are* different. An
interviewee said, "It *is* creating something, not creating it
in the imagination sense, but creating it in terms of bringing
it out as a fact." Fieldnotes are closest, perhaps, to nonfiction creations such as biographies and documentary films:

> You have to be very careful and sure and honest with yourself
> that what you're recording has to be objectively true, and
> along with the personal satisfaction you have to have a

responsibility to the environment you're treating, . . . to be aware of a kind of hubris that would lead you to impose yourself on the material.

Yet interviewees seemed to feel that ethnography has an additional problem, one not encountered by conventional documentary filmmakers in their attempts to translate observed and felt reality into a film to be comprehended by an other: the problem of translation from another culture and language. Fieldnotes, at least stereotypical anthropological ones, are supposed to aid in the revelation of truths that emerge out of quite foreign contexts, even though a given truth might be felt to be universal. Fieldnotes are supposed to reveal an other that is not the other created by a novelist or portrait painter, for the former is incomprehensible without the translation and interpretation which the ethnographer must provide. It is the ethnographer who quintessentially creates this kind of representation:[22]

Malinowski . . . says [when] he's coming into Kiriwina, "It's me who's going to create them for the world."

We do more than historians . . . we create a world.

Although many kinds of human creations may be initially viewed by their intended audience only through a glass darkly, traditional ethnography is, perhaps, a different kind of creation because its translation tasks precede and dominate its other goals.[23]

Conclusions

Many of my interviewees were all too aware of their mixed feelings about fieldnotes, indicating their unease by using familiar words from the anthropological lexicon of ritual, such as *sacred, exorcism, fetish,* and *taboo.* They also commented on our tendency to *avoid* talking about fieldnotes or to only *joke* about them.[24] Fieldwork *is* a kind of ritual, a rite of passage. In Turner's (1985) terms, fieldwork has some of the qualities of *comunitas,* a period during which people negate, affirm, and create meaning[25] and (at times mystically) participate in native life. Fieldnotes can be seen to assume a heavy emotional valence and sacredness because they are objects crucial to the performance of the rite.[26]

Furthermore, if fieldwork is a coming-of-age process, then writing fieldnotes would seem to be a remarkably well-designed and effective ordeal that tests the anthropologist's mettle. One can rely on advisors only so much in these trials, for it is eventually necessary to forge ahead into unchartered territory, if a genuine transformation in the initiand is to be achieved. One's first fieldnotes are a link to one's advisor, and for some interviewees these fieldnotes are both a sign of this link and a sign of having successfully broken it. The confusion and resentment many anthropologists express about their training regarding fieldnotes and about professional canons perhaps is necessary, given the socialization function that fieldnote-taking performs. Perhaps this is why anthropologists delight in jokes about "rules" for doing fieldwork, complaining on the one hand about a lack of rules and yet on the other how inadequate, if not downright stupid, are the rules that they were told to follow.[27]

Indeed, the overall confusion noted by the vast majority of interviewees surrounding the doing and meaning of fieldnotes suggests the feature found in ritually liminal situations of a suspension of rules.

Fieldnotes are intimately tied up, then, with the fieldworker's transition to a new state; returning from fieldwork, fieldnotes in hand, is a kind of graduation. Fieldnotes can be seen as a diploma and a license to continue to practice anthropology:

> I remember reading a novel by Barbara Pym of an anthropologist burning his fieldnotes in a ritualistic bonfire in the back yard. It was inconceivable of someone doing that and remaining an anthropologist. I found this passage to be fascinating and very provocative.

One source of provocation undoubtedly is the nagging doubt that many anthropologists have regarding whether or not the ethnographer would have the *right* to burn fieldnotes: if a larger community helped produce them (e.g., funding agencies, native informants), shouldn't this community have some say in their disposition?

Another way that fieldnotes are chameleonlike for some interviewees involves fieldnotes' ability to take on the romance and the exotic, grubby character of the field and yet also represent the colonialist, statist, literocentrism of the West from which the fieldworker must flee[28] in order to do successful research.

Fieldnotes are not only liminal in the sense of "betwixt and between," they are a mediator. They accompany the fieldworker home and provide the means to be symbolically transported back to the field during write-up. They are materially of the field, with their "dirt, blood, and spit." They also index the field. Yet they serve to remind the researcher while in the field that he or she stands apart, and they often remind the native of this as well. They are betwixt and between perceived reality and the final version intended for the public. They are a translation from one meaning system to another, and they provide the means (and often the incentive) to continually retranslate.

Hence fieldnotes mediate between worlds and between the personas that the anthropologist assumes in different

places and at different times. Fieldnotes also straddle the
fence between sacred and profane, being seen by some
interviewees as holy and taboo, with associations made
between fieldnotes and rituals ("writing them up every
night"), involving fetishes, ordeals, and high affect, and yet
also seen as a matter-of-fact, nuts-and-bolts task that must
be attended to every day.

For some anthropologists, fieldnotes symbolized the crucial period of seclusion in this particular initiation rite's
bush school. Other anthropologists spoke of fieldwork as a
chance to leave school behind and to go out into the wide
world and live. For some interviewees, fieldnotes signaled
their adult, scientist, and professional status. For most,
fieldnotes represented a problem between research via living and doing and research via writing.

In sum, many characteristics associated with liminality
emerged in these interviews: the theme of embarking on a
quest; the notion of undergoing an ordeal which, if done
correctly, will bring about a transformation in the individual; a suspension of rules; high affect; and, at times, an
association with the sacred. Fieldnotes, in short, are both
déjà entendu because they are so linked to the anthropologist who created them and evidence of just how mysterious
and *jamais entendu* "the field" can be.

Notes

1. To protect the confidentiality of my interviewees, any potentially
identifying details in the quotations that follow have been altered.
2. Given the sample's lack of systematic representation, this chapter
should be seen in qualitative terms. The reasonably large sample size
guards against bias in only the crudest fashion because so many complex
variables are present. Although I cannot *claim* to represent any group, I
do feel the sample represents practicing anthropologists living in the
United States. Some are famous, others obscure; some have reflected

about fieldwork and fieldnotes extensively (a few have written on these topics), whereas others describe themselves as having been fairly unconscious (or even hostile) to such matters. My sample is thus more representative of the profession than if I had written a chapter based on published comments about fieldnotes—the last thing many of my interviewees contemplate undertaking is writing on this topic.

I should comment that although this chapter is inspired by the current interest in "ethnographies as text" (see Marcus and Cushman 1982; Clifford 1988) my methodology necessarily produces findings differing from these and similar work in two crucial respects. One is the fact that most of the anthropologists I interviewed are not enamored of the "anthropology as cultural critique" (Marcus and Fischer 1986) trend, even though all of them had very interesting comments to make about fieldnotes. The other is that, given the frankness and strong feelings —especially the ambivalence and negativity—that emerged in the interviews, I doubt if my interviewees, even those who might be inclined to write about fieldnotes some day, would ever say in print some of what they said to me. For all I know, some interviewees might later have regretted being so frank with me (something that often surprised me at the time), although this does not necessarily make what they said any less true. While I certainly do not think I got the *entire* truth from anyone, given that a confidential interview setting can elicit ideas and feelings people might not come up with by themselves, I believe that the material I obtained from my interviews is different—complementary—to material acquired from the literature on fieldnotes.

3. My interview procedure was the following: I first asked interviewees to tell me whatever they have to say about the subject of fieldnotes. Almost all were willing to do this. Then I asked about the following topics: (1) their definition of fieldnotes, (2) training—preparation and mentoring, formal and informal, (3) sharing fieldnotes, (4) confidentiality, (5) disposition of fieldnotes at death, (6) feelings about fieldnotes, particularly the actual, physical notes, and (7) whether "unlike historians, anthropologists create their own documents." I also tried to query those who had more than one field experience about any changes in their approach to fieldnotes.

Interviews lasted at least an hour. Lacking funds for transcription, I did not use a tape recorder, but I did try to record verbatim as much as possible.

Along the way, of course, I discovered other issues I wish I had been covering systematically —for example, the interdependence of "headnotes" (remembered observations) and written materials. In later interviews I asked about the mystique of fieldnotes and whether fieldnotes are connected to anthropologists'—or anthropology's—identity.

Several people initially asked why I chose such a nuts-and-bolts topic, but they all seemed interested in the subject (no one declined to be interviewed). In fact, fieldnotes seems to be a remarkably good entry point for obtaining opinions and feelings about bigger issues, probably better than asking point-blank questions about them.

4. Why liminality exists as a concept has been explained with reference to the presumed need a society has to order experience by classifying the universe—both to allow its members to think and interpret and to use such classifications for society's own ends. Such a system of classification allows a society's members to not only "make sense" of the myriad of stimuli assaulting the five senses but to be able to judge some as more beautiful or better than others. Since this is achieved by highlighting some attributes of certain phenomena and ignoring others, so the argument goes, possible confusion and conflict threaten when instances of boundary-straddling become apparent. Gluckman (1963) argues that ritual, and formal behavior in general, serve to keep potentially confused, ambiguous, and conflictive roles distinct by highlighting their differences. Also see Babcock (1978).

5. See Crocker (1973) and Morris (1987) for discussions of various social, cognitive, and affective/emotional theories explaining why, under certain circumstances, liminality is highlighted and exaggerated.

6. In a sense moving between two different social systems; see Weidman (1970, 262).

7. Sojourners of all kinds are in a geographically liminal state and are often liminal in other respects, especially those undertaking pilgrimages. Fieldwork can be likened to pilgrimages and quests.

8. See Rabinow (1977):

> Fieldwork, then, is a process of intersubjective construction of liminal modes of communication. Intersubjective means literally more than one subject, but being situated neither quite here nor quite there, the subjects involved do not share a common set of assumptions, experiences or traditions. (p. 155)

He also refers to fieldnotes as liminal since a process of mutual construction of a hybrid world by both ethnographer and informant takes place (p. 153). Kondo (1982) speaks of this hybrid world as "the conspiracy my informants and I had perpetrated" (p. 6).

9. I have vast amounts of statements linking fieldnotes with dirt and mess. One possible interpretation comes from Crocker who points out that liminal social roles are associated with liminal symbols. Hence, just as prophets or boys undergoing initiation are expected to be dirty, so would fieldnotes. Dirt is liminal because it is matter out of place (Crocker 1973, 70; see Douglas 1966).

10. Compare:

> When I look back at them, the 500 or so pages or notes are
> clearly my own. I see here where I spilled my coffee and there
> where my pen was running out of ink. My mind goes back to
> the sounds and smells of a New Guinea morning, and insights
> surface from somewhere in the cobwebbed depths of my mem-
> ory. Certainly it was necessary to sift and sort through the
> data, but the intimate relationship which had developed be-
> tween the fieldnotes and myself made it a very different
> phenomenon from the research I was to take on next. (Podo-
> lefsky 1987, 15)

11. Which, of course, can be found in any long-term, intense
participant-observation fieldwork even though not undertaken by an
anthropologist. See Van Maanen (1988).

12. See Pratt (1986):

> To convert fieldwork, via fieldnotes, into formal ethnography
> requires a tremendously difficult shift from the latter discur-
> sive position (face to face with the other) to the former. Much
> must be left behind in the process. Johannes Fabian charac-
> terizes the temporal aspect of this contradiction when he
> speaks of "an aporetic split between recognition of coevalness
> in some ethnographic research and denial of coevalness in
> most anthropological theorizing and writing." (p. 32)

13. Of course, the opposite situation can obtain when informants
demand that their words be written or taped: "Write this down! Isn't what
I'm telling you important enough?"

14. Some interviewees, however, contrasted fieldnotes with diary in
their definitions

15. This quote from a female interviewee is a very "emphatic" and "interpretive" kind of statement. See Kirschner (1987) concerning "sub-
jectivist" and "interpretive" approaches to fieldwork and how these
correlate with the gender of the ethnographer. An interpretive view of
such attempts at empathy, according to Kirschner, would see them as
leading to a "false sense of mystical communion with the inner life of the
Other, and therefore a projective illusion" (p. 217).

16. Goffman (1989), the patron saint of many fieldworking sociologists, says the test of penetrating the society you're supposed to be
studying involves getting to the point where "the sights and sounds
around you should get to be normal. You should be able to play with
people, and make jokes back and forth. . . . You should feel you could

settle down and forget about being a sociologist" (p. 129). But sociologists cannot "go native" either, for the same reasons my interviewees gave.

17. Some interviewees spoke of potential value to the natives, especially if the fieldwork had applied to activist aspects.

18. The fieldnotes themselves vary in this regard, of course; informants commented on how fieldnotes contain material that represents several stages of the transformation of observed interaction to written, public communication: "raw" data, ideas that are marinating, and fairly done-to-a-turn diagrams and genealogical charts to be used in appendices in a thesis or book.

19. Crapanzano (1977) might agree that because fieldnotes are between the "reality" perceived in the field and a published ethnography they are also a mediator between the ethnographer as deconstituted self in the field and reconstituted self acquired through writing an ethnography, which will " 'free' him to be a professional again" (p. 71): "The writing of ethnography is an attempt to put a full-stop to the ethnographic confrontation" (p. 70).

20. Freilich (1990) notes that

the sparsity of writings on anthropological field methods and field experiences is explained by . . . the "rewards" field workers receive for keeping their errors and their personalities hidden and for maintaining a romantic attachment to the fieldwork mystique. (p. 36)

Note that this statement preceded the explosion of writings about fieldwork beginning in the mid-1970s. Also see Geertz (1988) on "the oddity of constructing texts ostensibly scientific out of experiences broadly biographical" (p. 10).

21. A reminder: The meaning of some of these statements depends on a specific definition of fieldnotes; definitions varied substantially among the interviewees.

22. "Even experimental ethnographies which are self-conscious accounts of the evolving process of understanding in the field, must also in some sense BE an understanding of another cultural form, to qualify as ethnography" (Kondo, 1982, 6).

23. I would argue that this is a crucial distinction between what stereotypical sociology and stereotypical anthropology would bring to the same fieldwork situation—regardless of where it occurs and the social scientific goals of the research.

24. Joking and avoidance behavior are frequently encountered ways of dealing with conflicting, difficult relationships and subjects of conversation.

25. Compare Crapanzano's (1977) comment that "indeed, the 'movement' of fieldwork can be seen as a movement of self-dissolution and reconstitution" (p. 70).

26. See Crapanzano (1987): "For Kondo, as for many anthropologists, fieldwork becomes a sort of Faustian voyage of discovery, of descent and return" (p. 181). Also see Jackson (1990).

27. See Bowen (1964, 4) on advice about cheap tennis shoes.

28. We are talking about the stereotypical fieldwork situation, which has not represented the majority of fieldwork situations for quite some time (see Pelto and Pelto 1973) and is much less representative today.

References

Babcock, B. A., ed. 1978. *The reversible world: Symbolic inversion in art and society.* Ithaca, NY: Cornell University Press.

Bowen, E. S. 1964. *Return to laughter: An anthropological novel.* New York: Doubleday.

Clifford, J. 1988. *The predicament of culture: Twentieth-century ethnography, literature, and art.* Cambridge, MA: Harvard University Press.

Crapanzano, V. 1977. On the writing of ethnography. *Dialectical Anthropology* 2 (1): 69-73.

Crocker, J. C. 1973. Ritual and the development of social structure: Liminality and inversion. In *The roots of ritual,* edited by J. D. Shaughnessy, 47-86. Grand Rapids, MI: William Eerdmans.

Douglas, M. 1966. *Purity and danger.* Harmondsworth, England: Penguin.

Freilich, M., ed. 1970. *Marginal natives: Anthropologists at work.* New York: Harper & Row.

Geertz, C. 1988. *Works and lives: The anthropologist as author.* Stanford, CA: Stanford University Press.

Gluckman, M. 1963. Rituals of rebellion in south east Africa. In *Order and rebellion in tribal Africa,* edited by M. Gluckman, 110-37. London: Cohen & West.

Goffman, E. 1989. On fieldwork. Transcribed and edited by Lyn H. Lofland. *Journal of Contemporary Ethnography* 18 (2): 123-32.

Jackson, J. E. 1986. On trying to be an Amazon. In *Self, sex, and gender in cross-cultural fieldwork,* edited by T. L. Whitehead and M. E. Conaway. Urbana: University of Illinois Press.

Jackson, J. E. 1990. "I am a fieldnote": Fieldnotes as symbol of professional identity. In *Fieldnotes: The makings of anthropology,* edited by R. Sanjek, 3-33. Ithaca, NY: Cornell University Press.

Kirshner, S. R. 1987. "Then what have I to do with thee": On identity, fieldwork, and ethnographic knowledge. *Cultural Anthropology* 1 (2): 211-34.

Kondo, D. K. 1982. Inside and outside: The fieldworker as conceptual anomaly. Paper presented at the annual meeting of the American Anthropological Association, Washington, DC.

Malinowski, B. 1967. *A diary in the strict sense of the term.* London: Routledge & Kegan Paul.

Marcus, G., and R. Cushman. 1982. Ethnographies as texts. *Annual Review of Anthropology* 11:25-69.

Marcus, G., and M. Fischer. 1986. *Anthropology as cultural critique: An experimental moment in the human sciences.* Chicago: Chicago University Press.

Morris, B. 1987. *Anthropological studies of religion: An introductory text.* Cambridge: Cambridge University Press.

Ottenberg, S. 1990. Thirty years of fieldnotes: Changing relationships to the text. In *Fieldnotes: The makings of anthropology,* edited by R. Sanjek, 139-60. Ithaca, NY: Cornell University Press.

Pelto, P., and G. H. Pelto. 1973. Ethnography: The fieldwork enterprise. In *Handbook of social and cultural anthropology,* edited by J. J. Honigmann. Chicago: Rand McNally.

Podolefsky, A. 1987. New tools for old jobs: Computers in the analysis of fieldnotes. *Anthropology Today* 3 (5): 14-16.

Pratt, M. L. 1986. Fieldwork in common places. In *Writing culture: The poetics and politics of ethnography,* edited by J. Clifford and G. Marcus, 27-50. Berkeley: University of California Press.

Rabinow, P. 1977. *Reflections of fieldwork in Morocco.* Berkeley: University of California Press.

Turner, V. 1967. Betwixt and between. In *The forest of symbols: Aspects of Ndembu ritual,* edited by V. Turner, 93-111. Ithaca, NY: Cornell University Press.

Turner, V. 1974. *The ritual process.* Harmondsworth, England: Penguin.

Turner, V. 1985. *On the edge of the bush: Anthropology as experience.* Edited by E. L. B. Turner. Tucson: University of Arizona Press.

Van Maanen, J. 1988. *Tales of the field: On writing ethnography.* Chicago: University of Chicago Press.

Weidman, H. H. 1970. On ambivalence in the field. In *Women in the field,* edited by P. Golde. Chicago: Aldine.

3

Making a Study
"More Ethnographic"

◩

HARRY F. WOLCOTT

hy ethnography has gained widespread acceptance among social researchers to become the label of choice for much of the qualitative/descriptive work currently being reported remains something of a mystery. Whether ethnography is the appropriate label for some of this work is even more questionable. Nevertheless, the times are right for encouraging an ever widening circle of interested researchers to inform themselves about, and become more discerning toward, things ethnographic.

AUTHOR'S NOTE: This chapter was originally drafted as part of a monograph on *Writing Up Qualitative Research* prepared for the Qualitative Research Methods Series published by Sage. The monograph was growing too large, and the focus a bit too ethnographic, when the editor of that series, who is also editor of this volume, suggested rewriting the material as a separate article. In its early drafts, the material benefitted from critical readings of colleagues and students. In its present form, it benefitted from the careful reading of Philip D. Young and the careful editing of John Van Maanen.

My purpose here is to raise questions about how studies "become" ethnographic, how a "slightly" ethnographic study might become more so, and how to assess whether making a study "more ethnographic" seems an appropriate course to follow. Growing interest in ethnography outside its original arenas of practice may account, in part, for a newly awakened self-consciousness among producers and consumers of ethnography alike. Producer or consumer, if you employ terms like semiotics, poststructuralism, deconstructionist hermeneutics, and critical or postmodern ethnography in an informed way—and individually, rather than in the safety of a list as I have done here—then you are keeping up with current debate. I hope you include traditional ethnographies as well as recent critique in your canvass so that you are as well-tuned to what has been accomplished in the past as you are alerted to possible directions and adaptations we may see in the future. My focus here is on the former: ethnography past and present.

The audience I presume to address includes anyone who has neither studied nor worked in an "ethnographic tradition" but feels drawn to it and wonders how (and perhaps whether) ethnography can be achieved in modest increments instead of requiring the full-time commitment of a cultural anthropologist or close disciplinary ally. How does qualitative, descriptive, or naturalistic research, broadly conceived, become "ethnographic," and how do qualitative researchers become ethnographers?

Although ethnography provides my example, underlying issues about research approaches and strategies are of concern to qualitative researchers of all persuasions, not just to ethnographers, would-be ethnographers, and shouldn't-be ethnographers. What are the risks and benefits of keeping one's focus as broad as possible for as long as possible while conducting a field study? How do disciplinary traditions function to set our research problems, shape the course of our fieldwork and presentations, and provide a cloak of legitimacy for our endeavors? Returning to the case at hand, what are the consequences of labeling a study "ethnographic"? The need to label our studies or identify ourselves as working within particular scholarly traditions is partly self-imposed, partly the result of institutional requirements and academic posturing. While ethnography itself may thrive on its newfound attention, the consequences for individual researchers are not always beneficial. Faulting a study because of an unwarranted claim to be ethnographic may overshadow the fact that, labeling error aside, the research is thorough, informative, and insightful. We might be better off to employ only generic labels such as "case study" or to eliminate labels altogether, at least when their purpose accomplishes little more than academic claims-making. However, as Ward Goodenough observes in *Culture, Language, and Society,* "The human approach to experience is categorical" (Goodenough 1981, 63). What we don't label, others will, leaving us at their mercy. We are better off to supply labels of our own and to be up front about the identifications we seek.

A lesson in claims-making came early in my career in the somewhat ambivalent status I occupy as an educational anthropologist. I pressed a colleague in anthropology (Alfred G. Smith) to look at a paper I had drafted for an educator audience and to render an opinion as to whether it was "good anthropology," worthy of the ethnographic tradition. His immediate reaction was, "You don't really care whether it's 'good anthropology,' do you? What you really want is a good study!"

Given the tone of his reaction (and for the first time fully appreciating what mavericks anthropologists can be), I felt obliged to respond, "Of course I want it to be a good study. Still," I persisted, "I do wonder whether the case as presented and analyzed seems solidly grounded in anthropology."

I doubt that he heard me even then. As requested, however, he agreed to critique my paper, a chapter-length draft based on fieldwork for a study of an elementary school principal. As a result of Smith's reading, the piece probably became less rather than more anthropologically oriented, for I incorporated his provocative suggestion of viewing administrative styles in terms of "variety reducing" and "variety generating" behaviors, notions drawn from his wide-ranging interests in communication and culture, including the then timely topic of general cybernetic systems. Since I could not get him to utter the magic words I longed to hear ("anthropology," "ethnography"), I cautiously subtitled the paper a "field study" (Wolcott 1974) but confidently submitted it for inclusion in George Spindler's edited volume, *Education and Cultural Process: Toward an Anthropology of Education.*

In subsequent years, the question "What makes a study ethnographic?" has been a recurring one, not only among cultural anthropologists but among others anxious to appropriate an "ethnographic approach" for problems closer to home and for settings in which cross-cultural and comparative considerations cannot simply be taken for granted. Let me say something about ethnography from the perspective (or, more accurately, "a" perspective) of anthropology before discussing its applications and appeal for qualitative researchers more generally.

What Distinguishes Ethnography as a Particular Form of Qualitative Research?

Ethnography contributes in its own way to the confusion surrounding it. The term refers both to the *processes* for accomplishing it—ordinarily involving original fieldwork and always requiring the reorganization and editing of material for presentation—and to the presentation itself, the *product* of that research, which ordinarily takes its form in prose. My traditional, conservative, discipline-oriented view (spelled out in more detail in Wolcott 1987) is that the research process deserves the label ethnography only when the intended product is ethnography. Therefore, a claim to be "doing ethnography" is also a proclamation of intent.

In observing fieldworkers in action as they, in turn, observe, participate, conduct interviews, make their audio and visual recordings, or pursue archival research, another observer would not necessarily have the least clue as to which of several individuals working side by side might eventually lay claim to having conducted a journalistic inquiry, a case study, an oral history, or an ethnography. The fieldnotes, interview questions, even the apparent focus of their attention might be remarkably similar, at least in the short run. In order to discern critical differences, we would have to be party both to the researchers' own thought processes and to whatever aspects of their informants' deeds and accounts they were attending most carefully.

Anyone who engages in ethnography also assumes responsibility to participate in the continuing dialogue to define and redefine it both as process and as product. This entails seeking satisfactory ways to explain ethnography to others, including members of the group among whom the fieldworker proposes to study as well as local officials and allied researchers. Because ethnography undergoes the constant buffeting of critical analysis, it can appear not only remarkably adaptable but maddeningly ambiguous, except that *in its discipline of origin* the underlying rationale for doing ethnography is understood to be cultural interpretation. To commit to ethnography traditionally has meant to commit to looking at, and attempting to make sense of, human social behavior in terms of cultural patterning. To pursue ethnography in one's thinking, doing, and reporting is to engage simultaneously in an ongoing intellectual dialogue about what culture is *in general*—and how, paraphrasing Michael Moerman (1988, 56), culture influences without controlling—while attempting to portray specific aspects of the culture of some human group *in particular.*

I am aware of arguments that the culture concept is moribund, but I join others who recognize and defend its heuristic value not only for ethnographers but for social scientists in general (see, e.g., Wuthnow et al. 1984). Yet I concur with Clifford Geertz about the importance of "cutting . . . the culture concept down to size, therefore actually insuring its continued importance rather that undermining it" (Geertz 1973, 4). My understanding of culture as the orienting concept for doing and writing ethnography has been influenced by two statements written a decade apart, the first by Charles Frake in the sixties, the second by Ward Goodenough in the seventies.[1]

Charles Frake has described the ethnographer's task as one of rendering a *theory of cultural behavior* for members of the society under study. He explicitly contrasts the centrality of such theory building with the tendency of uninformed fieldworkers to become preoccupied with recording and recounting events:

> To describe a culture, then, is not to recount the events of a society but to specify what one must know to make those events maximally probable. The problem is not to state what someone did but to specify the conditions under which it is culturally appropriate to anticipate that he, or persons occupying his role, will render an equivalent performance. This conception of a cultural description implies that an ethnography should be a theory of cultural behavior in a particular society. (Frake 1964, 112)

From conception to final account, the implications of Frake's statement for the conduct of ethnographic research are enormous. He draws attention away from the gathering of seemingly endless detail—what elsewhere has been dubbed "haphazard descriptiveness" evident in the work of such anthropological luminaries as Malinowski and Margaret Mead (noted in Marcus and Fischer 1986, 56)—to address the analytical sense-and- meaning-making taken by many to be the essence of cultural interpretation.

Let me provide an example of "haphazard descriptiveness" drawn from a qualitative study describing the work and role of secondary school headteachers in Great Britain that I was asked to review. I hope the authors forgive my taking them to task once again by focusing on a single paragraph of text that displays their considerable talents as observers but raises the critical issue of purpose. I do not recall a comparable brief passage that better illustrates what I take to be descriptiveness gone awry for any researcher who forgets even for a moment that facts cannot speak for themselves. The quotation is drawn from a discussion of how the four headteachers who were the focus of the study dealt with everyday routines:

> Mr. King rarely took work home. Mr. Dowe loaded his attache case every evening, and accounted for most of his evening work as being related to his examining or on the phone—mostly to parents or his deputy. Mr. Shaw always took work home. Mr. Mercer took work home mainly at the weekends. (Hall, Mackay, and Morgan 1986, 118)

In a richly contextualized case study, as I noted in my review (Wolcott 1988), any one of these idiosyncratic styles might be described in far greater detail, for not only would we recognize individuals constructing their own work patterns, priorities, and preferences, we also should acquire a sense of how a multitude of discrete behaviors fit together in some integrated way. Reporting four diverse ways of handling the problem of what and how work gets done does not give us four times as much insight; rather, it raises the question of why we need to know any of this. A well-intended effort at thoroughness serves instead to distract researcher and reader alike from seeking out systematic relationships among the ways that different headteachers define and execute their assigned role.

Frake's words provide the underlying rationale for capturing and reporting detail in an ethnographic presentation: not to recount events, as such, but to render a theory of cultural behavior. Goodenough addresses the issue of where and how the artifacts and behaviors that observers observe and record are transformed into culture. Culture is not "there," waiting demurely to be discovered. Instead, culture—an explicit conceptual orientation that provides the purpose and rationale for doing ethnography—gets there because *the ethnographer puts it there*. Culture is an abstraction based on the ethnographer's observations of actual behavior, coupled with insights and explanations of the order "That is our way," "We've always done it like that," or "If that happened, I guess my reaction would be . . . ." Attempting to pull all that together into some comprehensive (although not necessarily logical—human behavior isn't all that logical) blueprint, or archetype, or "code," or set of implicit "rules" or "standards" for behavior—is the assignment ethnographers define for themselves.

Goodenough has described the ethnographer's task as *attributing* culture to the group being studied:

> The culture of any society is made up of the concepts, beliefs, and principles of action and organization that an ethnographer has found could be attributed successfully to the members of that society in the context of his dealings with them. (Goodenough 1976, 5)

Hardly a coincidence, then, that ethnographers invariably "discover" culture. Rather than looking to see whether culture is "there," they seek out confirming evidence to support the assumption they accept as fact. Culture is imposed, not observed, and there is no ethnography until culture makes an entry, no matter how tenuously. Ethnographers do tend to be cautious in their statements about culture. They do not bandy the term about or attribute mysterious powers to it, more often referring to their work as cultural *interpretation* rather than cultural *explanation*. Geertz notes a necessary tentativeness to all cultural description, a sense of having accepted an assignment destined to remain elusively beyond reach:

> Cultural analysis is intrinsically incomplete. And, worse than that, the more deeply it goes the less complete it is. It is a strange science whose most telling assertions are its most tremulously based, in which to get somewhere with the matter at hand is to intensify the suspicion, both your own and that of others, that you are not quite getting it right. (Geertz 1973, 29)

The details recorded in ethnographically oriented fieldwork fall into convenient *etic* categories that have evolved in standard conventions of reporting (e.g., economic organization, social organization, social control, technology and cultural ecology, political organization) or can be presented in more *emic* fashion through informants' own words. But somewhere in their accounts, ethnographers eventually tip their hands as they begin weaving the descriptive strands together to speculate how the members of some particular group organize their lives to manage everyday routines, communicate what they know and what they expect of others, and cope with forces within and beyond their control.

This "ethnographic presence" may reveal itself in the structure implicit in the organization of the account or in the selection of illustrative detail. It may be addressed boldly in the effort to discern cultural themes, patterns, or configurations. Or, it may become evident as the ethnographer broaches topics such as a group's projective systems, religion and beliefs, or worldview. Discerning and describing the problems as defined and dealt with by any human group—some shared in common with all humanity, others unique to smaller subsets—are the stuff of ethnography.

Such questions intrigue me. They also orient me, providing a reassuring sense of what I am about, whether actively engaging in fieldwork or reflecting about it at my desk. In a cultural orientation I find the sense of structure I need to guide my research and focus my interpretations. And, broad mandate though it be, ethnographically oriented fieldwork does not insist that I attend to "everything."

I would hardly propose ethnography to be such a good thing that the world needs more of it. That argument is difficult enough to make on behalf of all social research, and ethnography is but a small part of what is being done. Among the vast array of qualitative/descriptive approaches, traditional ethnography is too culture and context oriented, too holistic, and too time-consuming for most purposes. Further, as Kenneth Burke (1935, 70) observed years ago, "A way of seeing is always a way of not seeing." Current debate reminds us that, in our enthusiasm for turning a critical eye on everyone else, we have attended rather little to ethnography's own assumptions and blind sports or considered, for example, the ethnographies we dare not initiate or that simply do not occur to us.

An argument I do make on behalf of ethnography is that, as an approach informed by decades of experience and critical review, it can be salutary *for the researcher.* It can help in explaining one's purposes and approach to others. It

helps orient research in the field. And it guides the transformation of data collected in field experience into the
information of ethnographic presentation, offering the researcher an intellectual filter that highlights what people
attend to in awareness of each other rather than what they
do that is idiosyncratic.

Not every qualitative researcher needs to be doing ethnography. But every qualitative researcher needs some structure or conceptual framework through which to view, record, and interpret social action. That structure may be
derived from a question related to the research setting or
problem, from a well-honed tradition for recasting problems
in terms of established disciplines or practices, or from an
informed blend of new problems and old traditions. There
must be some basis on which we attend to and subsequently
report some things rather than everything. Otherwise, it
does not matter a fig that Mr. King rarely took work home
and Mr. Shaw always did.

I recognize a distinction between being well-versed in a
major tradition and necessarily following its every tenet to
the letter. Not every setting in which ethnographers *might*
have something to contribute deserves such painstaking
effort at cultural interpretation. There is a time and a place
for everything: ethnographers do not have to be holistic,
cross-cultural, and comparative, nor meet ordinary expectations of a year or two in the field, every time they set out
to explore a problem or are asked a question. Ethnography
is not always the answer, even for ethnographers.

Suppose, however, as in my case, that you want not only
to do a "good" study but would like to make a warranted
claim that it *is* ethnography. Perhaps you have been bold
enough to announce your study as ethnographically oriented or have identified "culture" as your locus of concern
(e.g., adolescent culture, nurse culture, organizational culture, changing culture, acquiring cultural competence). To

what extent can you justify or strengthen a claim to be "doing" ethnography? And what are some consequences of making that claim (and commitment) at different stages in the research, especially if not from the outset? Let me begin with a "worst scenario," a virtually completed study over which a researcher belatedly wishes he or she could wave a magic wand: "Poof. Ethnography!" (That might be a good nickname for it. Also easier to spell than *blitzkrieg,* à la Rist 1980.)

Making a *Completed* Account
"More Ethnographic"

Labels are important. One quick and easy way to make a descriptive account appear "more ethnographic" is to tack that label onto your title or subtitle and see if you get away with it. You just might!

As noted, a precedent exists among qualitative researchers for affixing descriptive labels rather indiscriminately, although not necessarily out of mischievousness. The underlying rationale seems to be that "minor" differences among labels are of relatively little consequence compared to critical tasks of conducting solid descriptive studies and gaining acceptance for them (see, e.g., Smith 1979). If calling a study ethnographic helps legitimate or dignify one's research, goes the argument, then by all means do it.

Ironically, Geertz's well-known 1973 essay entitled "Thick Description" provided a "quick description" of ethnography as well. Geertz's purpose in that writing is revealed in his subtitle "Toward an Interpretive Theory of Culture," but it is the short, catchy phrase "thick description" that has lingered to become the critical attribute of ethnography in many minds. When I pressed a graduate student about an implicit distinction she was making between two types of qualitative study, ethnographic versus case study, she explained that to her ethnography implies "more depth—some kind of hard core observation." I am glad to be counted on the side of thick (hard core?) description rather than thin, but by itself thick description offers a thin basis for ethnographic claims-making. Better perhaps to label any study grounded in solid description but lacking the requisite attention to cultural interpretation for just what it is—thick description. If *ethnography* is what you want, go the extra mile. Follow Geertz if his notions of an "interpretive theory of culture" seem appropriate. Follow some alternative "meanings and symbols" approach, or some alternative to it, if they do not.

This confusion between degree (level of detail) and kind (direction one takes with the interpretation) has fostered the mistaken idea that ethnography is achieved by staying on site longer, taking "more complete" notes, or conducting some extra interviews. In danger of being lost is the fact that ethnography is different *in kind* from related approaches like phenomenology, ethnomethodology, or even "participant observer" study. Qualitative research and researchers alike are better served, I firmly believe, when critical distinctions among approaches are recognized and respected rather than allowed to blend into one vast but undifferentiated celebration of the range of human possibility. As more and more researchers in professional and applied fields discover and adapt ethnography to their own problems and purposes, the likelihood that it might someday mean no more than observer-present research looms large.

One way to maintain an awareness of important distinctions among the various research traditions is to keep an eye on those arenas where academic boundary-maintaining issues are raised. Questions about ethnography are aired in the meetings and journals of such organizations as the American Anthropological Association and the Society for

Applied Anthropology. More vigorous debates often occur on interdisciplinary frontiers (such as in the *Anthropology and Education Quarterly, Qualitative Sociology,* or the *Journal of Contemporary Ethnography*) where questions arise over how to define ethnography-in-use or where to situate ethnography within the broad spectrum of qualitative approaches (for discussions of ethnography vis-à-vis other qualitative approaches in applications for *educational* research, see Erickson 1984; Jacob 1987, 1988; Jaeger 1988; Lancy 1993; LeCompte, Milroy, and Preissle 1992; Spindler 1982; Wolcott 1982a).

I believe I myself precipitated a bit of boundary redefining by adding the subtitle "An Ethnography" to *The Man in the Principal's Office* (Wolcott 1973). Originally I did that in response to the question of whether my study was all that ethnographic. I was prepared to claim it as ethnography, although I did not restrict myself to anthropology in my search for relevant analytical concepts. Had I anticipated that the study would serve as a model for a spate of similar studies in years to come, I would have endeavored to make it more ethnographic, as I have explained elsewhere (Wolcott 1982b). My intent at the time was to hold a figurative mirror that would allow educational administrators to look at themselves, following the notion of ethnographers as "silverers" of what Clyde Kluckhohn (1949) called anthropology's *Mirror for Man.* Reviewers nested my study with a new subgenre they called "micro-ethnography" (Basham and DeGroot 1977), to be discussed below.

If, upon completing your study, you believe you have contributed to or expanded the definition of ethnography, albeit in some new and unconventional way, step into the fray, not simply to say so but to say why. If you choose early-draft readers with care, they may help you assess the strength of the case you present for ethnography before you have to make a public declaration. The question of "ethnographicness" also can be raised as a methodological one by the researcher within the pages of a study. Doing so helps foster the dialogue about definitions and purposes. It may also produce some consciousness raising about the claims, the labels, and the sometimes uneasy status surrounding the work and careers of those of us who employ so-called alternative methodologies. As qualitative researchers, we forget that typically we ourselves are perceived as working within a common, unified tradition (or, as often, working in no tradition at all).

Another way to grapple with the ethnographicness of a completed study is to invite someone else to address that question for you, perhaps in a foreword or introduction. That has become standard practice in series heralded as ethnographic in the burgeoning field of educational research. If you entertain doubts or do not want your work to be judged *solely* on its merits as ethnography, you are better off letting someone else tout it as such.

On the other hand, neither anthropologists nor sociologists have been all that protective of their field-oriented approaches. Many have seen and seized the opportunity to encourage colleagues in other fields to pose their research problems in a broader context that captures more of the complexity of human life. Further, the sometimes offhand definitions of ethnography are not always helpful for those seeking authoritative proclamation, such as the too casual observation that ethnography is what (social) anthropologists do (Geertz 1973, 5), or, looser still, "any written report that is based on fieldwork" (Werner and Schoepfle 1987b, 42, and attributed to Robert Launay).

The bottom line on post hoc labeling seems to be this. In the wave of excitement surrounding qualitative/descriptive approaches, studies are being labeled ethnography on the basis of the depth of the reporting rather than the nature of the interpretation. That studies are passed off as ethnographies attests to the aura currently surrounding the term and its implied assurance that fieldwork has been conducted "in depth," although the label *thick description* would convey that message more modestly and more accurately. If the data or the research problem cry for cultural interpretation, then offering it—or at least pointing the reader in that direction—stakes a more legitimate claim to ethnography. If the bias toward ethnography is more a function of researcher enthusiasm than the nature of the interpretation, maybe that's a clue to the kind of approach to follow next time.

Making an Account "More Ethnographic" During Analysis and Write-Up

Much better if you decide to make a study "more ethnographic" while the analysis is in progress. Although not particularly *efficient* (think how an even earlier decision would have helped focus fieldwork as well as deskwork!), there *may* be opportunity to infuse a study with a strong ethnographic orientation while analysis and writing are still under way. Regardless of potential, an account does not take shape as ethnography (or criticism, or history, etc.), until the processes of analyzing and writing are in motion. In whatever transformation researchers make of their data, what has been observed of everyday life is recast into an account that sacrifices *most* of those data in order to feature *some* data with untoward attention. To the extent your fieldwork has focused on the contextual variables with which ethnographers are ordinarily concerned, the account based on that fieldwork can assume an ethnography orientation. If you have been preoccupied with a survey or questionnaire, it probably cannot.

Presumably, an unanticipated pull toward cultural interpretation (or any other recognized tradition) reflects a researcher's own self-conscious search (*re*-search?) for relevant ways to conceptualize and report data already collected. As John Van Maanen noted in correspondence about this topic, although most fieldworkers gather good data, few produce good ethnographies. If that is true, we should concern ourselves not with promoting better fieldwork but with fostering a clearer understanding of ethnography itself and how successful ethnographers derive ethnography from the fieldwork experience.

If you are at a loss for how to orient your analysis in an ethnographic vein, try slipping the adjective "cultural" into your every thought and most of your sentences: *cultural* barriers, *cultural* context, *cultural* setting, *cultural* (or *culturally appropriate*) behavior. The phrases you generate may not always make sense, but the exercise will keep your commitment to cultural interpretation paramount in your thinking. I also suggest that you use only the adjective form "cultural" and avoid the habit of making vague, unspecified references to "culture." There is a tendency to assign mystical explanatory power to culture whenever it gets separated from its locus of practice among individuals (e.g., "That is part of their culture" or "Their culture requires them to . . ."). Whenever I find individual students becoming overly dependent on the term culture I urge them to excise it in every instance where it appears in their writing and to replace it with another word or phrase that points more precisely to what they mean.

Because ethnography is inherently cross-cultural and comparative, another way to enhance ethnographicness is to draw on the comparative literature relevant to a problem or setting. In a study of directed social change, for example —a problem of seeming interest for practitioners in every professional field—it may be useful to examine how anthropologists have interpreted change processes studied in other settings and to ask whether something comparable may be occurring in the case under analysis. Of course, anyone may draw on anthropological perspectives without such self-conscious efforts to rub shoulders with ethnographers. Outside the discipline of anthropology, ethnography as method seems to receive too much attention and the content of the ethnographic literature too little. It is always disconcerting to find accounts written by "gonzo ethnographers" (as one student called them) whose citation lists suggest that they are totally oblivious to prior reported fieldwork.

Enhancing one's *own* understanding of how social science works or simply wanting to engage in fieldwork for its own sake is often an important corollary to other research objectives. After presenting a broadly descriptive account, a researcher might propose, in a parallel set of interpretive sections or chapters, an analysis and interpretation consistent with each of several disciplines or traditions. The result would be a sort of *Rashomon* effect, to borrow the title of the Japanese film classic in which viewers witness an event through the eyes of different parties to the scene. We do not ordinarily develop interpretations along more than one disciplinary path (consistent with our own traditions in academia), but a recognition of multiple interpretations is a reminder that we *impose* our analytical structures upon the social world we endeavor to describe. There is nothing to prevent a would-be ethnographer from presenting a descriptive account and then posing—and pursuing—the question "Now, what sense might an ethnographer make of all this?"

If the fieldwork is substantially completed, however, and cultural interpretation is a latecomer onto the scene, the researcher's options cannot help but be narrowed simply because data are no longer available to provide what Geertz (1973, 23) refers to as the "complex specificness" that characterizes good ethnography. You cannot do an anthropological life history if you have not been working with an informant. You cannot build an emic account of "meanings" for people in a setting unless you have been interviewing to learn how insiders view their world. You cannot proceed with conversational analysis if you have not been recording natural conversation. Nor need you lament that your mistake was in failing to record everything. You cannot get it all. You will do well to get enough of the "right stuff" even *after* you decide what the right stuff is.

If you are well along with your fieldwork before making a decision about a framework for analysis, an alternative to slapping on the label "ethnography" as afterthought is to proceed with the interpretation on the same intuitive basis that guided you thus far. That could free you to discuss how a more rigorously informed and discipline-oriented approach *might* have proceeded, without having to lay claim to offer it. If you believe in your capability as an intuitive observer, you may take a certain delight in identifying possible blinders that a strict adherence to tradition might have imposed. But do not boast of an "atheoretical" approach that has allowed you to achieve greater objectivity, or tout your eclecticism as evidence of being "open to everything." Without some idea of what you were up to, you never could have set out for your research site in the first place or known what to look at once there. A saying attributed to William James and noted in Michael Agar's helpful introduction to ethnography, *The Professional Stranger,* captures the underlying point: you can't even pick up rocks in a field without a theory (Agar 1980, 23).

Some eminent qualitative researchers work on a highly intuitive basis, and all research depends on intuition to a greater extent than anyone ever seems to acknowledge. I hope there always will be brave souls willing to come forward and state the case for intuition. Remain ever mindful, however, that data never speak to anyone, not even the most intuitive of researchers. Whatever sense is to be made is made because some human observer attempts to make that sense. Those who do it convincingly get published; those who appear to make the most sense receive the most attention—although, in time, that attention invariably gets redirected to demonstrating how and why they went astray. (Posthumously, Margaret Mead has caught a lot of flak, but there are indications [e.g., Feinberg 1988] that she will not have to continue to take the rap for us all.)

Making an Account
"More Ethnographic" During Fieldwork

What does an ethnographic orientation look like when the decision is made sufficiently early to shape not only the analysis but the fieldwork as well? How can a neophyte researcher decide whether ethnography is an appropriate strategy?

The question of a research approach does not mean identifying *the* approach to a problem. As George Homans observed more than four decades ago, "People who write about methodology often forget that it is a matter of strategy, not of morals" (Homans 1949, 330, cited in Smith 1979, 317). But, you are a remarkable strategist indeed if you can confidently, competently, and committedly exercise even a few of the options from the vast array of techniques employed by all ethnographers. Any choice of strategy entails not only an assessment of what you are going to study but a realistic appraisal of your capabilities and limitations for studying it. And clearly your interpersonal skills as a field researcher are critical if you accept the idea of *yourself* as your most sensitive and important instrument.

Each individual's range of strategy options is narrowed further by countless external factors that we take for granted. Everything from prior decisions about the institutions you attended, the classes you selected, the research problems that interest you, and the kinds of people whom you have chosen (consciously or not) for role models as researchers and professional associates influence the course you are setting. Economists, law professors, and exercise physiologists are not big producers of ethnography; historians and ethnographers don't conduct many experiments.

If you happen to be pursuing graduate study in cultural anthropology, for example, odds are you've already thought a great deal about *where,* but the question of *whether* to do an ethnographic study may never have occurred to you. If your graduate training has included a strong dose of quantitative methods, offered with disdain for "softer" approaches, your research problem will probably prove amenable to statistical treatment unless you deliberately (even daringly?) rebel in order to pursue an "alternative" strategy. Alas, alternative strategies may not prove realistic, for you may find yourself stymied not only by a lack of training but by the absence of a support group among students or faculty. *Not* liking statistics and *not* being interested in experimental design are hardly adequate as a foundation on which to base a qualitative study, and one's dissertation is not the place to reeducate faculty.

Time, money, nature of the research problem, expectations as to what should result from your work—all kinds of external constraints influence the extent to which ethnography is a realistic alternative. Further, ethnography is time-consuming and, for the time invested, a low-yield research approach, well-suited to some scholarly careers but rather too broadly focused for the targeted questions often posed in funded research or "quickie" dissertations.

Another problem already noted is lack of familiarity with the ethnographic literature. I refer not only to the recent outpourings dealing self-consciously with ethnographic research but also with published ethnographies, both pre- and postmodern. If your attraction to ethnography is based more on enthusiasm than information, exhibit restraint in your claims. Describe the *specific ethnographic techniques* you intend to employ and refrain from an untutored claim that you will be "doing ethnography." Eventually you may want to make that claim, but if there is any tentativeness, approach fieldwork with ethnography as a potential outcome, not a promise. (That might be nicknamed "Perhaps Ethnography.")

Most certainly there are advantages if you are able to set ethnography as your goal from the outset of your research, not the least of which is the opportunity to reflect on the crucial issue of whether you have focused on a crucial issue. Ethnographers are remarkable in their openness to openness, their insistence on pondering what the important questions *are* rather than becoming preoccupied too early with highly manageable but sometimes monumentally inconsequential topics. Qualitative research often earns a measure of approval from otherwise dyed-in-the-wool psychometricians because of its hypothesis-generating capacity, which, they concede, can be invaluable in early stages of problem definition, leaving the serious business of confirmation for their more systematic approaches.

Quite right: descriptive study can make an important contribution through assessing whether questions are properly posed or address relevant and significant issues. It is unfortunate, however, to view qualitative research *only* as a precursor or auxiliary to quantitative research rather than to recognize the contribution each has to offer. One characteristic suggested for distinguishing between them is to regard qualitative methods as "procedures for counting to one" that address the underlying *interpretive* issue "where meanings rather than frequencies assume paramount significance" (Van Maanen, Manning, and Miller 1986, 5). What counts as a unit of analysis is the critical question in qualitative research.

That is not to set qualitative and quantitative approaches in opposition, however. Studies are only *relatively* more qualitatively or quantitatively oriented, not exclusively one or the other. A precondition for every quantitative study is a qualitative judgment about what is to count (i.e., be studied), and, as the old saw goes, even the most resolute of qualitative researchers have been known to number their pages.

From the outside looking in, ethnography may present a seductive appeal as a go/no-go decision that, once made, puts an entire research program neatly into place. Quite the opposite is true: ethnography is only a broad prescription for research. Another advantage of an early decision, therefore, is that in the problem-setting and early fieldwork stages the researcher has ample time for exploring and selecting *within* ethnography's spectrum of possibilities.

One such alternative, in an approach never self-conscious about small *N*s, is to work with key informants and as few as one. An informant's account may serve not only as a critical data source but also provides the structure for organizing the research as an anthropological life history (described in Langness and Frank 1981; Watson and Watson-Franke 1985). The search for a key informant must begin early, although that is not to say the first person who happens along is suited for the role. On the other hand, failure to identify such an individual, or early recognition that a life history approach may be inappropriate (problems with confidentiality, status conflicts within the community, etc.), needs to be recognized and resolved early on while time remains for pursuing an alternative or modified approach.

One might, for example, collect and report several brief case histories instead of one life history reported in depth or create composite characters who exhibit observed behavior without pointing to particular individuals.

Another way to present an ethnographically oriented account—one seen increasingly in educational research—is through microethnography (also known as focused or specific ethnography). Microethnography zeroes in on *particular* settings (cultural events or "scenes," as Frake 1964 refers to them at p. 112), drawing on the ways that a cultural ethos is reflected in microcosm in selected aspects of everyday life but giving emphasis to particular behaviors in particular settings rather than attempting to portray a whole cultural system.

My impression is that microethnography has more appeal for hybrid and hyphenated ethnographers than for the "pure" types. Researchers in professional and applied fields typically work under constraints of time and scope. The prefix *micro* recognizes necessary accommodation to such limits through narrowed focus and manageable objectives. Anthropologists themselves are inclined toward studies that might be labeled "macroethnography," although we do not ordinarily hear that cumbersome phrase. To the anthropologist, the prefix "micro" may imply something inadequately attended to—perhaps even a contradiction in terms for scholars accustomed to exploring broad categories like worldview or cultural themes.

Frankly, I was not overjoyed to have *Man in the Principal's Office* cited as an example of microethnography in an essay review that appeared in the *American Anthropologist,* although my feelings were assuaged when reviewers proceeded to describe it as "urban microethnography at its best" (Basham and DeGroot 1977, 428). I never regarded my work as a "micro" study at the time. Yet the account is not "macro" and not community study; it is too focused to warrant those labels. Microethnography will have to do. Now that I have learned to live with it, I boldly suggest that it might prove a satisfactory orientation, goal, and label for others.

An early narrowing of choices among ethnographic possibilities for organizing and writing an account has implications both for how fieldwork is to proceed and how the data—and the researcher's experience gathering that data —will be reorganized, reduced, and relayed. Think how differently one proceeds in following a *life history* approach, including such variations as life cycle, rites of passage, or everyday events; or pursuing the focused study of *microethnography;* or attempting the broad cultural description of *traditional* (macro) *ethnography.*

Nor should we overlook that for anyone except perhaps professional ethnographers—and under some circumstances even for them—the underlying question of whether ethnography is appropriate for a particular set of circumstances also ought to remain under review. Ethnography isn't the only scholarly work anthropologists do. Central as ethnography is, as the field arm of cultural anthropology, not every cultural anthropologist does it well, and some do not attempt it at all. Thus another advantage of giving early and serious thought to "doing" ethnography is that, on reflection, ethnography may *not* be a workable strategy, may *not* be appropriate, and may *not* be feasible. On the other hand, ethnography is *invariably* inefficient and time-consuming, a roundabout way to obtain needed information if the nature of what is to be ascertained can be specified in advance. Ethnography aptly defines the ambitious goal of describing a group's "culture." It also describes more modest goals, such as exploring the range and variation of social behaviors in a particular setting or presenting highly contextualized cases. It is a dumb way to conduct a survey, census, or opinion poll. It is not intended as a manipulative way to do anything.

The better focused the problem in problem-oriented research, the less likely ethnography may prove an appropriate strategy for pursuing it. The legendary ethnographic broadsides of the past (e.g., Evans-Pritchard's 1940 *The Nuer,* which has also been catching flak recently) are giving way to so-called systematic procedures found not only outside cultural anthropology but within it (e.g., Bernard 1988; Spradley 1979; Werner and Schoepfle 1987a). Ethnography is more ambitious than seems warranted for topics both too modest and too broad in scope. Practically speaking, there ought to be more compelling reasons for anyone to engage in a long-term, traditionally oriented ethnography than the appeal of the label.

The earlier that possible options can be narrowed to plausible ones, and priorities set among those, the more effective the data collection, the more efficient the progressive focusing, and the sooner a tentative structure can be proposed and the initial writing begun. True, little may be lost in holding open the *possibility* of doing a traditional ethnography, but fieldwork is inefficient enough without collecting additional data simply because one is there.

One of the least commendable practices of the early ethnographers was their self-defined obligation to try to record everything—everything their fellow ethnographers were recording, that is—not only customs and language but Rorschach protocols, skin color, hair types, and even cranial circumferences. Today's ethnographers do not always recognize that modern technology invites a comparable dilemma with fast film speeds, easy-to-use audio and video recorders, and laptop computers for quicker and thus more comprehensive note-making. Neophyte fieldworkers still approach their sites grimly determined to "record everything." Although such determination does not assure their accounts will be ethnographic, it can raise doubts whether they will be completed at all. Paradoxically, a complementary chapter to this one, "Making a Study *Less* Ethnographic," would probably prove helpful to all but the most seasoned of ethnographers still inclined to cover their bases by recording (and reporting) far more than they need, "just in case."

Making a Study
"More Ethnographic" From Inception

Scientific method (and George Homans) to the contrary, approaches can and do go looking for problems. Our research talents and skills are never so extensive that we have more than a handful of ways to address a problem. Most researchers, ethnographers included, work within variations on a single theme. It is hardly a coincidence that the problems I address invariably "call" not only for ethnography but for ethnography in the very way I have come to understand and practice it. (Anthropologically trained or not, we are *all* self-styled ethnographers. There is no other kind.)

Let me conclude with a personal instance in which my ever ready ethnographic approach led the way to the study of the elementary school principalship mentioned earlier. I initiated that project in 1966. Prior to any consideration of focus, I had resolved to employ an ethnographic approach in conducting school-based research. My first step was to define a problem in such a way that ethnography was the answer. For career purposes, I needed to validate myself—among anthropologists and educational researchers alike—as an anthropologically oriented researcher. Although my Ph.D. program, completed at Stanford University two years earlier, included a formal minor in cultural anthropology and two years of cross- cultural fieldwork and writing, my doctorate was earned in education, leaving me with anthropologically "thin" credentials that needed bolstering through further ethnographic research. Among my cohort of doctoral students in education, virtually all of whom were trained in and committed to experimental or quasi-experimental design, there was some question whether I was a researcher at all. In their eyes (and the jargon of the day), my dissertation proposal merely required that I "go off for a year to live with the Indians."

My initial postdoctoral appointment, also in 1964, was as Research Associate in one of the new research and development centers funded by the U.S. Office of Education. The mission of the University of Oregon's center was educational administration (thus CASEA, the Center for the Advanced Study of Educational Administration, under whose auspices I conducted the work). Anthropological kit-bag figuratively in hand, I proposed an ethnographic inquiry into the day-to-day life and work of an educational administrator. Specifically, I intended to follow one elementary school principal through a year of his (most principals were male) professional activities. My approach was literally to regard and observe him "as though he were an Indian chief."

I was revising my dissertation for publication at the time and was becoming increasingly aware of the role Chief Henry Bell had played in my life at, and my understanding of, the tiny village on the Northwest Coast of British Columbia described in *A Kwakiutl Village and School* (Wolcott 1967). I proposed studying how one goes about "being" a principal the same way I would have gone about learning more about—and from—Henry had he, rather than the village school and children, been the focus of my inquiry.

My formal rationale (not to be confused with my real reason) for proposing an ethnographic study was that the literature in educational administration is essentially hortatory, telling principals what they ought to do. What they actually do had received little attention.

Heralding the study as "ethnographic" immediately raised questions—in those days any nonquantifiable procedure was suspect in educational research—but my forthright tactic helped. My commitment was exactly that: a determination to *demonstrate* the contribution of an ethnographic approach. For all the concern about method, always a major preoccupation among educational researchers, it may be of interest to note that I was never pressed for the content of what I expected to find, only for the generalizability of my findings: "What can we learn from a study of just *one* principal?" (It took two decades for me to recognize the obvious answer: All we can!)

Describing the study as ethnography from its inception provided an opportunity to explain what ethnography is, to outline what I hoped to achieve, and to secure approval and sponsorship for a "new" approach. I wanted it clear that I was allying myself not only with *interdisciplinary* inquiry (which was "in" during the 1960s) but with a *particular* discipline, a *particular* approach, a *particular* body of concepts and literature. For anyone able to distinguish between archaeology and cultural anthropology, my brief explanations often produced the response, "Oh, sorta like Margaret Mead, eh?" A challenge was created that continues to this day to find ways to describe and define ethnography and to continue to adapt for contemporary settings in modern societies a research tradition developed for long and typically solo encounters among small groups of people with "exotic" customs.

In Conclusion

Defined as "What cultural anthropologists do," ethnography virtually falls into the lap of the anthropologist and, by the same definition, might conveniently exclude everyone else. But neither anthropologists nor field-oriented (Chicago School) sociologists have been all that covetous toward ethnography. The label, the fieldwork approach, and ethnography itself continue to command greater interest among qualitative researchers and greater respect among researchers in general. I trust you realize that not all qualitative researchers concur with the position expressed here that a genuinely ethnographic approach provides both a sense of structure for conducting fieldwork and a commitment to cultural interpretation. But I hold that ethnography promises more than "being there," "thick description," or "case study" broadly defined. Like culture itself (and again paraphrasing Moerman 1988, 56), an ethnographic approach should also "influence without controlling." We can rightly expect to see evidence of that cultural influence if the finished product is labeled ethnography. Qualitative researchers need not have ethnography in mind as they embark on descriptive/interpretive studies, but they must have *something* in mind to guide their work, whether a well-established fieldwork tradition, a strong conceptual orientation, or a trustworthy sense of intuition.

Ethnographers concern themselves with cultural interpretation. If cultural interpretation adequately conveys the underlying purpose of your research, then the earlier you recognize and orient your focus, the more ethnographic the study that ought to result, the more satisfying the outcome, and the more appropriately the research problem can be set. If cultural analysis is not your goal, then ethnography is a misnomer, although you may draw upon ethnographic *techniques* in conducting your fieldwork and you can claim with impunity to be doing exactly that. But the opportunity is there, not only for borrowing field techniques but for making studies more genuinely ethnographic by attending to what ethnographers have traditionally attended to, even under remarkably nontraditional circumstances.

Note

1. I recognize that more than another decade has passed and further increments in my understanding may be overdue. Currently, I am attracted to a constructionist perspective (e.g., Handwerker 1989; Peacock 1986) in which culture is viewed as dynamically constructed and individually negotiated. Recent dialog addressing underlying conceptions of culture and the persona and role of the ethnographer has been lively, but my sense is that fieldwork practice itself remains little changed. Nor is fieldwork itself where ethnography "happens," the underlying point of this chapter.

References

Agar, M. H. 1980. *The professional stranger: An informal introduction to ethnography.* New York: Academic Press.

Basham, R., and D. DeGroot. 1977. Current approaches to the anthropology of urban and complex societies [Essay review]. *American Anthropologist* 79:414-40.

Bernard, H. R. 1988. *Research methods in cultural anthropology.* Newbury Park, CA: Sage.

Burke, K. 1935. *Permanence and change.* New York: New Republic.

Erickson, F. 1984. What makes school ethnography "ethnographic"? *Anthropology and Education Quarterly* 15 (1): 51-66.

Evans-Pritchard, E. E. 1940. *The Nuer: A description of the modes of livelihood and political institutions of a Nilotic people.* London: Oxford University Press.

Feinberg, R. 1988. Margaret Mead and Samoa: *Coming of Age* in fact and fiction. *American Anthropologist* 90 (3): 656-63.

Frake, C. O. 1964. A structural description of Subanun religious behavior. In *Explorations in cultural anthropology,* edited by W. H. Goodenough, 111-29. New York: McGraw-Hill.

Geertz, C. 1973. Thick description: Toward an interpretive theory of culture. In *The interpretation of cultures,* edited by C. Geertz, 3-30. New York: Basic Books.

Goodenough, W. H. 1976. Multiculturalism as the normal human experience. *Anthropology and Education Quarterly* 7 (4): 4-7.

————. 1981. *Culture, language, and society.* 2d ed. Menlo Park, CA: Benjamin/Cummings.

Hall, V., H. Mackay, and C. Morgan. 1986. *Headteachers at work.* Milton Keynes, England: Open University Press.

Handwerker, W. P. 1989. The origins and evolution of culture. *American Anthropologist* 91 (2): 313-26.

Homans, G. C. 1949. The strategy of industrial sociology. *American Journal of Sociology* 54 (4): 330-37.

Jacob, E. 1987. Traditions of qualitative research: A review. *Review of Educational Research* 57:1-50.

————. 1988. Clarifying qualitative research: A focus on traditions. *Educational Researcher* 17 (1): 16-24.

Jaeger, R. M., ed. 1988. *Complementary methods for research in education.* Washington, DC: American Educational Research Association.

Kluckhohn, C. 1949. *Mirror for man: The relation of anthropology to modern life.* New York: McGraw-Hill.

Lancy, D. F. 1993. *Qualitative research in education: An introduction to the major traditions.* New York: Longman.

Langness, L. L., and G. Frank. 1981. *Lives: An anthropological approach to biography.* Novato, CA: Chandler & Sharp.

LeCompte, M. D., W. L. Millroy, and J. Preissle, eds. 1992. *The handbook of qualitative research in education.* San Diego: Academic Press.

Marcus, G. E., and M. M. Fischer. 1986. *Anthropology as cultural critique: An experimental moment in the human sciences.* Chicago: University of Chicago Press.

Moerman, M. 1988. *Talking culture: Ethnography and conversation analysis.* Philadelphia: University of Pennsylvania Press.

Peacock, J. L. 1986. *The anthropological lens: Harsh light, soft focus.* New York: Cambridge University Press.

Rist, R. 1980. Blitzkrieg ethnography: On the transformation of a method into a movement. *Educational Researcher* 9 (2): 8-10.

Smith, L. M. 1979. An evolving logic of participant observation, educational ethnography, and other case studies. *Review of Research in Education* 6:316-77.

Spindler, G. D. 1982. General introduction. In *Doing the ethnography of schooling,* edited by G. D. Spindler. New York: Holt, Rinehart & Winston. Reissued 1988 by Waveland Press.

Spradley, J. P. 1979. *The ethnographic interview.* New York: Holt, Rinehart & Winston.

Van Maanen, J., P. K. Manning, and M. M. Miller, eds. 1986. Series introduction. In *Reliability and validity in qualitative research,* by J.

Kirk and M. L. Miller, vol. 1, 5-6. Sage University Paper series on Qualitative Research Methods. Beverly Hills, CA: Sage.

Watson, L., and M. Watson-Franke. 1985. *Interpreting life histories: An anthropological inquiry.* New Brunswick, NJ: Rutgers University Press.

Werner, O., and G. M. Schoepfle. 1987a. *Systematic fieldwork, vol. 1: Foundations of ethnography and interviewing.* Newbury Park, CA: Sage.

Werner, O., and G. M. Schoepfle. 1987b. *Systematic fieldwork, vol. 2: Ethnographic analysis and data management.* Newbury Park, CA: Sage.

Wolcott, H. F. 1967. *A Kwakiutl village and school.* New York: Holt, Rinehart & Winston. Reissued 1989 by Waveland Press with a new afterword.

—————. 1973. *The man in the principal's office: An ethnography.* New York: Holt, Rinehart & Winston. Reissued 1984 by Waveland Press with a new introduction.

—————. 1974. The elementary school principal: Notes from a field study. In *Education and cultural process: Toward an anthropology of education,* edited by G. D. Spindler, 176-204. New York: Holt, Rinehart & Winston.

—————. 1982a. Differing styles of on-site research, or, "If it isn't ethnography, what is it?" *Review Journal of Philosophy and Social Science* 7 (1,2): 154-69.

—————. 1982b. Mirrors, models, and monitors: Educator adaptations of the ethnographic innovation. In *Doing the ethnography of schooling,* edited by G. Spindler, 68-95. New York: Holt, Rinehart & Winston.

—————. 1987. On ethnographic intent. In *Interpretive ethnography of education,* edited by G. Spindler and L. Spindler, 37-57. Hillsdale, NJ: Lawrence Erlbaum.

—————. 1988. Review of *Headteachers at work,* by V. Hall, H. Mackay, and C. Morgan. *International Journal of Qualitative Studies in Education* 1 (4): 371-73.

Wuthnow, R., J. D. Hunter, A. Bergesen, and E. Kurzweil. 1984. *Cultural analysis: The work of Peter L. Berger, Mary Douglas, Michel Foucault, and Jürgen Habermas.* London: Routledge & Kegan Paul.

4

Literary Journalism
as Ethnography

Exploring the Excluded Middle

MICHAEL AGAR

Ethnography is an ambiguous term; it refers both to a research *process* and to a textual *product*. The process/ product link is not unique to ethnography, but seldom does lexical ambiguity so neatly index a fundamental disciplinary problem. Historically, in cultural anthropology, the problem was benign neglect. Both research process and ethnographic text were taken-for-granted aspects of the professional world. Things have changed. First, the process came under self-conscious scrutiny in the 1960s and 1970s, and then the 1980s brought an equally intense concern with the product. The ethnographic text will never again be taken for granted. Conventions of representation of self and other, inclusion of political economic context, genre constraints like the distribution of narrative and descriptive passages—these and other textual issues have been converted from out-of-awareness tradition into matters of conscious debate.

The "new" ethnography—the second "new" I have been through—serves a consciousness-raising function that, in the long run, will benefit the field. But I worry that the text-oriented celebration of the neglected product will cause us to lose sight of the process side. Process and product then stand in danger of loosing the ties that the ambiguity encoded in the first place. They become separate rather than related problems. Van Maanen's (1988) quote (with an embedded Marcus citation) exemplifies the tendency to make the split:

> Ethnography as a written product, then, has a degree of independence (how a culture is portrayed) from the fieldwork on which it is based (how a culture is known). Writing ethnography is office-work or deskwork, not fieldwork. (Marcus 1980, 4)

As an unintended consequence of broken ties between process and product, theories of the text can develop in isolation from the research processes whose results they supposedly represent.

I am not alone in my concern over the split. In his introduction to what is probably the founding volume for the new textual concerns, Clifford wrote,

> Clearly our sharp separation of form from content—and our fetishizing of form—was, and is, contestable. It is a bias that may well be implicit in modernist "textualism." (Clifford and Marcus 1986, 21)

Ironically enough, the book in which this introduction is found offers a comment on the separation of method from text. The cover depicts Steve Tyler taking notes during his fieldwork in India, but the chapters in the book deal with published works. The two activities, writing in the field and writing the book, have something to do with each other, but fieldwriting is by and large ignored.

In this chapter I want to restore both sides of the ambiguity to their proper intimacy. A speedy restoration is critical. First of all, many—not all, but many—of the questions raised in the name of textuality also apply to the research process. Problems of representation of political economy, of selection and display of voices and locales, of ethnography in a fragmented posttraditional world—when one asks if these are textual or field research issues, the answer is "yes" to both.

Second, a focus on text to the exclusion of research process risks the development of twin theories—one for writing and one for research—that are seriously out of sync. Geertz (1988) wrote at the end of a book subtitled "The Anthropologist as Author,"

> It's not clear just what "faction," imaginative writing about real people in real places at real times, exactly comes to beyond a clever coinage; but anthropology is going to have to find out if it is to continue as an intellectual force in contemporary culture. (p. 141)

The recent history of one form of "faction"—known as creative nonfiction—shows what it may come to when fiction form is laid over a "fact oriented" research process. In a moment, that recent history will be described as a case study in process/product discontinuity and the problems it can lead to.

Finally, ethnography—at least my practice of it—has always had a tie between field texts and published text, as the relationship between cover and chapters in the Clifford and Marcus book suggests. At the end of this chapter, I sketch that traditional relationship as a source of ideas for textual awareness integrated with, rather than distinct from, concerns with the research process.

Creative Nonfiction

First, I look at a kindred field to examine the dilemma that occurs when process and product turn problematic. That field, journalism, is another with a history of commitment to "fact" that, in the sixties, moved into experiments with a new textual form—realistic fiction. Whether it is called "new journalism," "literary nonfiction," or "creative nonfiction," the friction caused by the blend of documentary report and fiction form exposed a nerve—credibility. With the exception of Van Maanen (1988, 131-36) creative nonfiction has not been discussed in the ethnographic writing literature. In the spirit of the comparative method, I examine the story of creative nonfiction (CN) as a candidate parable for ethnography's current struggles.

CN is a child of the 1960s, a recent American genre whose initial classics were authored by Tom Wolfe, Truman Capote, and Norman Mailer. Now CN includes numerous articles and books, its own academic critical literature, and practical guides for working writers. The story of how the 1960s produced CN runs something like this: The social order caved in and reality turned into fantasy. Within a couple of years, Martin Luther King had a dream, the Beatles appeared on American TV, the Free Speech Movement began, Kennedy was assassinated, the Student Non-

Violent Coordinating Committee (SNCC) started its voter registration drive in Mississippi, Students for a Democratic Society (SDS) was founded, the Gulf of Tonklin resolution was passed, the citizens of Watts rioted, and LSD worked its way out of the lab. Among other things.

American writers responded in different ways. Journalists—like Tom Wolfe, Gay Talese, and Jimmy Breslin at the New York *Herald Tribune*—looked at the chaotic American scene and chafed against the traditional objective journalistic bit. They worked in an industry where competition for readers was turning cutthroat; a few editors were willing to gamble on new writing styles. People did not want more facts, the writers argued, facts that were stranger than fiction anyway. They wanted someone to go out and show them what was going on and make sense of it all. To convey the immediacy of experience and give it coherence and significance, the journalist turned to the *novelist*. According to Wolfe (1973), the new style fit in with their aspirations to move up the literary status ladder anyway.

Novelists, on the other hand, were bemoaning the lackluster state of postwar American fiction. Some, like Philip Roth, complained that America had changed so rapidly that the stable base of "manners and morals" for the realistic novel no longer existed (quoted in Hollowell 1977). Novelists wanted a role in the social action when the sixties broke out, wanted to comment on the revolutionary events of the American scene. They set out to gather the facts not as an end in themselves but as raw material for their art. The name for writers who set out to gather facts about people and events is *journalist*.

In 1965, Tom Wolfe's *Kandy-Kolored Tangerine Flake Streamlined Baby* and Truman Capote's *In Cold Blood* appeared. Wolfe's work was called "new journalism"; Capote said he had written a "nonfiction novel." Journalist and novelist met one another in the new genre. Wolfe and

Capote were showmen; public appearances and claims for the new literary form institutionalized it. Other names were added to the roster—Norman Mailer, Hunter Thompson, Joan Didion, and, more recently, John McPhee, Jane Kramer, Sara Davidson, Michael Herr, Tracy Kidder, and many others. Most novelists and journalists stayed with their traditional ways. But the new CN writers, in spite of their many differences, shared a new writing program—to blend factual content and fiction form, to play the roles of both observer/ reporter and textmaker, to commit equally to artistic and empirical truth, and to research fact not as an end in itself but as a means to art.

Writers and critics alike noted that CN was not completely new. The list of elders includes Dana, Twain, Dreiser, Dickens, Balzac, and even Voltaire and Defoe. More recent ancestors are James Agee, John Hersey, George Orwell, and Lillian Ross, among others. CN had its antecedents, but something new jelled in the 1960s. The crisis in fiction, the loosening of genre in journalism, the growing taste for nonfiction among American readers, the editors who supported experiments in writing, the hankering for a piece of the action among novelists and for a literary identity among the journalists, and the events of the 1960s that defied objective description and rivaled the imagination— conditions were right for CN to take hold and flourish, which is what it did.

Fiction in Form

CN is fiction in form but factual in content. The "contract with the reader," to use Hellman's (1981) phrase, is that *all this actually happened.* Commitment to fact is essential, according to the guides (Franklin 1986; Cheney 1987). But the events are dramatized using fiction techniques rather than reported. What does it mean to use fiction techniques? Several things, including at least the following:

The scenic method. The writer *shows* rather than *tells.* Situations are recreated for the reader, so that he or she can see and hear, smell and touch, listen to the dialogue, feel the emotional tone. Detailed scenes pull the reader in, involve him or her in the immediacy of the experience. In CN there is an added draw—the scenes are real, not imagined.

Character development. The writer centers the story on a few "rounded" characters, real and complicated characters that the reader gets to know and watches develop as he or she follows them from scene to scene. Readers may also slip into and out of different points of view. The use of "internal monologue" to express characters' points of view—their "subjective reality," in Wolfe's terms—is controversial in CN. The writer may also be a character in the story, an issue that is elaborated below.

Plot. The writer selects and arranges details to build dramatic tension. Parallel narratives, foreshadowing, and flashbacks are among the devices used. Structures vary from the Aristotelian to John McPhee's "e" and "Y"s (Sims 1984). So critical is the structure that my colleague at Maryland, Jon Frederick, entitled his CN advice book *Writing for Story.*

Authorial presence. Like a novelist, the CN writer is the voice behind—or perhaps in—the story. He or she is the Jamesian "organizing consciousness," the force that makes coherent meaning through skillful rendering of the details, a coherent meaning that, like good literature, should offer moral advice on one of the eternal human dilemmas. The writer's presence in the story varies from Capote's "recording angel" hovering in the background to Mailer's use of self as central character in books like *Armies of the Night.*

To find "real" detailed scenes and in-depth characterizations or "real" people, the CN writer does "saturation" or "immersion" reporting. They "live with their characters" to acquire the "true" details out of which they will produce their art. CN writers invest substantial time in research; in a forword or note they will tell the reader the general amount and type of research they have done.

No one questions their thoroughness or integrity. But, right from the beginning, some critics suspected that aesthetic concerns dominated the factual, that the structured, scenic presentation of powerful new events led to loose play with what had actually happened. What about the "scenic reconstructions" based on documents and interviews, the "interior monologues" that laid out what a character was thinking, the foregrounding of certain details to bring out significance—often a similar significance from one author's story (fiction or nonfiction) to the next, and the representations of characters that did not jibe with other views of the actual person? Fiction form, argued the critics, requires writing that factual content may not meet.

John Hollowell (1977), in the appendix to his overview of CN, added comments on CN books up to the date of publication. In the appendix he checked the recent work to see if the problem had been solved. It had not. The newest books waffled. Thomas Thompson said his *Serpentine* was "in essence, a true story"; and of *The Executioner's Song* Norman Mailer wrote that it "*does its best* to be a factual account" (emphasis added).

The problem is *still* current. Consider a brief item in the *Washington Post* book review section, December 20, 1987. In an interview with Bruce Chatwin, he talked about the "inventions" that went into *Songlines* and concluded that the book in general "added up to a fictional work." The reviewer noted that this exemplified the blurry lines between fiction and nonfiction and called into question the classification of *Songlines* as a travel book.

Could the problem be fixed with a statement of relationship between factual experience and fictional form? How
does a CN writer go from "immersion" to book? As it turns
out, it is not an easy question to answer.

Factual in Content

CN authors report their methods in forewords or notes to
the reader; they discuss "their original involvement in the
events, (their) sources' extremely vivid memories, or (their)
characters' reactions to their first reading of (the) manuscript" (Hellman 1981, 14). But even in Kramer's "model of
the kind of information on methods the writer of literary
nonfiction in the form of fiction owes the reader," according
to Weber (1980, 112), she focuses for the most part on the
writer's relationship to the subject. The critics clearly have
a problem with CN, and that problem is clearly one of the
possible "sacrifice of journalistic truth for dramatic effect,"
as Hellman (1981) put it.

There are slippery slopes all over the place. Tom Wolfe
(1973) wrote, "The basic reporting unit is no longer the
datum, the piece of information, but the scene, since most
of the sophisticated strategies of prose depend upon scenes"
(p. 52). This, he explains, highlights the importance of "saturation reporting," where you go out "combing the chaos for
the details; the creamy stuff you can use" (p. 52). Combing
chaos for cream doesn't solve the problem, it suggests it.

Perhaps interviewing is more straightforward. Brady's (1977)
The Craft of Interviewing treats interview technique for
journalists in general. His twelfth chapter is called "Pasting
It Together." Interviews, he says, are routinely cut up by
topic and rearranged for logical flow and smoothed for clarity
and comprehension. He reports that it is a point of controversy as to whether one can make up a quote that accurately

represents in effect what a person said. The resolution to the writer's doubts is simply to check with the subject. Then there's *researched* fact presented as *observed* fact, the problem of "scenic reconstruction." Capote's *In Cold Blood* is a favorite example of research converted into scenes with questionable accuracy. Bryan tells the reader his guidelines for *Friendly Fire:*

> I have assumed that if any individual recalled what was said and this recollection was confirmed by a second individual and there was no obvious advantage to be gained from a depiction of the conversation as recalled, then a reconstruction using the dialogue as remembered might be accepted as true. (quoted in Weber 1980, 158)

He does not explain where the other scenic details come from, but he tells the reader that he showed the finished manuscript to the main characters and they agreed that it was accurate.

Authorial presence in the story is another device to bolster credibility. Sims (1984) describes how "shared manners and morals" can no longer be taken for granted, so showing the reader one's role in the book helps them evaluate what one says. Weber adds that author as character helps solve the technical problem of how to be both "observer" and "maker," of how to let the reader get to know the reporter and evaluate the material accordingly.

CN authors reflect different positions on the issue. Mailer, in *Armies of the Night* and *Fire on the Moon,* turns himself into a character and converts his stuggle to understand and write into a centerpiece. Capote, on the other hand, lurks in the background as omniscient recording angel. His *In Cold Blood* is presented as polished "true fiction"; there is no Capote in sight. Wolfe is between the two; he's present in the *Electric Kool-Aid Acid Test* as an omniscient authorial voice inhabiting other characters' points of view, and his writing shifts from dramatic scene to impressionistic description when he flips from observed to researched material. Hunter Thompson's unique solution is to present himself as a drug-crazed maniac in an insane world; he can write most anything he wants.

Capote is criticized for hiding behind the lines, but some are skeptical of just how much the author as character really reveals. The reader learns the author's public description of his or her struggle with the material as well as his or her moral stance and vision of the world. But the relation between polished presentation and actual experience is as vulnerable to the critics' skeptical questions as everything else in CN.

Structure is also critical, although Sims (1984) notes that authors do not talk about it much. Once a writer has the structure, he or she seeks material that will play a role in the overall "architectonics," the "structural design that gives order, balance, and unity to a work, the element of form that relates the parts to each other and to the whole" (p. 14). Brady (1976) gives similar advice to interviewers: "Devise your angle, and build your interview around it" (p. 72), and later, decide the "dominant chord, and the details should then fall into place" (p. 214).

The material on method provided by CN critics and authors tells us that an account of fact/fiction relations is elusive at best; their methodological discussions suggest the discontinuity between process and product rather than resolving it. Readers with social-behavioral science backgrounds can add a long list of problems that have not been mentioned, problems that are routinely considered in the course of social research.

The critics have institutionalized the confusion. Zavarzadeh (1976) calls CN "bireferential"; it refers both to its own internal coherence and to an actual world. Hellman (1981) says CN is a type of fiction that "ultimately points inward" while also pointing outward "toward the actual world without ever deviating from observations of that world except in forms—such as authorial speculation or fantasy—which are immediately obvious as such to the reader" (p. 27). Weber (1980) says CN will never measure up to fiction; it is too constrained by the facts to achieve the fullness of character and plot that a fiction author provides. CN is either fact and fiction, fiction full of fact, or fact that will never make fiction.

Hollowell (1977), in a postscript to his analysis of CN, contrasts Woodward and Bernstein's two books to illustrate the problem. First, he describes *All the President's Men:* "In contrast to the atmospheric license of the new journalism, the day-by-day revelations in the *Washington Post* demanded rigorous and strictly accountable investigative reporting" (p. 148). Events were "simply too urgent" to allow the "fictionalized reconstruction of the new journalism." In a footnote, he says that Woodward and Bernstein's *The Final Days* had just appeared, a dramatic reconstruction in the new journalism style. All the predictable issues of methodology and ethics were raised, reactions that had not appeared with their first book.

No one doubts that CN authors put in substantial amounts of time in their research. No one doubts that they master the material before they produce a finished book. But, as Weber (1980) summed it up, "The basic critical problem with literary nonfiction cast in the form of fiction is always credibility" (p. 53). It was so in the beginning and still is.

The history of CN shows that the blend of journalism and fiction comes at some cost. From its birth in the 1960s to the present, the enduring problem of CN has been credibility, the question of just how much of the account the reader can believe. The problem, according to the CN critics, is a consequence of packing factual content into fiction form, where the form requires some details and structures that readers and critics plausibly suspect the world did not provide.

Fieldwriting

The discussion of CN is meant as a case study in credibility problems generated by a process-product conflict. It is now time to round up the usual hedges. First of all, several CN works, in reviews by both insiders and outsiders, are held up as powerful narratives that represent some fundamental truth about a group's situation. Tom Wolfe's *The Right Stuff* is an example. My guess is that the truth comes through as it would in good fiction, that the credibility problem would remain at the level of detail, but I cannot test that argument here.

A second important hedge is that the CN discussion of "fact" and "fiction"—I echo the terms that the CN literature uses—is naive because "fiction" signals the tradition of realistic fiction and, of course, many others and because "fact" flags an epistemological problem that would fill a library.

So let me try to circumvent the hedges and bring the issue back home. I started this chapter by claiming that the "new ethnography" literature tended to separate product from process, form from content, writing from research. Then I used CN to show that, in one case at least, the shift to a new product (or form of writing style), based on imaginative construction and dramatic representation of a world, persistently raised issues of credibility when laid over a process (or content or research style) whose fundamental claim was that the story was about real people doing real things.

Ethnography also makes the claim of credibility. The old positivist spirit of unique descriptions objectively verified through context-free methods has lost its charm. But, like many, I argue that the world sets constraints on credible ethnographic interpretation, that—with respect to some group—several ethnographic interpretations are possible but not all possible ethnographic interpretations are credible. Without the old positivist yardstick, how is one to know the difference?

One way is to restore the process/product ambiguity to ethnography, from start to finish. In one classic version—described first in *The Discovery of Grounded Theory* (Glaser and Strauss 1967) and now formalized in software like Ethnograph—data collection, analysis, and writing are dialectic and ongoing rather than being separate steps in a linear process. Ethnographers differ in the kinds of field texts they use as foundations, but, in principle, the approach applies to any of them—interviews, notes, or what have you—or any other text for that matter—archives, media, or other literature.

The process works like this. One takes interview transcripts, for example, and marks them off by major topic shift. One then takes topically similar segments from different material, abstracts them out, and places them together. These piles of topic-related text are the core for a "working memorandum," as Glaser and Strauss (1967) call it, within which one looks for patterns of similarity and variation in how members talk about topic X. Working memoranda—samples of raw material together with a discussion of patterns seen in them—become chapters or sections of chapters in ethnographic reports.

Van Maanen (1988), in a footnote (p. 69 n. 8), notes that such a research process underlies what he calls "reality tales." The process is, of course, not so simple and mechanical. One looks at a couple of interviews before doing the third; one is using field texts other than interviews; more than one content category might apply to an interview segment; mountains of other ethnographic data—recorded, experienced, and intuited—interact with interview conduct and analysis; and no old-time science claims are made for the result—coding and analysis are interpretive rather than positivistic. But this simplified sketch does show how, in one classic ethnographic style, the structure of the ethnographic text grows out of the structure of data gathered during ethnographic research. By and large the process and product are more intimately related than contemporary discussions of textuality suggest.

Lately, I have thought about argumentation as an appropriate genre for this style of research. Argumentation is a form that is receiving increasing attention in the discourse analysis literature, either in theoretical comparisons with other discourse genres like narrative and conversation or as a framework for modeling discourse in legal settings. In fact, some time ago, Ricoeur suggested legal reasoning as a model for the hermeneutic method.

The coding, sorting, searching for pattern, and organizing text that presents and evaluates it are part of what traditional ethnography represents. The final book will not read like a novel, but it will offer some raw material and reasoning so that an outsider can evaluate its credibility. The "new ethnography" literature calls this endpoint into question. On the one hand, if you are writing an argument, what is an argument anyway, and how is what you have written a result of the form rather than anything else, and what other forms of argumentation might be possible? On the other hand, why can't the book read like a novel, or a poem, or a plurivocal collage, or a political tract?

A break with "reality tales" is fascinating to consider, and the new literature brings the possibility of such breaks to consciousness. The problem I have is the lack of discussion over the research process and how it would change in harmony with the new product. Van Maanen's "impressionist tales" are interesting to consider because they use the scenic method to describe what actually happens. But then I start ticking off problems: How does one integrate and legitimate the expository writing to enable comprehension of the scene? How does one structure the scenes—simple chronology, thematically, topically, theoretically—and how does one mark the structure so the reader knows what is going on? How does one organize multiple potential interpretations of a scene and support some and rule out others? How does one weave theoretical frames into the discourse? These problems do not strike me as impossible, just difficult and neglected.

Ethonographic texts are more about making a case out of collected material than they are about creating entertaining art. I have become sensitive to the difference over the past few years with my own experiments in popular fiction and nonfiction writing—there are times when I think of it as fieldwork in the land of representation. Good fiction requires control over the text so that plot, story, character, theme, and style work tightly together to yield powerful and entertaining art. Good ethnography requires control over the data so that a skeptical outsider can see how a pattern is grown to enable comprehension of member-produced social action in the context of one world from the perspective of another.

I conclude this chapter with a personal example of the conflict between textual form and research process: a commercial nonfiction article I wrote. The article concerned the cotton industry. I knew it had to be in a dramatic form that would reach a wide readership. I was searching not only for a representation that avoided academic domination and elitism, as the new literature would put it—sometimes in a domineering, elitist way—but also for a way to report research so that it would connect with nonacademic readers, a problem that is notable by its absence in that same literature.

To get back to basics, I needed a good opening scene, but the few days of research had not provided the one I wanted. So I took an interview with a cotton merchant who had reminisced about the old days, a place—the area where his father started the business—and an activity he engaged in—going to lunch in that area—and constructed a plausible scene. This occurred before I had read the CN literature, but what I had done was to discover the controversies over "scenic reconstruction" and "interior monologue." I showed the article to the person involved, and he was delighted with it; it was, he assured me, right on target.

I was paid for the article, but shortly after its acceptance the editorial staff was fired and replaced, so it never appeared. The world of commercial writing is chaotic, but this is not the place to go into that story. The point is that the textual form required a structural piece that I did not have, so, given the commitment to form, I decided to construct it. If I had been doing ethnography, the problem would never have come up. I would have transcribed the interview with the cotton merchant, divided it into content-oriented segments, and added it to the pool of similarly segmented field texts from other interviews or notes or documents. The content structure of the material would have driven the textual form rather than the other way around.

Textuality as a consciousness-raising concept is long overdue. But textuality as the primary focus for what ethnography is all about is, I think, a mistake. When process and product tug against each other, ethnographic credibility turns sour—credibility in the sense of making a good argument that displays and accounts for samples of group life. At a time when interest in ethnographic research is growing, when our sense of what it is and how it works is improving, a move to new textual forms without more attention to the research processes that ground them would be a serious ethnomistake.

References

Brady, J. 1976. *The craft of interviewing.* New York: Vintage.

Cheney, T. A. R. 1987. *Writing creative nonfiction.* Cincinnati: Writer's Digest Books.

Clifford, J., and G. E. Marcus. 1986. *Writing culture: The poetics and politics of ethnography.* Berkeley: University of California Press.

Franklin, J. 1986. *Writing for story.* New York: Mentor.

Geertz, C. 1988. *Works and lives: The anthropologist as author.* Stanford, CA: Stanford University Press.

Glaser, B., and A. Strauss. 1967. *The discovery of grounded theory.* Chicago: Aldine.

Hellman, J. 1981. *Fables of facts: The new journalism and the nonfiction novel.* Chapel Hill: University of North Carolina Press.

Hollowell, J. 1977. *Fact and fiction: The new journalism as new fiction.* Urbana: University of Illinois Press.

Marcus, G. E. 1980. Rhetoric and the ethnographic genre in anthropological research. *Current Anthropology* 21:507-10.

Sims, N. 1984. The literary journalists. In *The literary journalists,* edited by N. Sims. New York: Ballantine.

Van Maanen, J. 1988. *Tales of the field: On writing ethnography.* Chicago: University of Chicago Press.

Weber, R. 1980. *The literature of fact: Literary nonfiction in American writing.* Athens: University of Ohio Press.

Wolfe, T., ed. 1973. *The new journalism.* New York: Harper & Row.

Zavarzadeh, M. 1976. *The mythopoetic reality: The postwar American nonfiction novel.* Urbana: University of Illinois Press.

5

On Acknowledgments
in Ethnographies

◪

EYAL BEN-ARI

One of the passages most often turned to by anthropologists in their initial run-through of ethnographies is the acknowledgments. This section, which rarely extends for more than a page or two, is considered to be among the less serious, less substantial parts of ethnographic texts. Nevertheless, acknowledgments—especially in ethnographies that are thought to be major signposts in anthropologists' careers—appear to arouse considerable interest among professional readers. This interest is related, no doubt, to the preoccupation of anthropologists with their professional community: specifically, with its past history

EDITOR'S NOTE: Adapted by permission from *Journal of Anthropological Research,* vol. 43, no. 1 (1987), pp. 63-84.

and personages and with its present social relations and members.

Candid admissions of the fervor with which this preoccupation is pursued can occasionally be found in the literature. In the early 1960s for example, Gluckman (1963) confessed that he believed he was "not alone among senior anthropologists in finding it more interesting to teach students about anthropologists than about anthropology" (p. 314). A decade later Needham (1974) remarked that, though bored by ethnographic facts and even analysis, anthropologists did like to hear about "other anthropologists" (p. 15).

Yet since the 1970s such observations and comments have increasingly come to be coupled with an explicit theoretical focus on the exploration of the ways in which anthropological work is related to and generated by its social and intellectual contexts. In other words, communal self-absorption has begun to be paired with a more critical and informed professional reflexivity.

This professional reflexivity is rooted in three interrelated trends. The first finds its source in a combination of calls for a "history of anthropology" and some of the newer attempts at biography and autobiography (Darnell 1974, 289-90; Hallowell [1965] 1974, 305; Hymes [1962] 1974, 297; Jarvie 1975, 263-64; Langham 1981). The appeals for a history of the profession have been phrased, for example, as the necessity for understanding the intellectual organization and "culture" of anthropology (Gruber 1975, 5) or for analyzing the social processes that underlie the formation of theory (Silverman 1981, ix). The biographical approach, for its part, has been justified by its value in uncovering the problematics of fieldwork (Powdermaker 1966, 9-15) or in analyzing the complex ways by which self-definitions and doubts are "translated" into public professional influence (Modell 1983, chap. 1; 1975). Within this historical-biographical trend, the accent has been on the personal and institutional processes involved in the creation and maintenance of anthropological communities: for instance, the interaction of personalities, career making, professional socialization, or mobilization of resources and personnel. The second trend is rooted in the concern with the political and ethical implications of anthropologists' involvement in research settings. This concern has been formulated either as part of a critique of the profession's role in colonialism (Asad 1973) or as part of an examination of the ethical problems associated with fieldwork (Jansen 1973). The problematics dealt with within this trend have, especially at the beginning, focused on the ties between anthropologists and informants and between ethnographers' "home" and "host" societies. Of late however, some of the questions about these relations have been directed inward towards the ties within the anthropological community (Nader 1976; Gertrude 1977; Whitaker 1981, 439ff.): ethnography's determination by institutional and political interests, the creation and control of professional norms and expectations, or the ethical implications of interpersonal relations among anthropologists.

The third trend toward professional reflexivity began in the late 1970s in the debate about how ethnographic texts are produced. Drawing upon developments in linguistics, philosophy, and literary criticism, this trend initially concentrated on the textual creation of ethnographies and on the place of anthropologists within and outside their documentary creations. More recently, scholars have called for an awareness of the dangers posed by the hermetical isolation of the text's analysis from the traditional realist goals of ethnographic inquiry (Fischer, in Marcus and Clifford 1985, 269). More specifically, they have demanded that an institutional analysis of the microrelations within the professional community be turned into an integral part of the examination of how ethnographic texts are produced (Rabinow, in Marcus and Clifford 1985, 270). The emphasis on textuality has driven scholars taking this line of inquiry to focus on the processes by which ethnographic authority and authenticity are created and projected, the methods used for the display of individual originality and creativity, or the ways that oral discourses are inscribed in representational accounts.

Despite their differences, the three trends appear to agree on certain theoretical assumptions and concerns. All accept the assumption "that ethnography—writing about other people and their societies—is a constructive, historically contingent activity" (Marcus and Clifford 1985, 267). Also basic to all three trends is an awareness of the need to examine not only the processes which bind ethnographers to their "people" but also the processes by which they are tied to different institutions, collectivities, and interpretative communities within their "home" societies.

But why acknowledgments? With rare exceptions—like Bateson's ([1936] 1958) *Naven* or the recent spate of "experimental ethnographics"—ethnographic texts published in the past five decades or so suppressed or neutralized the existential dimension of the ethnographic situation (Scholte 1980, 56). The dominant mode of presentation was that of the "dispassionate, camera-like observer; the collective and authoritative third person" (Marcus and Cushman 1982, 32). The most common textual locations for a limited treatment of such matters were marginal and relatively unintegrated passages like appendixes, footnotes, prefaces, forewords, or acknowledgments. Yet even there the concern was with one overriding matter: fieldwork.

It is precisely in this regard that material found in acknowledgments differs from that in other marginal textual locations; it is virtually only here that one finds reference to conditions affecting not only fieldwork but also all the other stages of the ethnographic project: formal and informal studies, preparation for fieldwork, procurement of funds and official permission, write-up, and publication. The expressions of debts and gratitude found in acknowledgments well bring out how anthropologists are enmeshed in webs of relations, belong to a variety of collectivities, and are subject to a range of duties and obligations not only in the field but *throughout* the development of their ethnographic projects.

A number of special social and literary constraints guide the writing of acknowledgments. They may be understood by contrasting them to another type of textual construction found in ethnographies. Acknowledgments that appear as parts of prefaces, introductions, and forewords or as separate pretextual sections are lists or inventories; they are fixing or ordering devices for enumerating certain categories and subcategories. In this sense, acknowledgments are akin to synopses, tables of contents, indexes, or lists of graphs and illustrations. The forms of all of these are governed by conventions that differ from the narrative and textual practices that guide the writing of the main parts of ethnographies.

Yet acknowledgments differ from tables of contents and similar lists that are designed chiefly as guideposts for the text that follows them. Acknowledgments, by contrast, are formulations that take on an intermediate position between the internal contents of the ethnography and the people and relationships outside it; they are both an introduction to an intellectual product and a reconstruction of the external contributions that have gone toward its realization. As will be seen, this dual quality determines much of the potentials and limits of these devices.

Another point is related to Goody's (1981) caution in regard to literary devices such as lists or tables. He warns against too facile an acceptance of the classificatory and knowledge-organizing function of such devices: "To accept that these devices somehow reflect the organization of knowledge in a social unit, may well lead one to an uncomplicated appreciation of the social reality to which they refer. For these fixed literary devices may well simplify the reality of human communication beyond reasonable recognition" (p. 206). Indeed, to regard them as direct "expressions of an underlying structure is to mistake metaphor for reality" (p. 220).

Thus I do not suggest that the categorization found in acknowledgments offers a direct expression of, or a key to, the order that underlies "anthropologizing." Acknowledgments should not be simply seen as documents contrived to portray or somehow to order the complex reality in which ethnographic projects are completed. Rather, I suggest that an understanding of such vehicles entails taking into account a much wider view of the relations between them and the social and cultural orders of anthropology.

A characterization of acknowledgments as "ritualistic" (see, e.g., Freilich 1977, v) provides a hint at what I am getting at, for a focus on rituals—or more generally on "special" social constructs—brings out not only the public nature of such passages but also how they may be designed to define or alter a new situation. As Lewis (1980) notes, "Ritual is not done solely to be interpreted: it is also done (and from the point of view of the performers this may be more important) to resolve, alter, or demonstrate a situation" (p. 35). Such a view leads to the wider realization that acknowledgments are part of the processes of "management of meaning" within anthropology. They may, in other words, be devised to do a whole range of things like show, report, camouflage, hide, command, beg, maintain, reason, qualify, or inform about a certain order or state. In short, we must examine textual phenomena like acknowledgments as constitutive of social action (Mulkay 1984, 547), that is, as procedures and practices by which anthropologists construct the social and cultural orders of their profession. The analysis that follows is based on an examination of about two hundred ethnographies and on discussions with anthropologists from the United States, Britain, Canada, Australia, France, Israel, and Japan. Its main focus, however, is on anthropology in North America and Britain.[1]

Acknowledgments to Anthropologists

NAME DROPPING: INTELLECTUAL GENEALOGIES AND BINDING

In their acknowledgments, anthropologists invariably make references to people within their professional community. These references often include remarks directed at "juniors" or "equals," but by far the most common statements are those addressed to "seniors": teachers and older colleagues, supervisors and mentors, guides and intellectual influences. Mentioning these kinds of people clearly has to do with the activities that underlie and structure anthropologists' intellectual and academic careers. According to a dominant approach to the sociology of the intellectual world, anthropologists' careers consist of getting themselves as much as possible into the center of conversation, into the center of arguments. As Collins (1975) graphically puts it,

> "a realistic image" of the intellectual world would be an open plain with men scattered throughout it, shouting. "Listen to

me! Listen to me!" The polite formulations of the sociology of science take scientific communication as an exchange of gifts of information. But men are interested in such gifts mainly to the extent that it helps them to formulate statements that will cause others to listen to them. (p. 480)

In securing other people's attention, intellectuals are dependent on certain crucial resources and their wielders. The resources include material and financial assistance, information, and validation and recognition granted to their work by their peers. In this respect the power of certain gatekeepers—members of academic committees, publishers, consultants, or journal editors, to mention only a few—is very important for they control or influence the routes of access to resources and the communications channels themselves.

The few works that have been devoted to a sociology of anthropology in Britain and America portray both the centrality of competition and communication and the continued operation of a patrimonial type social organization within anthropology. Kuper (1973, 136), for example, describes a few powerful individuals in British social anthropology and their importance in controlling the main research and teaching posts. Similarly, scholars from across the ocean note that American anthropology continues to be organized as a mentor system: whom a person studied with and in what theoretical tradition remain important status markers throughout a career (Marcus and Clifford 1985, 268). Darnell (1971) sums up her awareness of these circumstances through her conclusion that anthropological "paradigms"

have proved to be a composite of theories, men who believed in them, institutions which supported their research, and perhaps above all, scientific consensus within a community of scholars—a process heavily dependent on the social context in which men's ideas seek paradigmatic status. (p. 101)

This is why the mention of other, especially "older," anthropologists' names in acknowledgments may be viewed as a strategy for gaining professional attention. Along with picking arguments with more well known persons, opening up new topics for others to follow, or talking to a select audience, writing acknowledgments is used to improve an anthropologist's career chances.

In name dropping, of course, what is of importance is not just information about the acknowledged and their relations to the acknowledger. Of central significance are the accompanying metamessages that guide and direct the interpretation of the information being conveyed (Bateson 1972). In intellectual name dropping, the metamessage accompanying acknowl-edgments to well-known personages would follow these lines: "Listen to me because I am related to someone important enough not to be ignored." The acknowledger can attempt to "appropriate" some of the importance of the acknowledged by implicitly alluding to the latter's central position in the professional community. In this sense, intellectual genealogies are just as potentially amenable to manipulation as are the genealogies of people studied by anthropologists.

Conversely, by citing others' names, anthropologists repay them in the best of all possible mediums of exchanges, for such citations can be seen as introductions or reintroductions of the acknowledged people's names into the community's conversations and argumentations. It is in a similar light that acknowledgment to financing bodies or other such gatekeepers should be seen. Thus strategic choice in regard to textual construction is related to strategic choice involved in careering.

Another way in which acknowledgments imply a career strategy is related to the dynamics of debts and obligations found within the professional community. Goffman (1967, 60) hinted at this when he wrote of how the allusions to the past of a relationship and the promise of its future are involved in any communication about a relationship. What one finds in such communications are both an appeal to the vestigal meaning of the relationship and a pledge to treat the receiver in a particular way in the future. Acknowledgments thus bring together metamessages about the value of the ties binding author and acknowledged and about commitment to these ties in times to come.

Relating these exchanges of communication to Gouldner's (1960) seminal discussion of reciprocity points out their implications for the continuity and cohesion of the professional community. Gouldner illuminates both the mechanisms that constrain or motivate people to do their duty and pay off their debts and those that induce people to remain socially indebted to each other. He states that the strength of these binding mechanisms lies in the norms of reciprocity that inhibit the complete repayment of a social debt (Gouldner 1960, 175). This is because the ambiguity as to whether indebtedness has been repaid and the uncertainty about who is in whose debt that these norms entail are crucial for continued commitment to the relationship.

When seen as parts of ongoing relationships, acknowledgments function in much the same way. The introduction of an acknowledged person's name into the networks of professional communication is a repayment, but it is always an equivocal repayment, for it is impossible to define what kind of acknowledgment would be sufficient to repay the author's debts. In addition, acknowledgments may transform the author's repayment into the acknowledged individual's debt. In this sense, while ethnographers may be "merely" following the conventions of writing acknowledgments to elders, they may actually be employing these conventions to further their own career ends. As Scheiffelin (1980) puts it, through the management of meaning that is effected through communications, "exchange becomes a vehicle of social obligation and political manoeuvre" (p. 503). It is important to note that there is an element of complementarity here: A needs B's possession, which B is willing to give away, and vice versa. Complementarity is possible in a homeomorphic exchange, as in friendship, but it is more likely to be based on a heteromorphic exchange: the kind of exchange that usually characterizes ties between anthropologists and their superiors. As Lebra (1975) notes, both superior and inferior possess goods which are disposable and desired by the other:

> The superior can offer guidance, protection, and benevolence —material and non-material—which the inferior needs and is willing to take; whereas the inferior, in turn, can afford to give reliance, esteem, and loyalty which the superior wants. (p. 557)

Thus reciprocity involves two opposite pulls: one toward symmetry and balance and the other toward asymmetry and imbalance. The potential strain between symmetry and asymmetry is predicated, in turn, on the fact that the exchange of resources—not unlike that of the patron-client nexus (Eisenstadt and Roniger 1980, 50-51)—is a "package deal": that is, material, political, intellectual, and sentimental resources cannot be exchanged separately but only in combination. As Murphy (1981) eloquently puts it,

> The ties between our anthropological teachers and founders and ourselves may not be as primary as those of kinship, but

they are commonly modeled on these attachments and share some of their qualities. They are multistranded, or functionally diffuse, they are hierarchical and entail varying degrees of authority, they are incorporative, and they are ambivalent. We may not follow the paths set by the ancestors, but our very deviations have been conditioned by them. (p. 174)

But because these "package deals" are effected within intellectual settings, the strain basic to reciprocity is manifested in the structuring of communal argumentations. Two fundamental contrasts or tensions stand out: one between the inequality of hierarchical positions (and the resources at their disposal) and the normative equality of members to voice their ideas, and the other between guidance and continuity in intellectual traditions and an emphasis on creativity and innovation.

THE ARTICULATION OF TENSION
IN ASYMMETRICAL RELATIONS

Surely a prime focus of a professional reflexivity should be on the problematics posed by the asymmetries of power and position. But anthropologists have usually chosen the simplest way to handle them: the problematics have been ignored. This disregard fits well with a view that stresses competition and professional advancement as the primary processes that structure the anthropological community. According to this view, because these issues bear directly upon professional careers, one would expect few direct allusions to them in published works; one would hardly expect anthropologists to discuss matters that could jeopardize their professional lives.

In fact, a number of textual devices are used to channel away any forthright suggestion of these problematics. The use of politeness forms in acknowledgments, for example, clearly fits with careering and may be seen as an attempt to characterize relationships in ways that will not impair the future chances of acknowledger vis-à-vis acknowledged. As Esther Goody (1978) explains, "The communicative distress to which politeness forms are a response is the danger of threatening an interlocutor and thus jeopardizing the successful outcome of a speech act" (p. 6). At the same time however, acknowledgments do possess the potential to allude to problematical issues. This is achieved through the use of linguistic forms such as qualifications, apologies, and justifications and the downplaying or highlighting of criticisms. Peristiany (1939), for example, conjures up an image that is both distant and suggestive to characterize the relationship he had with his supervisor:

> Professor Malinowski, whose pupil I have been for nearly two years, has been for me a constant source of inspiration. His passionate devotion to Anthropology and the interest he takes in his pupils bring back to mind the medieval tradition of the Magister. (p. xvii)[2]

Handelman's (1977) evocation of a different type of image is directed toward another one of anthropology's strong personalities:

> The late Max Gluckman was often the anvil of support and the hammer of opposition between which many of my ideas first took shape. His death took from us an unusual mind, whose devotion to anthropology complemented the zest with which he pursued the complexities of daily life. (p. xiv)

Stirling (1965) provides a good example of a backhanded allusion, framed within a series of complementary phrases, to the inequality of many dyads within the intellectual world:

I should like to thank Professor Firth and Professor Gellner for reading the manuscript and making helpful suggestions, and Professor Schapera who performed this task twice on different versions, surely a rare service to a junior colleague. (p. ix)

Turnbull (1962) uses a combination of hints at the difficulties with his supervisor and compliments on his good qualities to communicate the tension that characterized their relations:

And then I must thank professor Evans-Pritchard, a more austere teacher, who teaches all his students that the study of man should be approached not necessarily without emotion but with careful scientific impartiality. (p. ix)

Closely related devices for alluding to the problematic nature of power relations in the professional community are "play messages" (Handelman 1982, 163): irony or sarcasm, for example. These mediums carry metamessages that serve both as releases and as concealments. They act as releases by triggering evaluation or reevaluation of the social order about which they are communicating. Concealment is involved because these devices do not openly display the hostility or critical posture that produced them.

Although Henry's (1965) comments are directed at grant-awarding institutions rather than individuals who hold powerful academic positions, his combination of "play upon form" and irony is hard to resist quoting:

It seems to me that, in the interest of encouraging younger people who may be dismayed by foundation "turn downs, I should acknowledge the foundations that have rejected my petitions. I believe the Wenner-Gren Foundation for Anthropological Research turned me down at least four times: and I have lost count over the years of the number of times I was rejected by Guggenheim. (p. ix)

Sarcasm can also trigger reflection upon the professional world and its underlying order:

> I should acknowledge, finally, the different committees on which I have sat beside infinitely eloquent and subtly resourceful colleagues, whose actions set me wondering why? (Baily 1969, xiv)

The special potential of acknowledgments for commenting about the basic tensions of asymmetry in the anthropological community is akin to the expressions of systematic strain uncovered by anthropologists in rituals of rebellion, *Naven,* role releases in total institutions, or joking relations. Thus the ambivalence and concealment found in some acknowledgments should not be viewed as literary defects or as outcomes of a lack of awareness of problematic issues. Rather, given the structural dependence of ethnographers on their superiors, it is only through the use of such means that tensions can be expressed at all.

INTELLECTUAL PEDIGREES:
INTEGRATION AND DIFFERENTIATION

In addition to expressing hostility or unmasking tension, acknowledgments may also perform integrating or differentiating functions by their creation of solidarity or exclusion (Zijderveld 1968, 303ff.). Illustrations culled from one older and one newer ethnography offer a good introduction to this function:

> Anthropology is a many-sided science. When the anthropologist has completed his or her fieldwork, there is still the problem of creating order out of the chaos. . . . It is impossible

within the compass of an introduction to trace the spiritual ancestry of a book in the making, but in the process of writing up my material I was particularly fortunate to be able to attend the seminars of two anthropologists, Professor Malinowski and Dr. Raymond Firth, whose writings and fieldwork have considerably moulded my own approach to anthropology, and proved a constant source of stimulus. (Kaberry 1939, xiv)

Hilda Kuper, with her love of anthropology, her imagination and profundity, was a splendid teacher and model. My friend and colleague Sally Falk Moore consistently deferred encouragement and criticism in a finely balanced mixture. Victor Turner is responsible not only for much of the theoretical substance of this work but for its existence in the present form as well. Though I have never studied with him formally, I consider myself his student. (Myerhoff 1974, 23)

The formulation of these excerpts is obviously guided by something more than individual calculation or political maneuvering. To view each transmitted communication merely as a strategically informed move disregards how any exchange is anchored in and reproduces wider symbolic systems. Scheiffelin (1980) brings this out in his discussion of how reciprocity

has as much to do with the symbolic basis for the formation of identities and differences and the adjustment of social distance and tension as it does with the distribution of material objects and the fulfillment of social obligations. (p. 515)

Seen in this light, name dropping in acknowledgments becomes a means by which ethnographers seek to establish various bases of their professional identity: for example, ties with intellectual ancestors or distinctions between subgroups in the community. Marwick's (1965) acknowledgment to Hoernle provides one of the clearest examples of this point:

The encouragement the late Dr. A. Winifred Hoernle has given South African anthropologists is legendary; and though I was not one of her students in a formal sense, her helpfulness and kindness to me made me appreciate why she had become known as the "mother" of social anthropology in South Africa, though I always felt that, owing to her knack of treating even her most junior colleagues as her intellectual equals, "grand mother" would, in terms of Radcliffe-Brown's principle of the combination of alternate generations, have been more appropriate. (p. xviii)

Acknowledgments, then, may sometimes exhibit fewer of the characteristics of manipulative strategizing or rituals of rebellion and more of the qualities of rituals of solidarity and integration; for by asserting membership in a group—Goody's groupies, Malinowski's minions. Radcliffe-Brown's retainers, Turner's trainees, or Geertz's graduates—not only is the group's internal collective identity built around a central person but its external boundaries are constructed as well.

This is not to assert that intellectual genealogies are never open to strategic manipulation on the basis of political realities, but to reduce the elaboration of all intellectual pedigrees to these terms is to miss the types of relations that are not built upon a direct interest in binding or effecting obligations. That such ties exist in the anthropological community is most evident in acknowledgments devoted to people with whom the author has no personal relations:

Rather by chance I had included among the books I carried into the bush two volumes which I turned to during the period of questioning, *The Phenomenology of the Social World,* by Alfred Schutz, and *The Phenomenology of Perception,* by Maurice Merleau-Ponty. Readers familiar with the philosophies of Schutz and Merleau-Ponty will be in a position to ferret out of my purported *description* of the Tswana the critical . . . arguments that I am making not only concerning the Tswana but also against much of contemporary empiricist anthropology and social science in general. (Alverson 1978, xii)

I have been influenced by the books of Gombrich, Wollheim, Frye, Cherry, and Huizinga. None of them was intended as a work for anthropologists and perhaps for that reason it is easier to single them out. (Lewis 1980, xvi)

These examples challenge conclusions such as Jorion's (1976): "Clearly, the acknowledgments that are to be found at the beginning of most books have more to do with the editorial and financial networks of the anthropological establishment than with any actual intellectual descent" (p. 23). Such a view ignores not only the variety of "operations" that such constructs may involve—manipulation as well as integration, strategizing in addition to identifying—but also the complex quality of intellectual descent.

As Said (1975) eloquently puts it, intellectual descent entails more than a linear (or vulgar) idea of influence (p. 15). It also involves a basic tension—between continuity and discontinuity, amplification and refinement, or repetition and rebuttal—that the stress on innovation and development infuses into the relations between intellectuals, particularly between teachers and pupils. Identity within an intellectual tradition is always problematical, and Bateson's ([1936] 1958) characteristically self-reflective comments are an example of how this is expressed in acknowledgments:

I wish to stress my admiration for Professor Malinowski's work. In the body of the book I have from time to time been critical of his views and theoretical approach. But, of course, I recognize the importance of his contribution to anthropology. (p. ix)

Acknowledgments to Others

THE "OTHER": TEXTUAL IMPRESSION MANAGEMENT

Social and cultural anthropology is distinguished from the other social sciences by its continuing reliance on fieldwork. Fieldwork, of course, is a social process that invariably involves the ethnographer in a heavy web of obligations toward the "other." Ethnographers express their awareness of this situation with thanks to those researched:

> An anthropologist's first debt is to the people who allowed him to study them, and I here wish to put on record my deep gratitude to them. (Gellner 1969, xii)

> An ethnographer's greatest debt is always to those who have allowed him to peer into their lives. For this I thank. . . . (Plath 1980, v)

The public documentation of such debts stands out immediately as problematical. Why are these debts and thanks to the "other" recorded in texts that are directed almost exclusively toward professional publics?

One answer may be related to the way anthropologists, like all intellectuals, can repay their debts with the tangible products they produce. The exchange of a book—a material object that can be shown, handled, or displayed—is a signal of the importance of a tie between the author and someone else. Yet a simple handwritten dedication on the inside cover would seem to do just as well. Another answer may lie in the growing literacy and international self-awareness of those researched. As Kuper (1973) observes, "Today virtually any anthropological monograph is bound to be read by some of its subjects. The country in which the study was carried out is in fact becoming a major market for the studies themselves" (p. 234).

But acknowledging the help of the people anthropologists study was a feature of ethnographies long before either widespread literacy became a characteristic of many Third World societies or the emergence of a global society transcended many social and political boundaries—witness Malinowski's acknowledgments to the Trobrianders he studied. A fuller explanation lies in an awareness of how acknowledgments to the "other" are directed toward professional readerships. The initial question, then, may better be rephrased "What professional conventions or expectations are served by recording an ethnographer's debts to his or her 'people'?"

Of importance in this regard is the recent interest in a long-neglected side of professional competence—what has been formulated as a preoccupation with literary style or aesthetic judgment (Scholte 1980, 61) but perhaps is more aptly termed textual "impression management." This concerns how the authenticity and plausibility of an ethnographic text are communicated to readers (Marcus and Cushman 1982, 38): that is, the ways by which the logic of an argument is "rhetorically ornamented" in order to make it persuasive to the specific audience in the anthropologist-author's mind (Marcus and Cushman 1982, 54).

Acknowledgments may establish the authority and credibility of an ethnographic text by including accounts of how intimate relations or ties of rapport were established in the field:

> My wife . . . and our offspring . . . attended the local schools, mingled with young Payaneses and Queretanos, and contributed many juicy personal items to our ethnological catalogue. (Whiteford 1964, viii)

The Ngologa . . . never allowed me to feel out of place . . .
[and] accepted me into the closest circle of friendship. (Kuper
1970, ix)

The list would be endless from the neighboring children who
told me their secrets, to the residents of the Communal Old
Folks' Home where I lived, who helped to map out the way
things had been. (Lander 1976, xi)

Several dozen Tswana opened their lives to me, making
possible all that follows. (Alverson 1978, xiii)

A related device is the use of fictive kinship terms to characterize relations between the ethnographer and key informants: for example, Turkish "parents" (Magnarella 1974,
4), adopted daughter (Lander 1976, xi), or "my Tswana
'Father' " (Alverson 1978, xiii).

One also often finds confessions of the ethnographer's
fallibility in carrying out fieldwork or recitals of the obsta-
cles overcome in completing research:

Although I could never wander about unnoticed, at least I was
ignored when engrossing matters were afoot. My awkward-
ness in handling *betel quid* was always a chance for diversion.
The clumsiness of my dance steps was politely ignored. . . .
    It is therefore to those friends in Alor, to their shrewd but
tolerant acceptance of my peculiarities and to their vigorous
engrossment in their own affairs that any contributions which
this volume may make . . . are primarily due. (DuBois 1944,
xi-xii)

The main difficulty I had to contend with was my linguistic
unpreparedness . . . and it is mainly through the goodwill of
my interpreter and friend . . . that I have made some small
progress in that most difficult language. (Peristiany 1939, xv)

Finally, take the place—or rather lack of it—of jargon. In the main ethnographic text, jargon communicates the professional competence of the author, for by using the generalizing and objective style of reportage (Boon 1982; Marcus and Cushman 1982, 35), the ethnographer communicates her or his mastery of the vocabulary and conceptual apparatus of the profession. In acknowledgments, the absence of professional parlance along with the personal appeals and individual statements, tales of rapport, confessions of fallibility, and use of fictive kin terms all serve to create the impression of a human, concrete, intimate—and *therefore* believable and genuine—experience.

Three expectations that form part of the "folklore" of anthropology, or what Freilich (1977, 14) terms "fieldwork culture," seem of particular relevance here: first, that fieldwork is a unique and partially untranslatable experience; second, that research in the field is an exacting business full of difficulties, tensions, and blunders; and third, that ethnographers will somehow overcome these predicaments and get close enough to the people researched for their purposes. The believability of the main text is thus established by communicating metamessages that fulfill these three expectations about fieldwork. But what is important here is that the satisfaction of shared expectations and experiences establishes a trust between reader and writer. As Young and his associates (1970) put it, "An element of trust must be present in every persuasive situation . . . [and] it arises at the precise point where sharing has occurred" (p. 209). In this respect, acknowledgments are a device for building trust between the ethnographer and her or his readers and for underpinning the authenticity of the main part of the ethnography.

SOCIAL SELVES:
THE ANTHROPOLOGIST AS PERSON

Acknowledgments in ethnographies rarely lack reference to another category of people with which anthropologists maintain close ties but which do not as a rule belong to the profession—family and friends:

> Throughout my apprenticeship my parents gave me unstinting support in every possible way. My wife, who shared only a brief part of the pleasures of fieldwork, cheerfully endured the long periods of analysis, writing, tension and proofreading. (Kuper 1970, ix)

> Finally, my most personal debt is to [my husband] and Jenny, Peter, and Hannah Kilson who endure the inconveniences of a part-time wife-mother on both sides of the Atlantic. (Kilson 1974)

> Finally, I mention the assistance of my family. My father, Arthur S. Gregor, is the ace of editors and critics to whom this book is dedicated. My wife Elinor accompanied me on the first trip to the Mehinaku, is gifted in languages, and has a natural talent for fieldwork. She maintained my good disposition as well as her own through occasionally trying conditions and times when the whole project seemed hopelessly mired. This book is therefore in large measure a joint endeavor. (Gregor 1977, xiv)

These selections hint strongly at the tensions that fieldwork and "writing up" generate for anthropologists and their intimates. It cannot be denied that family and friends play a role in helping ethnographers cope with these difficulties—and sometimes in exacerbating them. But why acknowledge—in a publication designed for professional consumption—the contribution of persons who participate only marginally in the anthropological community?

The answer lies in the potential of such passages to create images of ethnographers as social persons. Yet the concepts and standards for the evaluation of selfhood or appropriate behavior change over time: they cannot be understood apart from specific sociocultural contexts. Thus a close reading of the acknowledgments written before and after World War II reveals how anthropologists have reacted to shifts in the definitions of personhood and of proper social relationships within their societies. One major shift is the transformation of the definition of the spousal relationship from an attitude characterized by "gallantry" and a view of nonanthropologist spouses as fulfilling auxiliary roles to an emphasis on sharing, cooperation, and "equality."

The first emphasis comes across rather clearly in the following passages:

In preparing our materials for publication we had the assistance of—particularly with proofs and style—Mrs. Margaret Arensberg. Mrs. Arensberg's labor has made possible whatever grace the book may have. (Arensberg and Kimball [1940] 1968, xvii)

My wife, Irmgard, contributed, as usual, to the logistics of an impeccably run household, and provided me with an invaluable sounding board for ideas and research problems. (van den Berghe 1973, x)

It is customary to express one's debt to one's wife. But I can say truthfully not merely that this study owes its existence to my wife, but also that I owe my wife to this research. Also, during the crucial field trips which she joined, she did invaluable work as research assistant, secretary, nurse, cook, psychotherapist and PRO: in the words of my application for research funds, she performed services which, if purchased locally, might have been more expensive and less satisfactory.

Contrary to convention, however, she neither typed the MS nor read the proofs nor compiled the index. (Gellner 1969, xiv)

From the late 1960s, a greater diversity of forms is used to acknowledge the role of partners and the nature of the spousal relationship:

My wife Kazuko was an equal partner in the 1975 restudy, but I have been unable to persuade her to accept coauthorship of this book. Her help and criticism during this project, as in all my undertakings, were indispensable. (Smith 1978, xv)

[My wife] provided me emotional support and an intelligent, perceptive and sympathetic ear while we were in the field. . . . Because the field experience inseparably combines personal and professional life, [her] contribution to this volume has been inestimably great. (Brandes 1980, x)

Although not situated in an ethnography, Darnell's (1974) gentle quip also falls within this kind of emphasis:

Finally, I would like to thank my husband . . . who, although he does not type, has contributed in innumerable ways to the completion of this manuscript. (p. x)

The fact that anthropologists are sensitive to shifts in their society's conceptions of social ties and personhood highlights their rootedness in their "home" cultures and their persistent "need" to express something about their relations with others, but what is the underlying "need" or basic motivation that impels ethnographers to project images of themselves and their ties with intimate others? In the past, the influence of family and friends on ethnographic projects has received attention only in biographies (e.g., Simpson 1973; Steward 1973; Lipset 1980; Modell 1983),

autobiographies (e.g., Powdermaker 1966; Mead 1972), theoretically minded works like Cesara's (1982), or special
segments of journals like *Annual Review of Anthropology*
(e.g., Leach 1984). Recently, however, a number of studies
have begun to illuminate these issues by examining the
place of anthropologists' "social selves" both within and
outside their professional projects.

An underlying theme of these studies is "care." Care
subsumes not only the more technical or instrumental aspects of assistance but also a special kind of human concern
for others and their needs. This concern is illustrated in the
following excerpts:

> To my wife, my co-worker on both projects, I owe a debt of
> such dimensions that acknowledgment seems but a vain and
> meager gesture. (Geertz 1963)

> Lee, Nicolas and Matthew Myerhoff were usually patient and
> always devoted. They cared about this work because I did and
> let me go even when they wanted to be with me. (Myerhoff
> 1974, 24)

> Yet it must be said as it is all too easy to take the greatest
> acts of generosity and kindness quite for granted until one
> looks around, discovering the opportunity for an expression
> of his deep appreciation in the manner that he would have
> liked, has slipped away. Thus it is to my mother and to the
> memory of my father—who always took an interest in my
> work and my experiences as if they were his own, and who
> passed away suddenly and unexpectedly as this book was in
> the final stages of completion—that I dedicate the present
> work. (Feinberg 1981, xviii)

The emphasis on caring involves an attempt to express
the difficulties and strains anthropologists experience in
trying to attain a "total" or "composed" self. Through the

transmission of messages about kith and kin, anthropologists strive to convey a sense of themselves as total persons not limited to their professional selves. The stress is not so much on utility or advantage as on "images of solutions to experienced stresses and problems" (Ortner 1984, 152). To use Cesara's (1982) philosophical parlance, "Anthropologists face constant difficulties in finding an 'existential unification,' a relief from constant contradiction and ambiguity, [which] is only possible for an authentic self, which is to say a self that cares" (p. 226).

By presenting communications about "caring," anthropologists hint not only at their awareness of these difficulties but also at their attempts at grappling with them. To be sure, given the textual conventions and limitations of acknowledgments, only indirect references are possible. To reiterate, this should not be viewed as a textual defect but, rather, as the result of the special potential of such textual constructs.

It is on this account that Scholte's (1971, 1980) or Diamond's (1971) assertions about the inevitable consequences of professionalization in anthropology should be rejected. According to Scholte (1971), "The anthropologist must turn himself into a detached voyeur, an amoral instrument, a mere shadow of a 'mensch.' " (p. 784). This process of professionalization entails the development of a "split personality," a situation in which the professional ethnographer "is unlikely ever to recapture a personal sense of existential reconciliation" (Scholte 1980, 64; see also Diamond 1971, 3). To judge by the stress that ethnographers have placed on the tensions and difficulties involved in integrating their various selves, such assertions seem too strong. While there are difficulties—rooted in personal inhibitions and textual conventions—in expressing these matters within the anthropological community, they nevertheless do come across.

Conclusion

Acknowledgments, as I have tried to show, are special textual constructs. They are "special" both because their formulation is governed by conventions which are different from those of the main text and because they involve a unique potential for expressing issues not usually addressed in standard ethnographies. A similarity was identified between these passages and other special social constructs like ritual, formal ceremonies, play, or joking behavior. All of these constructs are set apart from the "normal" social— or in our case also textual—order and operate to comment on this order.

Acknowledgments thus work on the basis of suggestiveness and indirectness rather than logical argumentation and direct criticism. On the one hand, suggestiveness—like ritual—create an attitude within which critical judgment is suspended; both the processes of data gathering on which the ethnography is based and the relations that form the basis of professional identities are accepted with little question.[3] On the other hand, suggestiveness—like humor or play—may communicate problematic issues: difficulties with kin or seniors or the tensions of integrating a number of social selves.

Yet acknowledgments also operate on the basis of principles that are different from those of special constructs like ritual and play. Because they are special, marginal texts, their operation is always twofold: social and textual, historical and literary. These passages stand between, and are directed toward, the external social frameworks of which the anthropologist is a member and the internal order and structure of the text. Marcus and Cushman's (1982) assertion about how certain issues, especially those related to fieldwork, are "relegated" to marginal textual locations can now be better understood. This "relegation" results from a choice among different textual constructs, each of which carries its own kind of communications and metacommunications. If, as Lewis (1980) notes, to know a culture is to know its alternatives for expression, then an analysis along the lines suggested here can uncover some of the options for communicating within the culture of anthropology. This refers not only to fieldwork culture but also to the set of norms, values, and expectations that cover all of what anthropologizing entails.

Yet an uncovering of the range of literary choices for expression that is open to anthropologists is not enough. To understand why a certain choice is made, we must also consider the social situation of the chooser, especially the configuration of power within the professional community. For example, because they cannot directly address the issue of asymmetry in resources, juniors resort to the use of special means, like acknowledgments, that are nonlogical and suggestive but are accepted as legitimate. Differences in status and position thus may constrain or facilitate the use of different modes of expression.

For these kinds of reasons, discussions of the problematics of the anthropological community have come from scholars who are somehow less hindered by the limitations of expression that confront most anthropologists. Within anthropology these issues have usually been considered only within historical cases, where chronological distance and experiential detachment buffer the writer from any direct career or identity implications. Where the treatment has been of a more contemporary nature, it has come from individuals—like Mead or Leach—whose powerful positions enable them to disregard their dependence on other anthropologists. Nevertheless, scholars outside the community—sociologists, philosophers, or historians—are likely to pay the most explicit attention to the current problematics of the anthropological community. Paradoxically then, as anthropology's self-reflexivity brings up issues that strike closer to home, the greater the need will become to go outside the discipline for critical approaches and viewpoints.[4]

The argument put forward here is not just for a multiplicity of approaches to understanding how anthropological work is related to its social and intellectual contexts. More specifically, the argument is for the need to go in two directions beyond the recent, fashionable stress on various aspects of textuality. The first is a movement toward seeing anthropological texts not just as products of social action but also as constitutive of social action—that is, as entities that are designed to work back on social relations. The second urges a movement beyond the examination of the complexities of fieldwork and the production of ethnographic projects toward consideration of all the other contexts that affect and contribute to such projects.[5] If a fuller and richer professional reflexivity is to arise within anthropology, our collective stocktaking must consider the whole gamut of these contexts.

Notes

1. I wish here to publicly, dutifully, amiably, and gladly record my thanks to the following people who read an earlier version of this chapter: A. Seligman, Y. Bilu, B. Siebzehner, R. Rosen, T. Rapoport, N. Ben-Ner, and D. Amir. In no small measure this work is also the outcome of discussions with Don Handelman, Haim Hazan, and Virginia Dominguez. The Harry S. Truman Institute—directors and staff—helped me with the completion of the manuscript.

2. Powdermaker's (1966) recollections of Malinowski underline this kind of characterization: "He was also a man of paradoxes: kind and helpful as well as cruel and sarcastic. . . . The atmosphere was in the European tradition: a master and his students, some in accord and others in opposition" (p. 36).

3. It is in this sense that the analysis sheds light on Marcus and Cushman's (1982, 35) assertions that critical judgment about the relationship between what the ethnographer knows and how he or she came to know it is inhibited in reading ethnographies. The coupling of a stress on the construction of trust and the lack of a logical and argumentative style, which is found in marginal textual passages like acknowledgments, creates something like a "ritual truth." The reader is invited to suspend critical appraisal of the information given and to accept it without further reflection.

4. Indeed, scholarly contributions that both reflect upon and stand outside anthropology may become more and more necessary in the coming years. A number of scholars have recently noted how the financial and institutional situation of the discipline is becoming increasingly more difficult (e.g., D'Andrade et al. 1975, 767; Lombard 1984, 717). Under these conditions it seems realistic to expect it to also become increasingly more difficult to critically reflect upon such matters as the microrelations within the anthropological community.

5. For lack of space I have not dealt with a number of other "contexts" of social and cultural anthropology to which there are allusions in acknowledgments: for example, the publishing world, political institutions, and financing bodies. Nor have I examined the "cultural" differences between subgroups within anthropology (e.g., Britons and Americans or archaeologists and cultural anthropologists). But these issues can, I believe, be examined along the lines proposed within this chapter.

References

Alverson, H. 1978. *Mind in the heart of darkness: Value and self-identity among the Tswana of Southern Africa*. New Haven, CT: Yale University Press.

Arensberg, C. M., and S. T. Kimball. [1940] 1968. *Family and community in Ireland*. Reprint. Cambridge, MA: Harvard University Press.

Asad, T., ed. 1973. *Anthropology and the colonial encounter*. London: Tavistock.

Baily, F. G. 1969. *Stratagems and spoils*. New York: Schocken.

Bateson. G. [1936] 1958. *Naven*. Reprint. Stanford, CA: Stanford University Press.

———. 1972. *Steps to an ecology of mind*. New York: Ballantine.

Boon, J. A. 1982. *Other tribes, other scribes: Symbolic anthropology in the comparative study of cultures, histories, religions, and texts*. Cambridge, UK: Cambridge University Press.

Brandes, S. 1980. *Metaphors of masculinity: Sex and status in Andalusian folklore.* Philadelphia: University of Pennsylvania Press.

Cesara, M. 1982. *Reflections of a woman anthropologist: No hiding place.* New York: Academic Press.

Collins, R. 1975. *Conflict sociology: Toward an explanatory science.* New York: Academic Press.

D'Andrade, R. G., E. A. Hammel, D. L. Adkins, and C. K. McDaniel. 1975. Academic opportunity in anthropology, 1974-90. *American Anthropologist* 77:767-73.

Darnell, R. 1971. The professionalization of American anthropology: A case study in the sociology of knowledge. *Social Science Information* 10:85-103.

———. 1984. Preface. In *Readings in the history of anthropology,* edited by R. Darnell, ix-x. New York: Harper.

Diamond, S. 1971. Anthropology in question. In *Reinventing anthropology,* edited by D. H. Hymes, 31-45. New York: Pantheon.

DuBois, C. 1944. *The people of Alor: A social psychological study of an East Indian island.* New York: Harper.

Eisenstadt, S. N., and L. Roniger. 1980. Patron-client relations as a model of structuring social exchange. *Comparative Studies in Society and History* 22 (1): 42-77.

Feinberg, R. 1981. *Anuta: Social structure of a Polynesian island.* Laie, HI: Institute for Polynesia Studies.

Freilich, M., ed. 1977. *Marginal natives at work: Anthropologists in the field.* New York: Schenkman.

Geertz, C. 1963. *Peddlers and princes: Social change and economic modernization in two Indonesian towns.* Chicago: University of Chicago Press.

Gellner, E. 1969. *Saints of the atlas.* Chicago: University of Chicago Press.

Gertrude. 1977. Postface à quelque préface. *Cahiers d'Etudes Africaines* 17 (1): 180-85.

Gluckman, M. 1963. Gossip and scandal. *Current Anthropology* 4:307-16.

Goffman, E. 1967. The nature of deference and demeanor. In *Interaction ritual,* edited by E. Goffman, 47-95. Harmondsworth, UK: Penguin.

Goody, E. N. 1978. Introduction. In *Questions and politeness,* edited by E. N. Goody, 1-16. Cambridge, UK: Cambridge University Press.

Goody, J. 1981. Literacy and classification: On turning the tables. In *Text and context,* edited by R. K. Jain, 205-22. Philadelphia: ISHI Press.

Gouldner, A. W. 1960. The norm of reciprocity: A preliminary statement. *American Sociological Review* 25 (2): 161-78.

Gregor, T. 1977. *Mehinaku: The drama of daily life in a Brazilian Indian village.* Chicago: University of Chicago Press.

Gruber, J. W. 1975. Introduction. In *Toward a science of man: Essays in the history of anthropology,* edited by T. H. H. Thoreson, 1-13. The Hague: Mouton.

Hallowell, A. L. [1965] 1974. The history of anthropology as an anthropological problem. Reprinted in *Readings in the history of anthropology,* edited by R. Darnell, 304-21. New York: Harper.

Handelman, D. 1977. *Work and play among the aged: Interaction replication and emergence in a Jerusalem setting.* Assen, Netherlands: Van Gorcum.

———. 1982. Reflexivity in festival and other cultural events. In *Essays in the sociology of perception,* edited by M. Douglas, 162-90. London: Routledge.

Henry, J. 1965. *Culture as against man.* New York: Vintage.

Hymes, D. [1962] 1974. On studying the history of anthropology. Reprinted in *Readings in the history of anthropology,* edited by R. Darnell, 297-303. New York: Harper.

Jansen, W. H. 1973. The applied man's burden: The problem of ethics and applied anthropology. *Human Organization* 32:325-29.

Jarvie, I. C. 1975. Epistle to the anthropologists. *American Anthropologist* 77:253-66.

Jorion, P. 1976. Anthropological fieldwork: Forerunners and inventors. *Cambridge Anthropology* 3 (2): 22-25.

Kaberry, P. M. 1939. *Aboriginal woman.* London: Routledge.

Kilson, M. 1974. *African urban kinship: The Ga of central Accra.* London: Hurst.

Kuper, A. 1970. *Kalahari village politics: An African democracy.* Cambridge, UK: Cambridge University Press.

———. 1973. *Anthropologists and anthropology: The British school, 1922-1972.* London: Allen Lane.

Lander, P. S. 1976. *In the shadow of the factory: Social change in a Finnish community.* New York: Schenkman.

Langham, I. 1981. *The building of British social anthropology.* Dordrecht: D. Reidel.

Leach, E. R. 1984. Glimpses of the unmentionable in the history of British social anthropology. *Annual Review of Anthropology* 13:1-23.

Lebra, T. S. 1975. An alternative approach to reciprocity. *American Anthropologist* 77:550-65.

Lewis, G. 1980. *Day of shining red: An essay on understanding ritual.* Cambridge, UK: Cambridge University Press.

Lipset, D. 1980. *Gregory Bateson: The legacy of a scientist.* Englewood Cliffs, NJ: Prentice Hall.

Lombard, J. 1984. The teaching of anthropology: A comparative study. *International Social Science Journal* 36 (4): 713-23.

Magnarella, P. J. 1984. *Tradition and change in a Turkish town.* New York: John Wiley.

Marcus, G. E., and J. Clifford. 1985. The making of ethnographic texts: A preliminary report. *Current Anthropology* 26 (2): 267-71.

Marcus, G. E., and D. Cushman. 1982. Ethnographies as texts. *Annual Review of Anthropology* 11:25-69.

Marwick, M. G. 1965. *Sorcery in its social settings: A study of the Northern Rhodesian Cewa.* Manchester, UK: University of Manchester Press.

Mead, M. 1972. *Blackberry winter: My earlier years.* New York: William Morrow.

Modell, J. S. 1975. Ruth Benedict, anthropologist: The reconciliation of science and humanism. In *Toward a science of man: Essays in the history of anthropology,* edited by T. H. H. Thoreson, 183-203. The Hague: Mouton.

————. 1983. *Ruth Benedict: Patterns of a life.* Philadelphia: University of Pennsylvania Press.

Mulkay, M. 1984. The ultimate compliment: A sociological analysis of ceremonial discourse. *Sociology* 18 (4): 531-49.

Murphy, R. F. 1981. Julian Steward. In *Totems and teachers: Perspectives on the history of anthropology,* edited by S. Silverman, 171-206. New York: Columbia University Press.

Myerhoff, B. G. 1974. *Peyote hunt: The sacred journey of the Huichol Indians.* Ithaca, NY: Cornell University Press.

Nader, L. 1976. Professional standards and what we study. In *Ethics and anthropology,* edited by M. A. Ryakiewich and J. P. Spradley, 167-82. New York: John Wiley.

Needham, R. 1984. *Remarks and inventions: Skeptical essays about kinship.* London: Tavistock.

Ortner, S. B. 1984. Theory in anthropology since the sixties. *Comparative Studies in Society and History* 26 (1): 126-66.

Peristiany, P. G. 1939. *The social institutions of the Idipsigis.* London: Routledge.

Plath, D. W. 1980. *Long engagements: Maturity in modern Japan.* Berkeley: University of California Press.

Powdermaker, H. 1966. *Stranger and friend: The way of an anthropologist.* New York: Norton.

Said, E. W. 1975. *Beginnings: Intention and method.* Baltimore: Johns Hopkins University Press.

Scheiffelin, E. L. 1980. Reciprocity and the construction of reality. *Man* 15 (3): 502-17.

Scholte, B. 1971. Discontents in anthropology. *Social Research* 38:777-807.

———. 1980. Anthropological traditions: Their definitions. In *Anthropology: Ancestors and heirs,* edited by S. Diamond, 53-87. The Hague: Mouton.

Silverman, S. 1981. Introduction. In *Totems and teachers: Perspectives on the history of anthropology,* edited by S. Silverman, ix-xv. New York: Columbia University Press.

Simpson, G. E. 1973. *Melville J. Herskovits.* New York: Columbia University Press.

Smith, R. J. 1978. *Kurusu: The price of progress in a Japanese village.* Stanford, CA: Stanford University Press.

Steward, J. H. 1973. *Alfred Kroeber.* New York: Columbia University Press.

Stirling, P. 1965. *Turkish village.* New York: John Wiley.

Turnbull, C. M. 1962. *The forest people.* New York: Anchor.

van den Berghe, P. L. 1973. *Power and privilege at an African university.* London: Routledge.

Whiteford, A. H. 1964. *Two cities of Latin America: A comparative description of social classes.* New York: Anchor.

Whittaker, E. 1981. Anthropological ethics, fieldwork and epistemological disjunctures. *Philosophy of the Social Sciences* 11:437-51.

Young, R. E., A. L. Becker, and K. L. Pike. 1970. *Rhetoric: Discovery and change.* New York: Harcourt.

Zjiderveld, A. C. 1968. Jokes and their relation to social reality. *Social Compass* 35:286-311.

6

Humor in Ethnographic Writing

Sarcasm, Satire, and Irony as Voices in Erving Goffman's Asylums

GARY ALAN FINE

DANIEL D. MARTIN

thnography abounds. Define ethnography as the description of a scene, setting, group, or organization, and one finds that, like Moliere's Monsieur Jourdain, amazed at being able to speak prose, we write ethnography without awareness. Yet only certain ethnographic texts are privileged. The academic guilds have a special slot for "ethnographic scholarship," and some works are so classified.

Within this classification reside styles of discourse (Geertz 1988; Van Maanen 1988); the possible voices are diverse, although perhaps not as diverse as within "nonfiction" or "realistic fiction." If not all ethnography can be classified as a "realist tale," all ethnography is "realistic" in another sense—the implicit claim is that what has been depicted "actually" happened, even recognizing that the story could be told in several ways, varying with the persona of the author, character of the audience, and attitudes toward the focus, or that in some cases the claims may reflect a composite reality.

One predominant characteristic of ethnography, and of scientific discourse generally, is its serious and sedate mien (Fine 1988). This diverges from modes of description that accord emotions (humor, passion, pathos, or tragedy) a respected place. Scientific writing "should be" emotion free. Emotion, if included, resides in segregated prefaces, acknowledgments, or methodological appendixes. Yet, despite the normative expectations, emotion does creep into ethnographic description. It should not be surprising that a discourse heavily dependent on the authorial presence (e.g., Clifford 1988) will incorporate the feelings of the author. Emotion presumes that the author's self is positioned in the text, and, so, we find echoes of fear, sadness, and exaltation.

In this chapter, we focus on a small corner of emotion-laden writing: the use of humor in ethnographic description. As is widely known, humor contributes to rhetorical effectiveness (e.g., Gruner 1979); yet this technique is infrequently employed in social scientific writing. To demonstrate potential uses of humor, and particularly a few subtypes—sarcasm, satire, and irony—we examine a single book: Erving Goffman's (1961a) *Asylums: Essays on the Social Situation of Mental Patients and Other Inmates.* Our goal is to demonstrate the possibilities of humorous ethnographic writing rather than to demonstrate the frequency of such writing. While sarcasm, satire, and irony are recognized categories of humor, they are by no means an exhaustive list. They are, however, three forms used vigorously by Goffman.

By virtue of its production, *Asylums* is a *book;* it is also a set of four essays, related but with different tones and with little explicit connection. All are based on Goffman's ethnographic research at St. Elizabeth's Hospital in Washington, D.C. *Asylums* is regarded as a classic work in medical sociology, deviance, and symbolic interactionism, and it has reoriented policy by helping demolish the justification for large state mental institutions (Goldstein 1979, 399; Price and Smith 1983, 413). Some of our homeless must thank and blame Goffman for their circumstances and for the circumstances they have avoided.

In this account, we focus on three humorous techniques: sarcasm, satire, and irony—forms that overlap more than slightly. For purposes of this chapter we argue inexactly that each characterizes one of Goffman's three humorous essays ("The Moral Career of the Mental Patient" is serious and more "scholarly" than its mates). "On the Characteristics of Total Institutions" (pp. 1-124) is characterized by sarcasm; "The Underlife of a Public Institution: A Study of Ways of Making Out in a Mental Hospital" (pp. 125-70) is largely satiric; and "The Medical Model and Mental Hospitalization: Some Notes on the Vicissitudes of the Tinkering Trades" (pp. 321-86) should be seen as ironic. Goffman does not use any one mode exclusively in any essay, but a certain tone predominates each one. We make no claim for what might or might not have been intended by Goffman in his act of writing.

Humor is a technique for persuading an audience, even when relying on the presentation of ethnographic data.

Humor admits a challenging authorial stance while avoiding explicit political commitment and a need to state one's own solution. That persuasion is a concern of Goffman's is evident in his prefatory comments about focusing on patients as opposed to other denizens of a mental hospital:

> The world view of a group functions to sustain its members and expectedly provides them with a self-justifying definition of their own situation and a prejudiced view of non-members, in this case, doctors, nurses, attendants, and relatives. To describe the patient's situation faithfully is necessarily to present *a partisan view.* (For this last bias I partly excuse myself that the imbalance is at least on the *right side of the scale,* since almost all professional literature on mental patients is written from the point of view of the psychiatrist, and he, socially speaking, is on the other side.) . . . Finally, unlike some patients, I came to the hospital with no great respect for the discipline of psychiatry nor for agencies content with its current practices. (Goffman 1961a, x; emphasis added)

The emphasized phrases suggest a double meaning. On one level, Goffman claims that the perspective of the mental patient has not been considered sufficiently but simultaneously charges that *they are morally preferable* to their keepers. Recall the meanings of "partisan" as defined in *Webster's* (1965): "1: one that takes the part of another: SUPPORTER 2a: a member of a body of detached light troops making forays and harassing an enemy b: a member of a guerilla band operating within enemy lines" (p. 614). Perhaps Goffman relished definition 2b. Goffman's role as an assistant to the athletic director (at St. Elizabeth's) and as a grant recipient (from the National Institute of Mental Health) suggest the significance of "partisan."[1]

Goffman's Ethnography

For a productive *empirical* sociologist, Erving Goffman did remarkably little research, and the quality of the research that he did conduct is open to question, given contemporary cannons of ethnographic research. Goffman conducted two long-term qualitative research projects[2] during his thirty years of scholarly engagement. Both studies were completed early in his career,[3] and we know Goffman for his secondary data analysis, cribbing the examples of others.

Between December 1949 and May 1951 Goffman (1955) spent twelve months on one of the Shetland Islands, north of Scotland, in which he claimed the role of "an American college student interested in gaining first-hand experience in the economics of island farming" (p. 2).[4] During 1954-1957 Goffman "did some brief studies of ward behavior in the National Institutes of Health Clinical Center" (p. ix), and in 1955-1956 he conducted a year's fieldwork at St. Elizabeth's Hospital, then the nation's largest mental institution with over 7,000 patients. Goffman describes his role:

> My immediate object in doing fieldwork at St. Elizabeths was to try to learn about the social world of the hospital inmate, as this world is subjectively experienced by him. I started out in the role of an assistant to the athletic director, when pressed avowing to be a student of recreation and community life, and I passed the day with patients, avoiding sociable contact with the staff and the carrying of a key. I did not sleep in the wards, and the top hospital management knew what my aims were. (p. ix)

There is a studied vagueness in this passage, Goffman's only description of his method. What did Goffman do *after* he was assistant to the athletic director, how did he avoid

sociable contact with the staff and how did their attitudes
shape the research, and what did the top hospital management think his aims were (did they know his attitudes
toward psychiatry)?

Beyond these technical questions there arise three issues
about the connection between Goffman's written reports
and his goals: (1) the lack of systematic description of the
social institution being studied, (2) the lack of perspective
on how participants view their worlds, and (3) the effects of
Goffman's theoretical goals on his collection of data.

1. One reading these essays gains little *systematic* knowledge about how St. Elizabeth's Hospital operates. For instance, one does not learn about the physical layout of the
hospital, its appearance, how many and what kinds of
personnel are employed (or incarcerated), what the typical
day is like for the patients or the staff, or which forms of
therapy are used (cf. Strauss et al. 1964). Rather, one is
exposed to a *tone* of life and some descriptive examples of
what happens (or might happen) but little that allows
outsiders to picture the routine patterns of behavior. In this
sense *Asylums* veers from the assumptions of "traditional"
ethnography in which the presentation of the "whole picture" of a culture is fundamental.

2. To Goffman, the goal is to discover how the world is
"subjectively experienced" by the patient. To the reader, the
book represents anything but. The essays represent how a
"sane" Goffman would *himself* experience a large mental hospital if he was incarcerated against his will. Readers learn
precious little about how patients experience their own
world or, at the least, how they report this experience. Only
rarely does one gain a sense that these are people whose
behavior was seen as sufficiently strange ("dysfunctional")
that they belonged at St. Elizabeth's. The assumption is

that these individuals use Goffman's own experiential categories. He rarely role-plays figures with "mental illnesses" himself but has these figures role-play sociologists:

> In actual practice almost all of the secondary adjustments I have reported were carried on by the patient with an air of intelligent down-to-earth determination, sufficient, once the full context was known, to make an outsider feel at home, in a community much more similar to others he has known than different from them. (p. 303)

St. Elizabeth's is filled with Goffman manqués. Part of the limits to the study's phenomenological validity stems from the fact that the patients and staff were unaware of Goffman's goals, and so he was forced to rely on behavioral traces rather than focused responses. The "lived experience" of the patients was as opaque to him as his was to them.

3. Free from a need to depict a scene or personal responses to that scene, Goffman's ethnography is grounded in theoretical concepts of social organization and interaction: total institution, moral career, underlife, and secondary adjustments. In order to make his theoretical points (and perhaps because his "hidden" role did not permit detailed data collection), Goffman rarely presents fieldnotes (one in "Characteristics of Total Institutions," pp. 71-72). He often relies on what we might term "as-if ethnography." Rather than detailing an occasion on which a set of events took place, he relies on typifications of what "might" or often does happen. Consider the following:

> In mental hospitals, there always seem to be some patients who dramatically act against their own obvious self-interest: they drink water they have themselves first polluted; they overstuff on Thanksgiving and Christmas, so that on these

days there are bound to be a few ruptured ulcers and clogged esophagi; they rush headfirst against the wall; they tear out their own sutures after a minor operation. (p. 82)

One wonders whether Goffman actually witnessed those things that "always seem to happen."[5] Precisely because these data caution us about accepting the normalized absurdity of the place, exact depiction seems particularly critical. This casual data presentation—data given en passant —helps Goffman rhetorically in asserting a theoretical point, free of the messy particulars of a situation, but also leads a reader to wonder precisely what is referenced and whether the data truly support the argument.

In sum, despite Goffman's status as one of the most important American sociologists of the twentieth century, he is not among the century's best ethnographers. His ethnography is casual, not methodologically thorough, and perhaps not to be trusted in providing a precise picture of this social institution. Ultimately, Goffman wishes to provide a perspective, not a photograph. For a "fair" reading of life in an institution, other ethnographies must be relied upon. In the theory and in the *presentation* of the theory we find the glories of Goffman the "ethnographer."

Goffman's Style

Goffman's literary style has been robustly critiqued by sociologists and other savants. His ability to communicate is one of his most distinctive traits when contrasted with much academic writing. As Manning (1976) remarks, Goffman's "conceptual approach, his use of metaphor and a literary method all contribute to the resonance of his work and to its essential ambiguity" (p. 13). The apotheosis of Goffman as man-of-letters reached its zenith in Marshall Berman's glowing tribute to *Relations in Public* on February 27, 1972. Berman claimed that Goffman was one of the greatest contemporary writers. He further suggested that, in his ability to communicate vividly the horror, anguish, and absurdity of modern life, Goffman is our generation's Kafka (Berman 1972). Berman is not alone in emphasizing that style plays off the substance of the Goffman's sermons. In contrast to reviews of most sociology (Reed 1989), it is commonplace for reviewers to comment on the quality of the writing. Some critics suggest that "his writing has always been more readable than his analysis memorable" (Ditton 1976, 331) and that "the fascination with Goffman rests . . . upon the peculiar way he goes about his work rather than on the mere naked content of what he is saying" (Lofland 1980, 24).

Underlying this is the belief that, as Berman suggests, style connects to content. Such a view has become increasingly accepted within literary criticism and anthropology (e.g., Clifford 1988; Geertz 1988) and even sociology (Gusfield 1976; Van Maanen 1988). Authors, even those tethered to the academic world, adapt personae in their writings, and these voices carry force beyond the words alone (Bazerman 1981, 378; Campbell 1975, 391). The style is both the person and the substance.

John Lofland and Peter Manning, writing in Jason Ditton's (1980) edited collection, *A View from Goffman*, refer to Kenneth Burke's concept "perspective by incongruity":

A method for gauging situations by verbal "atom cracking." That is, a word belongs by custom to a certain category—and by rational planning you wrench it loose and metaphorically apply it to a different category. . . . The metaphorical extension of perspective by incongruity involves casuistic stretching, since it interprets new situations by removing words from their "constitutional setting." . . . It is designed to "remoralize" by accurately naming a situation already demoralized by inaccuracy. (Burke 1964, 94-95)

The goal of this exercise is to make the familiar problematic, to violate expectations of readers, to capture a feeling of verisimilitude through use of metaphor, and to view the world with the eyes of a stranger (Lofland 1980, 26-27; Macintyre 1969, 447; Manning 1976, 19). As Davis (1971, 309) suggests, theories that are defined as "interesting" involve denying assumptions of their audience. Perspective by incongruity typically involves a humorous or ironic stance and provokes a risible response by the audience; in Burke's (1964) term, it relies on "a methodology of the pun" (p. 95).

The Comedic Goffman

Although the fact that Goffman (and *Asylums*) is *funny* has not been discussed in detail, it has been noted in passing. Rosenberg (1975) speaks of "the characteristically Goffmanian punch line" (p. 21); Pfautz (1962), reviewing *Asylums,* notes "Goffman's happy penchant for colorfully conceptualizing . . . salient latent structures and processes" (p. 556); and Dawe (1973) refers to Goffman as a "sociological jester" (p. 248).

His writings are laden with humor, but the humor is of a particular sort—a dark wit (Berman 1972) of sarcasm, satire, and irony. These voices are central to our treatment of *Asylums* as we shed light (or heat) on the effects of humor on Goffman's persona and argument. We claim that his humorous tones permit a "partisan view" but simultaneously lead to questions about his political commitments and concern about ambiguous meanings.

Sarcasm

Perhaps the least kindly form of humor (and, for many, the most annoying) is sarcasm. Sarcasm, often lumped with satire, has rarely been studied as a humorous phenomenon in its own right, but, according to Donald Ball (1965), sarcasm is a distinct style of discourse: a "societal form" in the Simmelian sense (p. 190). While Ball does not provide a formal definition of sarcasm, he notes it is "a common everyday linguistic form of biting communication" (p. 191). The core of sarcasm (as opposed to other forms of humorous expression) is open hostility or contempt,[6] and, because of its bitterness, sarcasm is not always experienced as funny. As incongruous communication, it is linked to humor (Berlyne 1969)—often involving saying the opposite of what is meant; that is, an "inversion" (Fowler 1926). Sarcasm announces a *position,* the attitude of the rhetor toward the target. This position is not often inherent in the denotative meanings of the words themselves. The context and persona (of writers) and the nonverbal and paraverbal expressions (of speakers) must convey the message. The person who disagrees may "sarcastically" respond "Right," when what is meant is "Wrong." Consequently, sarcasm may miss its target with an unsympathetic or naive audience.

With an audience that is potentially sympathetic or that identifies with the "sarcaster" (Ball 1965, 192), sarcastic comments have considerable power and can shape attitudes. Goodchilds (1959), in an experimental study of reactions to humor, discovered that a "sarcastic wit" was more influential, and less popular, than a "clowning wit." One trades one's halo to do the devil's business. Effective though it is, some negativity rubs off on the sarcaster.

The existence of a sarcastic tone in the works of Goffman has been noted in reviews. Caudill (1962), in his generally favorable review of *Asylums,* refers to Goffman's use of "biting concepts" (p. 368). Macintyre (1969) remarks on "Goffman's sometimes sour, sometimes bitchy . . . determination" (p. 447).

In "On the Characteristics of Total Institutions," Goffman attempts to demonstrate that total institutions of different emotional stripes have remarkable structural and interactional similarities. Yet his goal extends beyond a dispassionate comparative sociology. Goffman wishes to uncover the self-protective, altruistic ideologies that swaddle most of these institutions. The primary goal of total institutions is to protect the institutions, not to help their "clients." Goffman proposes no ameliorative solutions, no way of humanizing these sites. In the guise of analysis, he savages them.

UNPRIVILEGING

A common rhetorical technique in sarcasm is to remove the privileged status, uncovering taken-for-granted reality. In the case of mental hospitals, this means suggesting that one should accept their own justifications provisionally. All claims for which we lack personal empirical judgment (deriving from a third-party claim) could be treated in this way; in reality, only some are. Just as journalists use "allegedly" and "reportedly" to separate loony or self-serving statements from claims they consider "factual" and "legitimate," Goffman does the same with psychiatric practice, a realm that is accustomed to being treated with respect. Consider the following:

> The various enforced activities are brought together into a single rational plan *purportedly* designed to fulfill the official aims of the institution. (p. 6, emphasis added)

The process of entrance typically brings other kinds of loss and mortification as well. We very generally find staff employing *what are called* admission procedures. . . . Admission procedures might better be called "trimming" or "programming" because in thus being squared away the new arrival allows himself to be shaped and coded into an object that can be fed into the administrative machinery of the establishment, to be worked on smoothly by routine operations. (p. 16, emphasis added)

These statements undercut claims of unquestioned authority of the keepers of these institutions, and gain resonance from Goffman's own authority derived from having observed these practices in person.

ABSURD COMPLIMENTS

The "misplaced" adjective similarly conveys a skepticism of the target. This is harder to achieve in writing than in speech because of the difficulty in establishing cues conveying the intended frame. With a shared sense of context, it can be achieved.[7] While the text read seriously is complimentary, readers should not read "seriously." Consider the following:

Mental hospitals stand out . . . because the staff pointedly establish themselves as specialists in the knowledge of human nature, who diagnose and prescribe on the basis of this intelligence. Hence in the standard psychiatric textbooks there are chapters on "psychodynamics" and "psychotherapy" which provide charmingly explicit formulations of the "nature" of human nature. (p. 89)

"Charmingly" is a factious way to characterize claims that Goffman believes are unwarranted. This literary terrorism —an apparently innocent package is, in truth, a bomb.

THE CUTTING METAPHOR

Perhaps the most effective tool of the sarcaster is the metaphor that casts an admired target in a hostile light. Mark Twain's *mot* that "there is no distinctly native American criminal class except Congress" (Twain 1897) is a quintessential instance of sarcastic "guilt by association." Goffman uses this technique throughout his essay to discredit the standing of the mental hospital. Consider the following:

A total institution is like a finishing school, but one that has many refinements and is little refined. (pp. 41-42)

If the ordinary activities in total institutions can be said to torture time, [playful activities] mercifully kill it. . . . Every total institution can be seen as a kind of dead sea in which little islands of vivid, encapturing activity appear. (p. 69)

Many total institutions, most of the time, seem to function merely as storage dumps for inmates. . . . Given the physiological characteristics of the human organism, it is obvious that certain requirements must be met if any continued use is to be made of people. But this, of course, is the case with inanimate objects, too; the temperature of any storehouse must be regulated, regardless of whether people or things are stored. (pp. 74-75)

To refer to a mental institution as a storage dump, dead sea, finishing school, or Potemkin village (p. 103) skewers the privileged claim. The "hospital" is not what it alleges; its pretense is negated through rhetoric.

SARCASTIC ARGUMENTS

The previous examples have used dramatic imagery to undercut claims, but sarcasm can also be embedded in argumentation. The biting tone, while not to be found in a single word or phrase, is inherent in the text. The persona's hostility toward the target is made palpable by the dismissal of the target's argument. Consider the following:

> There is always the danger that an inmate will appear human; if what are felt to be hardships must be inflicted on the inmate, then sympathetic staff will suffer. . . . And, on the other hand, if an inmate breaks a rule, the staff's conceiving of him as a human being may increase their sense that injury has been done to their moral world: expecting a "reasonable" response from a reasonable creature, the staff may feel incensed, affronted, and challenged when the inmate does not conduct himself properly. (pp. 81-82)

> In mental hospitals we find the engaging phenomenon of the staff using stereotyped psychiatric terminology in talking to each other or to patients but chiding patients for being "intellectualistic" and for avoiding the issues when they use this language, too. (p. 97; see also Wiley 1989)

While one could not fairly claim that these passages raise laughter, they are sarcastic and sardonic. If one accepts that Goffman witnessed behaviors that led to these conclusions (the claim he puts forth by virtue of his presence in the hospital), then one is likely to be sympathetic to his lack of sympathy. His anger is not aimed at the practitioners who put this into place (see p. 124) but at the functional requirements of the system that "necessarily" gave rise to the dehumanization of patients.

Satire

The satirist has a painfully difficult task. By indirection he (satire, like much humor, has been a male domain) must undercut the self-satisfied. More than most humor, satire has the reputation of being subtle, so subtle that many miss it (a fate attributed to some writings of Jonathan Swift and Daniel Defoe). In its rhetorical force it overlaps with sarcasm, and some communications are both satiric and sarcastic, and others are either sarcastic or satiric. Satire is, at its root, profoundly moral; it opts for a morality that we all supposedly hold but which, as hypocrites, too often we ignore. By indirection it argues for moral "ought claims." The satirist is acutely aware of the gap between the way that things are and the way they should be (Pollard 1970, 3) and aims to correct this through the *weapon* of satire (Elliott 1960). The satirist is the minister of the mordant.

While definitions of "satire" are wondrously imprecise, and often not even attempted,[8] we shall define satire as "a playfully critical distortion of the familiar" (Feinberg 1963, 7). Satire is playful, critical, distorted, and familiar. Unlike sarcasm, it is not necessarily hostile or biting (e.g., gentle satire), and it always has a moral component.

That Goffman used his bully pulpit to condemn the falsity of society has not been missed (e.g., Sennett 1973, 31). When Hall (1977, 542) suggests that Goffman has a *disenchanted* view of society or when Davis (1975, 602) suggests that Goffman is a *social destructionist,* what is suggested is that Goffman will not accept the claims of the social system at their face value. Like any good satirist, he insists on holding up a mirror to society, showing hypocrisy. While this leads some to see him as cynical (Dawe 1973, 246; Rosenberg 1975, 21), it could also be taken as the howl of a true believer. As Berman (1972) suggests, Goffman's concern in "The Underlife of a Public Institution" is the ways and means of resistance to structured indignities of a totalistic institution (p. 2). No wonder Berman should link Goffman to Kafka as a corrosive critic of the immorality and inhumanity of modernism.

"The Underlife of a Public Institution" is a portrait of how the inmates run the asylum—and how they quite legitimately do so. Read in conjunction with his destruction of the moral basis of mental hospitals in "On the Characteristics of Total Institutions," Goffman's essay propounds the thesis that the patients' organization may be more humane than the nostrums their doctors prescribe. The "reality" of life in the hospital is a tonic for what should be occurring there.

Of all the essays in *Asylums*, "The Underlife" is the most ethnographically rich, as indeed it needs to be to present the behaviors and actions of the inhabitants of this underlife. It is also the most laughable, almost farcical in some of its "loonier" moments. It is within that tradition of accounts (e.g., *One Flew Over the Cuckoo's Nest; King of Hearts*) in which mental patients serve as moral exemplars for the rest of us. Unlike much satire (as exemplified by *Gulliver's Travels*) in which the satirist creates a world of his choosing, Goffman has his world, but it is a world that is known through such stereotypical and brutal visions that his implicit claim that these inhabitants are as normal as we strikes with immense force, for it carries the implication that we are as "mad" as they.

THE METAPHOR OF PLACE

One technique that Goffman borrows from other satirists is to suggest that what is officially one kind of place is "honestly" another quite dissimilar. Swift's treatment of the Grand Academy at Lagado (in Book Three of *Gulliver's Travels*) reveals it to be not a university but dilapidated hovels in which madmen reside. Goffman takes the mental hospital and turns it into a university, referring to the "campus" (p. 268) and "campus wheels" (p. 217). Elsewhere, the hospital is made a "drunk tank" (p. 216). Still again, it becomes a "poor house" in times of economic uncertainty:

> A considerable number of male patients who entered at a time when jobs were scarce and, being somewhat cut off from the flow of events outside, still believed that the "deal" they were getting on the inside was a good one. As one suggested upon receiving his free dessert, "You don't get apple pie like this on the outside for twenty-five cents, you don't." (p. 215)

The hospital becomes all things to all people with the support of the hospital structure:

> [One] group were Negroes: some of these who so wished were able to some degree to cross the class and color line, cliquing with and dating white patients, and receiving from the psychiatric staff some of the middle-class professional conversation and treatment denied them outside the hospital. [Another] group were the homosexuals: incarcerated for their proclivities, they found a one-sexed dormitory life awaiting them, with concomitant sexual opportunities. (p. 217)

What is "officially" one kind of place is transformed through metaphor (both satiric and sarcastic) to something unexpected.

THE METAPHOR OF PERSON

For the satirist, people are not always what they seem: the perfect become flawed, the flawed perfect. Just as a hospital is not always a hospital, so the mentally ill are not always mentally ill; they are really cagey actors out for rewards that make life bearable:

It was widely known by parole patients that at the end of charitable shows at the theater hall cigarettes or candy would probably be given out at the door, as the patient audience filed out. Bored by some of these shows, some patients would come a few minutes before closing time in order to file out with the others; still others would manage to get back into the line several times and make the whole occasion more than ordinarily worth-while. Staff were of course aware of these practices, and late-comers to some of the hospital-wide patient dances were locked out, the assumption being that they timed their arrival so as to be able to eat and run. The Jewish Welfare women apparently served brunch after the weekly morning service and one patient claimed that "by coming at the right time you can get the lunch and miss the service." (p. 212)

Such strategies convey slapstick, as one imagines a clever Charlie Chaplin cunningly sneaking into the theater only to file out again, as guards guard the door. The strategies became a game (p. 285).

Therapy was also transformed into something other than it was supposed to be as patients "made do" with their secondary adjustments:

Some patients even managed to find hidden values in insulin shock therapy: patients receiving insulin shock were allowed in bed all morning in the insulin ward, a pleasure impossible in most other wards, and were treated quite like patients by nurses there. (p. 223)

In Central Hospital the chief forms of psychotherapy were group therapy, dance therapy, and psychodrama. All were conducted in a relatively indulgent atmosphere and tended to recruit the kinds of patients who were interested in contact with the opposite sex. Psychodrama was especially workable because lights would be turned low during a performance. (p. 224)

Patients are skilled connivers, like the professional pick-pocket, who has too much self-respect to pay for what he might need (p. 183).

METAPHORS OF RELATIONS

Within Goffman's satiric vision is the belief that patients and staff are not striving for the same end but are in battle against each other: "[For some patients] the hospital represented a kind of game situation in which one could pit oneself against the authorities, and some of the relationships that flourished seemed to do so partly because the participants enjoyed the intrigue of sustaining them" (p. 285). The patients work the system, sometimes using their symptoms for their own ends and slipping in and out of them at will:

> Occasionally a patient *in the role* of someone out of contact would preferentially select a particular person as someone not to be out of contact with. (p. 258, emphasis added)

> Almost all patients in the hospital, with the exception of the few preadolescents, formed a single cigarette system involving the right to request and the obligation to grant a light from a lighted cigarette. Very surprisingly, patients on the worst wards, sick enough to be mute for years, hostile enough to decline the offer of a cigarette, and distracted enough to forget to extinguish a lighted cigarette which had begun to scorch their hands, observed this system. A function of this system, of course, was that it saved patients from having to beseech an attendant for a light. (p. 283)

Even muteness can be seen as a "defense" against staff, and was "grudgingly accepted as a legitimate mental symptom" (p. 257). Elements of mental dysfunction that might be seen as essential to the patient's character are presented as techniques for undercutting the staff, of denying the legitimacy of the institution.

Ultimately, the satire consists of a robust transformation of a privileged medical world into an illegitimate political world (pp. 299-300, 304-8). Recall the definition of satire as a playfully critical distortion of the familiar:

> Participants decline in some way to accept the official view of what they should be putting into and getting out of the organization and, behind this, of what sort of self and world they are to accept for themselves. Where enthusiasm is expected, there will be apathy; where loyalty, there will be disaffection; where attendance, absenteeism; where robustness, some kind of illness; where deeds are to be done, varieties of inactivity. We find a multitude of homely little histories, each in its way a movement of liberty. . . . From the patient's point of view, to decline to exchange a word with the staff or with his fellow patients may be ample evidence of rejecting the institution's view of what and who he is; yet higher management may construe this alienative expression as just the sort of symptomatology the institution was established to deal with and as the best kind of evidence that the patient properly belongs where he now finds himself. In short, mental hospitalization outmaneuvers the patient, tending to rob him of the common expressions through which people hold off the embrace of organizations . . . [w]hen a patient, whose clothes are taken from him each night, fills his pockets with bits of string and rolled up paper, and when he fights to keep these possessions in spite of the consequent inconvenience to those who must regularly go through his pockets, he is usually seen as engaging in symptomatic behavior befitting a very sick patient, not as someone who is attempting to stand apart from the place accorded him. (pp. 304-8)

This is brilliant, corrosive satire. That it is composed within the privileged tradition of academic style (as *Gulliver's Travels* was ostensibly a traveler's account) means that

Goffman plays off the genre and can report quite ludicrous happenings as if they are most ordinary. The emotion that some claim Goffman lacks (e.g., Berman 1972, 10) must be *read into* the text. Like much satire, the most absurd or outrageous events are depicted in a deliberately unremarkable style. That Goffman claims (like Lemuel Gulliver) that *he was there*—in reality, not in fiction—increases the power of the voice (see Geertz 1988). The measured academic style magnifies the attacks.

Irony

Irony, like satire or sarcasm, is difficult to define (Booth 1974, 2) and has numerous subtypes (Handwerk 1985). In general, irony refers to the technique of using incongruity to suggest a disjunction between reality and expectations; saying one thing and meaning another (with the audience aware of both). In this there is a close connection between satire and irony, so much so that irony is typically considered a major component of satire (Worcester 1969; Pollard 1970, 66). Yet, unlike satire, criticism of the status quo is not necessarily implied, just as satire need not be based on a verbal incongruity. Some satire is not ironic; some irony lacks satiric bite.

Discussions of Goffman's use of "perspective by incongruity" refer to his ironic stance. Manning (1976) describes Goffman's irony in seeking "to have the reader understand that [certain] phenomena are all that he suggests they are not" (p. 16). Hollingshead (1962) specifically notes Goffman's "delicate irony" in *Asylums* (p. 185), whereas Manning (1980) refers to this same collection as revealing "cutting irony" (p. 265). Cutting or delicate, Goffman uses an ironic stance throughout *Asylums*.

Perhaps the ironic stance is most evident in the final essay in *Asylums,* ironically labeled "The Medical Model and Mental Hospitalization: Some Notes on the Vicissitudes of the Tinkering Trades." This essay presents a decidedly off-kilter view of psychiatric practice. The essay, in its ironic persona, has two tonal segments. Goffman begins by describing the processes involved in repair, a metaphor he contends describes medicine. People, like cars, are brought into a workshop and fixed.

By the middle of the essay, Goffman's tone subtly shifts from seeing the doctor as Mr. Goodwrench to describing the psychiatrist as The Man. Patients are like autos, in part because they need to be fixed (comedic irony), but also because the fixer has total control over what can be done to them: a Buick has no privileged status in its relationship with the mechanic (satiric irony). Goffman glides from wry amusement to sardonic outrage. As Dawe (1973) notes, referring to the change in tone in Goffman's writing revealed in *Relations in Public* but equally applicable to "The Medical Model . . .", Goffman's writing shifts from "social comedy" to "sheer terror" (p. 249).

HUMOROUS IRONY

Consider, for lightness of tone, these incongruities suggested in the early pages of the essay:

The body is one possession that cannot be left under the care of the server while the client goes about his other business. (p. 341)

Due to medical ethics, a physician cannot advise a patient to junk the badly damaged or very worn object his body may have become (as can those who service other types of objects), although the physician may tacitly give such advice to other interested parties. (p. 342)

These passages are written with a gently ironic touch. The body may be a damaged object, but the ways in which it is not are theoretically rich for the sociologist. In these passages, one can not claim that Goffman is saying that the medical profession is other than what it must be, given bodily reality.

SATIRIC IRONY

When Goffman turns his attention from medicine to psychiatry his gaze becomes a glare. From his deep suspicion of psychiatry, Goffman is dubious that psychiatrists really fix these human machines:

> If we view the mentally ill as persons that others have had a special kind of trouble with, then the custodial role of the hospital . . . is understandable and, many would feel, justifiable; the point here, however, is that a service to the patient's kin, neighborhood, or employer is not necessarily . . . a service, especially not a medical service, to the inmate. Instead of a server and the served, we find a governor and the governed, an officer and those subject to him. (p. 353)

Here, Goffman is operating within that rhetorical domain in which sarcasm, satire, and irony are joined but is still sounding like a social scientist. His partisanship is clear and has gained legitimacy by his presence at the scene of the crime—the crime being the total domination of the patient by the psychiatrist, even when the patient is supposed to be a *client* of that psychiatrist:

> None of a patient's business, then, is none of the psychiatrist's business; nothing ought to be held back from the psychiatrist as irrelevant to his job. (p. 358)

Psychiatric staff share with policemen the peculiar occupational task of hectoring and moralizing adults; the necessity
of submitting to these lectures is one of the consequences of
committing acts against the community's social order. (p. 366)

Finally, there are heart-warming stories of impossible patients who finally came to form a good relationship with an
understanding doctor and thereafter dramatically improved.
As with the other of exemplary tales, these relationship
stories seem to center on proof of the rightness of the position
taken by staff. [Footnote: Patients, of course, have their own
set of exemplary tales almost equally discrediting of staff.]
(p. 374)

These announcements have undeniable power as typifications, but the real brutality of Goffman's satire comes when
he, as observer, describes the hideous falseness of the euphemisms and hypocrisy of psychiatric "rationalizations" in
this world "relatively uncontrolled in barbarity" (p. 378):

To cite a relatively extreme example I have seen a therapist
deal with a Negro patient's complaints about race relations
in a partially segregated hospital by telling the patient that
he must ask himself why he, among all the other Negroes
present, chose this particular moment to express this feeling,
and what this expression could mean about him as a person,
apart from the state of race relations in the hospital at the
time. (pp. 376-77)

The punishment of being sent to a worse ward is described as
transferring a patient to a ward whose arrangements he can
cope with, and the isolation cell or "hole" is described as a
place where the patient will be able to feel comfortable with
his inability to handle his acting-out impulses. Making a ward
quiet at night through the forced taking of drugs, which
permits reduced night staffing, is called medication or seda-

tive treatment. Women long since unable to perform such
routine medical tasks as taking bloods are called nurses and
wear nursing uniforms; men trained as general practitioners
are called psychiatrists. (p. 381)

Psychiatrists have endless tricks to make their patients fall
in line, and are facile with justifications for failure. It is all
a facade. The goal of the hospital is to uncover a crime that
fits the punishment and recreate the character of the in-
mate to fit that crime (p. 385). This is bitter writing—no
social comedy here. The irony is that what "allegedly" is
designed to perform moral acts has quite different effects.

Goffman as Partisan

It is a signal irony that both Alvin Gouldner (1968) and
Erving Goffman consider themselves to be sociological "par-
tisans." Equally ironically, Goffman is often seen as "on the
side of the system" (Dawe 1973, 251; see also Gouldner
1970). Collins and Makowsky (1978) wrote,

He explores the underside of life, but he is not really sympathetic to the underdog. *Asylums* does not condemn hospital
personnel for destroying the selves of mental patients, but
explains their behavior in terms of the exigencies of a necessarily bureaucratic total institution. (p. 235)

If the argument is that Goffman didn't experience hospital
employees as "evil," this is true enough and rather silly.
Instead, he presents the institutions as dehumanizing because of its structure and ideology. In *Asylums,* we read
both the corrosive power of his critique and some reasons
why it may not have been read as such. Consider these
passages from the Conclusion:

I do not mean to imply that the application of the [medical-service] model has not sometimes proved useful to those institutionalized as patients. The presence of medical personnel in asylums has no doubt served to stay somewhat the hand of the attendant. (p. 383)

The point is not that the hospital is a hateful place for patients but that for the patient to express hatred of it is to give evidence that his place in it is justified and that he is not yet ready to leave it. (p. 385)

Mental patients can find themselves in a special bind. To get out of the hospital, or to ease their life within it, they must show acceptance of the place accorded them, and the place accorded them is to support the occupational role of those who appear to force this bargain. This self-alienating moral servitude, which perhaps helps to account for some inmates becoming mentally confused, is achieved by invoking the great tradition of the expert servicing relation, especially its medical variety. Mental patients can find themselves crushed by the weight of a service ideal that eases life for the rest of us. (p. 386)

Like so many satirists, Goffman finds that this audience does not always "get" the message (at least not the message that *we* get). The problem, evident in these passages, is that Goffman writes with tongue in cheek, and perhaps in doing so overestimates his audience. It is not that Goffman doesn't care how he is viewed or that he presents both sides (Posner 1978, 67, 73) but that the connotations of irony, satire, and sarcasm can be misread (Johnson 1966). It is a subtle form of persuasion (Sutherland 1958, 5). The effective rhetor is the one who uses language in such a way that it speaks to an audience, a community (Overington 1977, 158).

Thus, in the first passage, Goffman admits the utility of the medical model. But why? To stay the hand of the attendant. The second passage doesn't deny that the hospital is a hateful place (we know from his ethnography that it is) but says that to admit it makes the patient's situation that much worse. In the final passage, acceptance of "the great tradition of the expert servicing relation" leads to confusion ("mental illness"), which implies that greatness adheres to the tradition, not to the relation. The text demands close reading and the active involvement of the reader.

We read *Asylums* as a political tract, aimed in part at unmasking the "fraud" of mental hospitals and psychiatric practice. It does not aim to demean individuals, but it does take on this system and those elements of the outside world that are being convenienced by the existence of the system. The mental institution is functional like the institution of slavery is functional; it makes life easier for some at the expense of others. Whereas Goffman adopts a "cooly detached" persona—a complaint that Gouldner (1968, 105) leveled at Becker—his role as partisan may be stronger for that. He has just emerged from "behind the lines" with his scalp intact and his evidence uncontaminated by the visions of others. The problem is for his readers to recognize the existence of his broad critique.

Ethnographic Laughs

As our discussion of *Asylums* has indicated, certain types of humor can be effectively used in ethnographic writing, although these techniques are not without their danger. Humor draws an audience and may be an effective rhetorical tool by which social and political arguments can be made. Yet, because these techniques often work by indirection, some audiences "misread" the argument.

The danger derived from indirection seems particularly relevant with regard to ethnographic writing. The standard mode of writing in ethnography is the "realist tale"—the account that purports to be "true" because of the presence and the objectivity of the author. In sarcasm, satire, and irony, objectivity is jettisoned. "Truth" represents a lower or higher ideal—humor is a framing technique of the kind in which Goffman luxuriates in the pages of *Frame Analysis*. This leads readers to question the fairness of the account as description and, unless the author can get us on his side, the wisdom of the charges. Given that sarcasm, satire, and irony do not present suggestions for change or ways to right the wrongs (Posner 1978, 72), those readers who might be sympathetic to the radicalness of the critique now see the argument, lacking a call for change, as supporting the status quo. As negative statements, such humorous techniques deny the ameliorative optimism that many social change agents share.

It is the power of satiric humor as a tool for memorable criticism, for denying us the possibility that the target can be seen as anything else but ludicrous, that ignores the possibility of a positive integration. That must come from the reader. Often, the humorist implies that there *are* no good solutions (and, here, the problem of the mentally ill may be just such an intractable issue).

Perhaps readers will now return to Goffman's *Asylums*, rereading it for its styles and for its power, seeing it as a literary experiment that depends on the triangulated relations between author, audience, and subjects. It would be more desirable still if other ethnographers would continue that experimentation evident in Goffman's oeuvre. Humor need not be inconsistent with academic writing. Ethnography is literature; let us hope that more of it can be good literature.

Notes

1. One recalls Alvin Gouldner's (1968) "The Sociologist as Partisan," penned in attack on Howard Becker's (1967) "Whose Side Are We On?" Gouldner uses "partisan" with the first meaning, without the hint of ironic subversion that one finds in Goffman. Goffman's "partisan," content to present sly, ambiguous calls to arms, is not Gouldner's street fighter.

2. In "Role Distance," Goffman (1961b) refers to "brief observations in the medical building of a mental hospital [presumably St. Elizabeth's] and the operating rooms of a suburban community hospital [presumably Herrick Memorial Hospital, Berkeley, California]" (p. 117). The references to this body of research were few and far between, and there is no clue as to what "brief" might mean. Apparently, Goffman also did some observations in Las Vegas casinos during the 1970s, but we are unaware of published analyses of these data.

3. Goffman (1989) avers that "you have to be young to do fieldwork. It's harder to be an ass when you're old" (p. 128).

4. This document, "Communication Conduct in an Island Community" (Goffman, 1953), is more traditionally ethnographic in tone and in use of data. It is like *Asylums* in that Goffman's primary goal is not the description of life in a small town in the Celtic fringe but to examine demeanor and interaction: questions that were pursued in *Presentation of Self in Everyday Life* (1959), which relies only occasionally on the material in the dissertation. Both the dissertation and the essays in *Asylums* are "theoretical ethnographies." Even in his dissertation one can occasionally see flashes of wit that are given free rein in his published writings.

5. Whatever else *Asylums* might be, it is not an instance of a "confessional tale" (Van Maanen 1988). The reader rarely sees Goffman in these adventures; thus it is a considerable shock when we read "I drank a few times on the grounds both with attendants and with patients" (p. 267). More typical is a coy reference to the same issue within the same essay: "I knew an extremely resourceful alcoholic who would smuggle in a pint of vodka, put some in a paper drinking cup, and sit on the most exposed part of the lawn he could find, slowly getting drunk; at such times he took pleasure in offering hospitality to *persons of semi-staff status*" (p. 313, emphasis added).

6. According to Ball (1965), "Etymologically, sarcasm comes from the Greek *sarkazein*, to speak bitterly—literally, to tear flesh" (p. 192).

7. Perhaps the classic instance of this is Freud's. When finally permitted to leave Vienna after the Anschluss, Freud was forced to sign a

document claiming no ill treatment by the German authorities. Freud asked to add a sentence to the document: "I can heartily recommend the Gestapo to anyone" (Jones 1957, 226).

8. Richter remarks, "Definitions of the comic serve the sole purpose of being themselves comic" (quoted in Worcester 1969, 10).

References

Ball, D. W. 1965. Sarcasm as sociation: The rhetoric of interaction. *Canadian Review of Sociology and Anthropology* 2:190-98.

Bazerman, C. 1981. What written knowledge does: Three examples of academic discourse. *Philosophy of the Social Sciences* 11:361-87.

Becker, H. S. 1967. Which side are we on? *Social Problems* 14:239-48.

Berlyne, D. E. 1969. Laughter, humor, and play. In *The handbook of social psychology,* edited by G. Lindzey and E. Aronson, 795-852. Reading, MA: Addison-Wesley.

Berman, M. 1972. Review of *Relations in Public. New York Times Book Review,* 27 February, 1-2, 10, 12, 14, 16, 18.

Booth, W. C. 1974. *A rhetoric of irony.* Chicago: University of Chicago Press.

Burke, K. 1964. *Perspectives by incongruity.* Bloomington: Indiana University Press.

Campbell, P. N. 1975. The personae of scientific discourse. *Quarterly Journal of Speech* 61:391-405.

Caudill, W. 1962. Review of *Asylums. American Journal of Sociology* 68:366-69.

Clifford, J. 1988. *The predicament of culture.* Cambridge, MA: Harvard University Press.

Collins, R., and M. Makowsky. 1978. *The discovery of society.* 2d ed. New York: Random House.

Davis, M. S. 1971. That's interesting: Towards a phenomenology of sociology and a sociology of phenomenology. *Philosophy of the Social Sciences* 1:309-44.

———. 1975. Review of *Frame Analysis. Contemporary Sociology* 4:599-603.

Dawe, A. 1973. The underworld-view of Erving Goffman. *British Journal of Sociology* 24:246-53.

Ditton, J. 1976. Review of *Frame Analysis. Sociology* 10:329-32.

———, ed. 1980. *A view from Goffman.* New York: St. Martin's.

Elliott, R. C. 1960. *The power of satire.* Princeton, NJ: Princeton University Press.

Feinberg, L. 1963. *The satirist: his temperament, motivation, and influence.* Ames: Iowa State University Press.

Fine, G. A. 1988. The ten commandments of writing. *American Sociologist* 19:152-57.

Fowler, H. W. 1926. *A dictionary of modern English usage.* London: Oxford University Press.

Geertz, C. 1988. *Works and lives: The anthropologist as author.* Stanford, CA: Stanford University Press.

Goffman, E. 1953. Communication conduct in an island community. Ph.D. diss. University of Chicago.

———. 1959. *Presentation of self in everyday life.* Garden City, NY: Anchor.

———. 1961a. *Asylums.* Garden City, NY: Anchor.

———. 1961b. *Encounters.* Indianapolis, IN: Bobbs-Merrill.

———. 1989. On fieldwork. *Journal of Contemporary Ethnography* 18:123-32.

Goldstein, M. S. 1979. The sociology of mental health and illness. *Annual Review of Sociology* 5:381-409.

Goodchilds, J. D. 1959. Effects of being witty on position in the social structure of a small group. *Sociometry* 22:261-71.

Gouldner, A. 1968. The sociologist as partisan. *American Sociologist* 3:103-16.

———. 1970. *The coming crisis of Western sociology.* New York: Avon.

Gruner, C. R. 1979. *Understanding laughter: The workings of wit and humor.* Chicago: Nelson-Hall.

Gusfield, J. 1976. The literary rhetoric of science: Comedy and pathos in drinking driver research. *American Sociological Review* 41:16-34.

Hall, J. A. 1977. Sincerity and politics: Existentialists vs. Goffman and Proust. *Sociological Review* 25:535-50.

Handwerk, G. J. 1985. *Irony and ethics in narrative.* New Haven, CT: Yale University Press.

Hollingshead, A. 1962. Review of *Asylums. Annals of the American Academy of Political and Social Science* 344:185.

Johnson, M. 1966. *The sin of wit.* Ann Arbor, MI: Gordian.

Jones, E. 1957. *The life and work of Sigmund Freud, Vol. 3.* New York: Basic Books.

Lofland, J. 1980. Early Goffman: Style, structure, substance, soul. In *The view from Goffman,* edited by J. Ditton, 24-51. New York: St. Martin's.

Macintyre, A. 1969. The self as work of art. *New Statesmen* 177:447-48.

Manning, P. K. 1976. The decline of civility: A comment on Erving Goffman's sociology. *Canadian Review of Sociology and Anthropology* 13:13-25.

————. 1980. Goffman's framing order: Style as structure. In *The view from Goffman,* edited by J. Ditton, 253-84. New York: St. Martin's.

Overington, M. A. 1977. The scientific community as audience: Toward a rhetorical analysis of science. *Philosophy and Rhetoric* 10:143-64.

Pfautz, H. W. 1962. Review of *Asylums. American Sociological Review* 27:555-56.

Pollard, A. 1970. *Satire.* London: Methuen.

Posner, J. 1978. Erving Goffman: His presentation of self. *Philosophy of the Social Sciences* 8:67-78.

Price, R. H., and S. S. Smith. 1983. Two decades of reform in the mental health system (1963-1983). In *Handbook of social interaction,* edited by E. Seidman, 408-37. Beverly Hills, CA: Sage.

Reed, J. S. 1989. Presidential address. Presented at the annual meeting of the Southern Sociological Society, Norfolk, VA.

Rosenberg, P. 1975. Review of *Frame Analysis. New York Times Book Review,* 16 February, 21-26.

Sennett, R. 1973. Two on the aisle. *New York Review of Books,* 1 November, 29-31.

Strauss, A., L. Schatzman, R. Bucher, D. Erlich, and M. Sabshin. 1964. *Psychiatric ideologies and institutions.* Glencoe, IL: Free Press.

Sutherland, J. 1958. *English satire.* Cambridge: Cambridge University Press.

Twain, M. 1897. *Following the equator.* Hartford, CT: American Publishing.

Van Maanen, J. 1988. *Tales of the field: On writing ethnography.* Chicago: University of Chicago Press.

Webster's seventh new collegiate dictionary. 1965. Springfield, MA: G. & C. Merriam.

Worcester, D. 1969. *The art of satire.* New York: Norton.

7

Narrative and Sociology

LAUREL RICHARDSON

L
ife histories, informants' oral accounts, in-depth interviews, case studies, historical documents, and participant observation are the major methods used by
qualitative researchers. An abundant literature discusses
how to gain entrée, ask questions, listen, take fieldnotes,
and tape record. The tapes and notes, however, do not
constitute the "findings." Rather, as part of our *research*
agenda, we fashion these accounts into a prose piece; we
transform biographical interviews and fieldnotes into a
sociological text. Although this stage of the research process
requires complex decision making, there is little in the
literature about the issues and their resolutions (but see the
literature review in Van Maanen 1988).

How *should* we write our research? The rhetorical, ethical, and methodological issues implicit in this question are

neither few nor trivial. Rather, the question reflects a central postmodernist realization: all knowledge is socially constructed. Writing is not simply a "true" representation of an objective "reality"; instead, language creates a particular view of reality. All language has grammatical, narrative, and rhetorical structures that "create value, bestow meaning, and constitute (in the sense of imposing form upon) the subjects and objects that emerge in the process in the inquiry" (Shapiro 1985-86, 192). How we choose to write, then, involves many major and minor rhetorical and ethical decisions (cf. Brown 1977; Edmondson 1984; Fisher 1987; Nelson, Megill, and McCloskey 1987; Van Maanen 1988). By what criteria should we evaluate the writing? Scientific soundness? Aesthetic resonance? Ethical rightness? What are our goals? Who is our audience?

Those questions are wrestled with from different vantage points in Richardson (1990). My goal in this chapter is the provision of an argument for the presence and value of *narrative* within sociology. In the process, I cover some familiar ground and touch on some new. Although narrative has been rhetorically marginalized, justified within conventional sociology during "exploratory" research or when used as human "filler" to "flesh out" statistical findings, I argue that narrative is quintessential to the understanding and communication of the sociological. All social scientific writing depends on narrative structure and narrative devices, although that structure and those devices are frequently masked by a "scientific" frame, which is itself a metanarrative (cf. Lyotard 1979). The issue is not whether sociology should use the narrative, but which narratives will be provided to the reader. Can we construct a sociology in which narrated lives replace the narrative of unseen, atemporal, abstract "social forces"?

What Is Narrative?

Narrative displays the goals and intentions of human actors; it makes individuals, cultures, societies, and historical epochs comprehensible as wholes, it humanizes time, and it allows us to contemplate the effects of our actions and to alter the directions of our lives. Narrative is everywhere; it is present in myth, fable, short story, epic, history, tragedy, comedy, painting, dance, stained glass windows, cinema, social histories, fairy tales, novels, science schema, comic strips, conversation, and journal articles. Children everywhere learn how to listen to and tell stories at very early ages. Roland Barthes comments, "The narratives of the world are without number. . . . [T]he narrative is present at all times, in all places, in all societies: the history of narrative begins with the history of [hu]mankind; there does not exist, and never has existed, a people without narratives" (Barthes 1966, 14).

Narrative is the primary way through which humans organize their experiences into temporally meaningful episodes (Polkinghorne 1988, 1). People link events narratively. "Narrative meaning is created by noting that something is a 'part' of a whole and that something is a 'cause' of something else" (Polkinghorne 1988, 6). The meaning of each event is produced by its temporal position and its role in a comprehensible whole. Narratively, to answer the question "What does something *mean?*" requires showing how the "something" contributed to the conclusion of the episode. The connections between the events constitute meaning.

Narrative is both a mode of reasoning *and* a mode of representation. People can "apprehend" the world narratively and people can "tell" about the world narratively. According to psychologist Jerome Bruner (1986), narrative reasoning is one of two basic and universal human cognition modes. The other mode is the logico-scientific. The two modes are irreducible to each other and complementary. Each mode provides a distinctive way of ordering experience and constructing reality, has its own operating principles and criteria of "well-formedness," and has radically different procedures for verification (p. 11). Causality plays a central role in both cognitive modes, but each defines it differently. The logico-scientific mode looks for universal truth conditions, whereas the narrative mode looks for particular connections between events. Explanation in the narrative mode is contextually embedded, whereas logico-scientific explanation is abstracted from spatial and temporal contexts. Both modes are "rational" ways of making meaning.

Not surprising, the two modes of reasoning rely primarily on different communication codes to get their messages across, although they borrow freely from each other's codes (Jakobson 1960). The narrative code "demonstrates" narrative reasoning, the type of reasoning that understands the whole by the integration of its parts, whereas the logico-scientific code demonstrates empiricist reasoning, the type of reasoning that "proves" statements. Both modes, however, are framed in metanarratives such as "science," "the enlightenment," or "religion." Narrative structures, therefore, are preoperative, regardless of whether one is writing primarily in a narrative or a logico-scientific code.

Conventional Social *Science* Writing

Sociology has constructed its writing practices so that the logico-scientific code is privileged and the narrative code suppressed. It acts as if it were untrammeled by narrative structure and conventions. Hiding behind the metanarrative of "science," conventional social science, however, deploys such master narratives as the impact of "social forces" or the "functional interdependence" of "complex systems." Literary devices flourish within social science, not only for adornment but to carry *cognitive* meaning. I briefly trace the historical roots of this social construction of sociological writing and then illustrate how the narrative code functions within social *science* writing.

From the seventeenth century onward, intellectuals have divided writing into two kinds: scientific and literary. Literature, a historical construction of the seventeenth century, was the repository of rhetoric, subjectivity, and fiction. Science was the repository of "plain" language, objectivity, and fact (Clifford 1986, 5). Truth value was denied literature because it "invented" reality rather than observing it the way science presumably did.

Drawing on Plato's distrust of poets, assaults on literary writing intensified during the eighteenth century. Science, in John Locke's estimation, had to be written in "plain style," in words that did not "move the Passions and thereby mislead the Judgement," in unambiguous words unlike the "perfect cheats" of poetic utterances (quoted in Levine 1985, 3). Adults, Locke contended, should avoid figurative language in order to leave the "conduit" between thoughts and things unobstructed. He urged parents to stifle any poetic tendencies in their children. David Hume depicted poets as professional liars. Jeremy Bentham proposed that the ideal language would be one without words, only unambiguous symbols. Samuel Johnson's dictionary sought to fix "univocal meanings in perpetuity, much like the univocal meanings of standard arithmetic terms" (Levine 1985, 4).

Into this linguistic world, the Marquis de Condorcet introduced the term "social science." De Condorcet contended that, with precision in language about moral and social issues, "knowledge of the truth" would be "easy and error almost impossible" (quoted in Levine 1985, 6). Both positivist and interpretive sociologists agreed. Emile Durkheim wanted sociology to cleanse itself of everyday language. Max Weber urged the construction of ideal-types as a way to achieve the univocity of science. The search for the unambiguous was "the triumph of the quest for certainty" (Rorty 1979, 61). By the nineteenth century, literature and science stood as two separate domains. Literature was aligned with "Art" and "Culture." It contained the values of "taste, aesthetics, ethics, humanity, and morality" (Clifford 1986, 6) and the rights to metaphoric and ambiguous language. Given to science was the belief that its words were objective, precise, unambiguous, noncontextual, nonmetaphoric. The "modernist" vision of science writing as "transparent"—simply reflecting, like a clear pane of glass, an objective "reality"—has dominated social scientific thinking. Only recently has this view been seriously challenged (cf. Gusfield 1976; Rorty 1979).

Rhetoricians have shown through concrete analyses that even the "plainest" science writing uses literary devices to *constitute value* and to *convey* meaning (cf. Bazerman 1988; Edmondson 1984; Nelson et al. 1987). All the social sciences, for example, have prescribed writing formats—none of them neutral or historically fixed, all of them value-constituting, and all of them narrative choices. The preferred style reflects the historically shifting domination of particular schools or paradigms.

How we are expected to write affects *what* we can write about. The referencing system in sociology (and most of the other social sciences) discourages the use of footnotes, a place for secondary arguments, novel conjectures, and related ideas. Knowledge is constituted as "focused," "problem" (hypothesis) centered, "linear," and straightforward. Other "thoughts" are "extraneous." Inductively accomplished research is to be reported deductively, the argument is to be "abstractable" in 150 words or less, and researchers are to explicitly identify with a "theoretical-methodological" label. Each of these conventions favors—creates and sustains—a particular vision of what constitutes sociological knowledge. The conventions hold tremendous material and symbolic power over sociological writers. Using them increases the probability of one's work being accepted within "core" social science journals but are not prima facie evidence of greater—or lesser—truth value of significance than social science writing following other conventions.

Even when social scientists think they are avoiding literary devices, they are using them. Literary devices are unavoidable for the communication of *cognitive* content. Of these devices, metaphor is arguably the most important one. "The essence of metaphor is understanding and experiencing one kind of thing in terms of another" (Lakoff and Johnson 1980, 5). This is accomplished through comparison or analogy. The metaphor can be carried implicitly in everyday, "plain" language. Consider the following statements: "These claims are *right* on *target*"; "Your point is *indefensible*"; "Don't *attack* my argument"; "He *shot* down *your positions*"; "*I* won." The italicized words are expressions that convey the metaphor "argument is war." The customary way of talking about arguments presupposes a metaphor that we are usually unconscious of using. Moreover, the metaphor structures "the actions we perform in arguing" (Lakoff and Johnson 1980, 4). We experience arguments as combative. Consider how differently we would experience arguing if the metaphor were "argument is a dance." Metaphors exist at the conceptual level, and they prefigure judgments about the truth value of a text. The truth value of conventional social science writing partially depends on a deep epistemic code regarding how knowledge is figured *in general* (Shapiro 1985-86, 198). Figures of speech and metaphors external to the particular piece of research prefigure the analysis with a code belonging to another domain (Jameson 1981). For example, the use of "enlighten" or "idea" for knowledge is a light-based metaphor, what Derrida (1982) refers to as the heliocentric view of knowledge, the passive receipt of rays. Imminent in these metaphors are philosophical and value commitments so entrenched and familiar that they can do their partisan work in the guise of neutrality passing as literal. Empiricism, the dominant philosophy behind the writing of conventional social science, *imagines* a datum as a "thing" removed from the temporal and human practices that produced it (cf. Taylor 1971). The technical mechanisms of explanation are quarantined from the human processes of interpretation. Consequently, the actual linguistic practices in which the researcher/writer is engaged are masked but are not eradicated.

Michael Shapiro (1985-86) identifies three guiding empiricist metaphors. First is the grammatical split between subject and object, which empiricists use as a wholly unnoticed metaphor for the separation between "real" subjects and "real" objects. The grammatical demarcation becomes "a Cartesian separation between the knower and the object of knowledge in the epistemology of empiricism" (p. 200). This metaphor is particularly powerful because it is a part of our language structure. It "fixes" objects in time and space, creating a static world. We write "about" things, as though they are "really" separable from us. The human practices that reified the objects are rendered invisible, irrelevant. "When objects are thus reified within a grammatical trope for knowing, human practices become a series of still lives, and the creation process, which within some models for knowing and understanding is the focus of inquiry, is forced into the silent background" (p. 200). Second, empiricism views language as a *tool*. While the empirical world of things is taken as "fixed and therefore open to instantaneous viewing," language is taken to be "instrumental, having no content that is lent to the reality of which it speaks" (p. 200). There is no comprehension that *what* we speak about is partly a function of *how* we speak. Like the grammatical metaphor, the tool metaphor reifies a radical separation between subject and object, the world and how it is apprehended. The two metaphors estrange the subject from the object and encourage the empiricist idea that inquiry, like master carpentry, is a matter of precision.

Third, empiricism uses a *management* metaphor. There are areas that need to be "controlled"; these are the "problems" and "research questions." Data are "managed," variables are "manipulated," research is "designed," time is "flow-charted," "tables" are "produced," and "models" (like toothpaste and cars) are "tested." Although much can be said about "good management," the management metaphor structures the activities of the researcher and eliminates other dimensions of knowledge.

Metaphor enters each stage of social scientific reasoning. The social scientific world is thought to be "like" a "complex model" whose measurements are "like" the "proxy variables" at hand. "The complex model is said to be like a simpler model for actual thinking, which is in turn like an even simpler model for calculation" (McCloskey 1985, 75). The analogic structure is aided by the use of other rhetorical devices such as the ordering of material, the use of examples to "prove" the general case, the construction of "ideal" or "test" "cases," repetition (e.g., of the hypothesis), appeals to authorities (citations), and so on (cf. Edmondson 1984).

Within sociology itself, metaphors are everywhere. "Functionalism," "role" theory, "game" theory, "dramaturgical analogy," "organicism," "social evolutionism," the social "system," social "structure," and "labeling" theory are obviously metaphoric. Conceptually, we talk about "equilibrium," "human capital," the "power elite," "resource mobilization," ethnic "insurgency," "developing" countries, "stratification," and so on. Methodologically, we talk about the "power" of a test and statistical "significance" (as distinct from sociological significance); we "sample" a "target" population that we "survey" and "probe." Some areas of the discipline are thought to be "core" or "mainstream." Metaphors are ubiquitous (cf. Lakoff and Johnson 1980). They organize the sociological work and affect the interpretations of the "facts"; indeed, facts are interpretable ("make sense") only in terms of their place within a metaphoric structure. To ignore the pervasiveness and power of literary practices within sociology is perverse and short-sighted—not to mention unscientific.

Given the unavoidability of narrative within the social sciences and given how human values, sensibilities, and ambiguities continuously reassert themselves in "plain" writing, we are propelled into taking seriously the relevance of narrative to the sociological enterprise. Narrative cannot be suppressed within sociology because it is ineluctably tied to the human experience; trying to suppress it undermines the very foundations of the sociological enterprise.

Time and Narrative

People everywhere experience and interpret their lives in relationship to *time*. Time is the quintessential basis for and constraint upon the human experience. Also everywhere, humans make sense of their temporal worlds through the narrative. The philosopher Paul Ricoeur has noted the relationship between the human experience of time and the universality of the narrative. Ricoeur's (1984-86) thesis is that the coexistence of the temporal nature of the human being and the activity of narrating a story are not accidental but represent a "transcultural form of necessity" (vol. 1, 52). Through the narrative, temporality becomes interpretable in human terms. Time is made human; narrative is a condition of temporal experience.

Unlike the clock and calendars that measure out life in moments, days, and years, people do not experience time as a succession of instants or a linear linking of points in space but as extended awareness of the past and the future within the present (cf. Husserl 1964). Sometimes, time is experienced as a concordant whole, such as when reading a familiar poem, where the whole piece is experienced despite the fact that some of it has already been read and more is yet to come. Other times, time is experienced as discordant, such as when regret about the past or fear of the future impinge on the present. This discordance cannot ever be totally overcome because human knowledge includes the knowledge that one's days are numbered. The future always becomes the past. The future is always death.

Narrative, I argue, provides powerful access to this uniquely human experience of time in five sociologically significant ways: the everyday, the autobiographical, the biographical, the cultural, and what I term the collective story. Although I present these ways as analytically separable, in practice they can overlap and intersect, as for example when an interviewee "tells" his or her autobiography that the interviewer "writes up" as a biography but "presents" as a part of a more general cultural or collective story.

In everyday life, narrative articulates how actors go about their rounds and accomplish their tasks. The narrative of "what we did today" assumes an experience of time. We "had time to," "we took time for," "we lost time." We organize our days with temporal markers, such as "first," "then," and "after." Our experience of daily time links us to others and to the public world. We meet people at particular times, we get caught in "rush hour" traffic, we watch the "six o'clock news." Social order is sustained through these collaborative efforts of individuals "timing" the logistics of their daily activities. People routinely talk to each other by accounting for how they spent their day—"What did you do in school today?" "What happened at work today?" Ethnomethodologists and conversational analysts have been especially attuned to these quotidian accounts, and a large research literature exists based on those perspectives. Few of these researchers, however, have explicitly analyzed and articulated how the individual's narrated experiences of daily time are linked to larger social structures, linking the personal to the public.

Second, autobiographical narrative is how people articulate how the past is related to the present. Events have a beginning, a middle, and an end. The past can be retrieved and relived in the present. Narrative organizes the experience of time into personal historicity. "Self-biography is the highest and most instructive form in which the understanding of life . . . is confronting us" (Dilthey quoted in Kohli 1981, 64). Telling one's story gives meaning to the past from the point of view of the present and future and "gives meaning to the past *in order* to give meaning to the present . . . life of the person" (Bertaux-Wiame 1981, 258).

People organize their personal biographies and understand them through the stories they create to explain and

justify their life experiences. When people are asked why
they do what they do, they provide narrative explanations,
not logico-scientific categorical ones. It is the way individuals understand their own lives and best understand the
lives of others. Experiences are connected to other experiences and are evaluated in relation to the larger whole.
Something does not make sense when it does not "fit in" with
the narrative. To make sense of the events in their lives, a
person reconstructs biography. The experience of (re)narra-
tivizing—like the experience of biographical time itself—is
open-ended and polysemous, allowing different meanings
and systems of meanings to emerge.

Narrative functions at the autobiographical level to mark
off one's own individual existence from all others by its
finitude. One's life is separable from others; it has its own
beginning and its own ending. But because of that separation one can be an integrated whole—a being with its own
unique past, present, and future. Narrative thus provides
the opportunity for the individual to make existential sense
of mortality and correlatively, through the narrative, the
profound experience of mortality becomes sociologically
accessible.

Autobiographies by historical, popular, and literary figures are a well-established genre. Anthropologists have
customarily written autobiographical statements—"tales of
the field"—in the margins of their ethnographies or as
separate books (for a review of these, see Van Maanen
1988). Although contemporary sensibilities question the
purposes and veracity of these tales, especially as they
inscribe the ethnographer as the "knower" and the culture
of the "other" as a known, they are exemplars of the ethnographer making autobiographical sense of his or her own
lived experience. More recently, sociologists have begun
writing autobiographies and writing narratives about soci-

ology as they write narratives about themselves (cf. Ellis 1989; Linden 1989; Riley 1988; Reinharz 1979).

Third, because people can narrativize their own lives, the possibility arises of understanding other people's lives as also biographically organized. Social and generational cohesion, as well as social change, depend on this ability to empathize with the life stories of others. Social interaction depends on actors making sense of others' actions and motivations from the *point of view* of the others, from their biographical perspective. Social cooperation relies on this human capability, a capability grounded in narrative. But the ability to understand another's biography goes beyond creating an interactionally presently shared world: it makes possible the understanding of people who are not present. Narrative creates the possibility of history beyond the personal. Contemporaries, predecessors, and successors communicate through the narrative (Schutz 1962). Passing on the biographies of heroes and villains links the generations and shapes the disorderly and chaotic, or boring and repetitive, into a communally shared world of experience. Through the communication of the past to present listeners, contemporary worlds are enlarged and grounded. Social scientists are now adding to the bounty of biographies written by historians, journalists, literary "biographers," and "factual-fiction" writers (cf. Deegan 1988; Stewart 1989).

The cultural story is the fourth way in which narrative is sociologically significant. Participation in a culture includes participation in the narratives of that culture, a general understanding of the stock of meanings and their relationships to each other. The process of telling the story creates and supports a social world. Cultural stories provide exemplars of lives, heroes, villains, and fools as they are embedded in larger cultural and social frameworks, as well as stories about home, community, society, and humankind.

Morality and cautionary tales instruct the young and control the adult. Stories of one's "people"—as chosen or enslaved, conquerors or victims as well as stories about one's nation, social class, gender, race, or occupation affect morale, aspirations, and personal life chances. These are not "simply" stories but are narratives that have real consequences for the fates of individuals, communities, and nations (cf. McClelland 1961). The cultural story is told from the point of view of the ruling interests and the normative order and bears a narrative kinship to functionalism. Since, for example, the central character in a patriarchal system is the male, a cultural story of "adultery" is about the normative status "marriage" and how an "other woman" tries to "ruin a family" by "stealing a man" from his wife. The central character in this story is the husband, and the storyline "blames" the minor characters, the women: the wife for her deficient sexiness/lovingness/understandingness and the other woman for her deficient morality. This particular cultural story, in the United States, transcends race and class lines, making it seem "true" and giving it a hold on the imaginations of men and women. Cultural stories thus help maintain the status quo.

There is, however, a fifth kind of narrative that gives voice to those who are silenced or marginalized in the cultural narrative. I call this narrative the "collective story." The collective story displays an individual's story by narrativizing the experiences of the social category to which the individual belongs rather than by telling the particular individual's story or by simply retelling the cultural story (cf. Richardson 1988). There are a multitude of such collective stories in contemporary society. Some arise through social movement activity, such as the civil rights movements, which resist the cultural narratives about groups of people and "tell" alternative stories. Others are about people who are not collectively organized. For example, there is the "new other woman" collective story (Richardson 1985), which takes the point of view of the "single" woman. In this collective story, the single woman is not cast as a villain in the "marriage plot," in combat with another woman over "having the love of a man." Rather, she is the central character in her own drama, struggling with old cultural plots and new possibilities of economic and emotional independence for women. Similarly, there are the "cancer survivor," "battered wife," "abused child," "coming out," "alcoholic," "diabetes," "chronic illness," "codependent," and "divorce" narratives, to name but a few (cf. Denzin 1987; Ferraro and Johnson 1983; Maines 1989). Although the narrative is about a category of people, the individual response to the well-told collective story is "That's *my* story. I am not alone."

Most significant are the transformative possibilities of the collective story. At the individual level, people make sense of their lives through the stories that are available to them, and they attempt to fit their lives into the available stories. People live by stories. If the available narrative is limiting, destructive, or at odds with the actual life, peoples' lives end up being limited and textually disenfranchised. Collective stories that deviate from standard cultural plots provide new narratives; hearing them legitimates a replotting of one's own life. New narratives offer the patterns for new lives. The story of the transformed life, then, becomes a part of the cultural heritage affecting future stories and future lives.

Transformative possibilities of the collective story also exist at the sociocultural level. People who belong to a particular category can develop a "consciousness of kind" and can galvanize other category members through the telling of the collective story. People do not even have to know each other for the social identification to take hold. By emotionally binding people together who have had the same experiences, whether in touch with each other or not, the collective story overcomes some of the isolation and alienation of contemporary life. It provides a sociological community, the linking of separate individuals into a shared consciousness. Once linked, the possibility for social action on behalf of the collective is present and therewith the possibility of societal transformation.

Collective Stories, Civic Discourse, and Societal Transformation

Civic discourse about societal identity, social goals, and societal transformation is largely constituted through social scientific language. The rhetorics of the social sciences identify and shape our social past, present, and future. They are nearly unavoidable in modern societies. At issue, then, is not the presence of social scientific rhetorics but *what* kind(s) of social-scientific representation we foster and with what consequences for whom. The logico-scientific paradigm has dominated public policy, but what might happen to our personal and civic discourses if narrative were valued as a way of acquiring and representing knowledge? The consequences of sociologists consciously attending to narrative structure, I contend, will empower individuals, contribute to liberating civic discourses, and support transformative social projects.

People make sense of their lives, for the most part, as has been earlier argued, in terms of specific events, such as giving birth, and sequences of events, such as the lifelong impact of parenting a damaged child. Most people do not articulate how the sociological categories of race, gender, class, and ethnicity have shaped their lives or how the larger historical processes such as the demographic transition, service economies, and the women's movement have affected them. Erik Erikson (1980) contends that only great people, people who see themselves as actors on a historical stage, tell their life stories in a larger and historical context. Yet, as C. Wright Mills (1959, 5) cogently argued, knowledge of the social context leads people to understand their own experiences and to gauge their "own fates." This is the promise of the "sociological imagination." What sociologists are capable of is giving voice to silenced people, presenting them as historical actors by telling their collective stories.

Sociologists tell the collective stories of constituencies to which they may not even belong; this, of course, raises central postmodernist problems about the researcher's authority and privilege. Narrative explanation means that one person's voice—the writer's—speaks for others (Roth 1989, 31). But what are the alternatives? To propose the stilling of the sociologist-writer's voice not only rejects the value of sociological insight but implies that somehow "facts" exist without interpretation. This presupposes a belief in essences and authenticity, a view that carries its own metaphysical and political baggage. Accordingly, "there is no principled resolution, no alternative, to the problem of speaking for others. There is no getting it right about who or what another is; there is no essence defining what 'right' is" (Roth 1989, 31). Narrativizing, like all intentional behavior (including the writing of conventional social science) is a site of moral responsibility. Further, because power differences are always being played out in personal and civic arenas, the most relevant issue, as I see it, is a practical-ethical one: how can we use our skills and privileges to advance the case of the nonprivileged? Telling collective

stories is an effective way in which we can do just that, a
way in which we can use our "sociological imagination" to
reveal personal problems as public issues, to make possible
collective identity and collective solutions.

Rhetorically, through curricula, grants, honorees, and
written exemplars of "core" sociology in "core" sociology
journals, the belief that narrative is (at best) of marginal
interest—and certainly nonproblematic for "practicing sociologists"—is reproduced and reconstituted term after term
in academic sociology. Yet, as the new rhetoric of the social
sciences has made clear and as this chapter has indicated,
rhetorical decisions are constantly being made, often uncon-
sciously, by the practitioners (cf. Nelson, Megill, and
McCloskey 1987). We choose how we write. Those choices
have poetic, rhetorical, ethical, and political implications.

All social science writing exists in the context of metaphors that shape the narrative. In addition to the deeply
burrowed ones, such as the "thingness," "tool," and "management" metaphors of empiricism, there are more easily
graspable and evocative guiding stories we tell about the
people we study. In the 1930s and 1940s, for example, the
social scientific narrative of Native Americans viewed the
present "as disorganization, the past as glorious, and the
future as assimilation." But now, as Edward Bruner (1986)
has pointed out, there is a new implicit narrative; "the
present is viewed as a resistance movement, the past as
exploitation, the future as ethnic resurgence" (p. 4). With
great rapidity, the guiding concepts of assimilation and ac-
culturation have been replaced with the concepts of exploitation, oppression, liberation, colonialism, and resistance.

The shift in story was more than a theoretical shift; it was
a shift in syntax and politics. As science is the child of
metaphor, metaphor is the child of politics. For the accul-
turation story, the writing problem was the description of

past culture. Indian life had no future, and the present was interpreted in light of this futurelessness as pathology and disintegration. The political action consistent with this metaphor was to send Native American children to Anglo boarding schools, to create urban relocation projects, to undermine tribal tradition. For the contemporary resistance narrative, however, the writing problem concerns the future: the resistance of indigenous people to exploitation in their struggle to preserve ethnic identity. The writing describes the resistance in the present to preserve the past for the future. Political action consistent with this narrative is intervention to prevent cultural genocide.

Analogous implicit narrative shifts have occurred in the collective stories of other groups of people. Within American society, certain sociologists have positioned blacks, women, gays and lesbians, the aging, and ethnic groups within a liberation narrative. And we have extended the liberation narrative to Third World countries, no longer conceptualizing them as "developing"—a metaphor that implies their current inferiority and their eventual Westernized future. Instead, the notion of ethnic nationalism is gaining ascendancy. The implicit liberation narrative is consistent with liberation movements. Indeed, the outstanding success of feminist scholarship across disciplines arises from its explicit link to the feminist movement, a continuity of purpose between research and activism, namely, the empowerment of women through personal and societal transformative projects. Sociologically grounded narrative thus can alter the shape and content of civic discourse by biographically, collectively, and politically enfranchising the previously disenfranchised. Because collective stories—including the ones written by sociologists, including this one—can become cultural stories, petrified and limiting, they too may be subject to future resistance and rewriting.

Conclusion

What social scientific writing has tried unsuccessfully to keep out of its writing may very well be the proper approach and subject matter of the discipline. No matter how "plain-spoken" sociologists try to be, the unavoidable human content keeps invading their thinking and shaping their writing. Marginalizing of the narrative may serve the political interests of entrenched sociological elites, but it does not serve sociology or society.

Narratives exist at the everyday, autobiographical, biographical, cultural, and collective levels. They reflect the universal human experience of time and link the past, present, and future. Narrative links sociology to literature and to history. The human experience of stability and transformation becomes sociologically accessible. Narrative gives room for the expression of our individual and shared fates, our personal and communal worlds. Narrative permits the individual, the society, or the group to explain its experiences of temporality because narrative attends to and grows out of temporality. It is the universal way in which humans accommodate to finitude. Narrative is the best way to understand the human experience because it is the way humans understand their own lives. It is the closest to the human experience and hence the least falsifying of that experience. Narrative rejuvenates the "sociological imagination" in the service of liberatory civic discourses and transformative social projects.

Finally, it suggests a path toward answering the question posed in this chapter: How should we write? If we wish to understand the deepest and most universal of human experiences, if we wish our work to be faithful to the lived experiences of people, if we wish for a union between poetics and science, or if we wish to use our privileges and skills to empower the people we study, then we *should* value the narrative.

References

Barthes, R. 1966. Introduction to the structural analysis of the narrative. Occasional paper, Centre for Contemporary Cultural Studies, University of Birmingham.

Bazerman, C. 1988. *Shaping written knowledge; The genre and activity of the experimental article in science.* Madison: University of Wisconsin Press.

Bertaux-Wiame, I. 1981. The life history approach to the study of internal migration. In *Biography and society: The life history approach in the social sciences,* edited by D. Bertaux, 249-65. Beverly Hills, CA: Sage.

Brown, R. H. 1977. *A poetic for sociology.* Cambridge: Cambridge University Press.

Bruner, E. M. 1986. Ethnography as narrative. In *The anthropology of experience,* edited by V. Turner and E. M. Bruner, 137-55. Champaign-Urbana: University of Illinois Press.

Bruner, J. 1986. *Actual minds, possible worlds.* Cambridge, MA: Harvard University Press.

Clifford, J. 1986. Introduction: Partial truths. In *Writing culture: The poetics and politics of ethnography,* edited by J. Clifford and G. E. Marcus. Berkeley: University of California Press.

Deegan, M. 1988. *Jane Addams and the men of the Chicago school, 1892-1918.* New Brunswick, NJ: Transaction.

Denzin, N. K. 1987. *The alcoholic self.* Newbury Park, CA: Sage.

Derrida, J. 1982. *Margins of philosophy.* Translated by Alan Bass. Chicago: University of Chicago Press.

Edmondson, R. 1984. *Rhetoric in sociology.* London: Macmillan.

Ellis, C. 1989. What are you feeling? Issues in the introspective method. Paper presented at the annual meeting of the American Sociological Association, San Francisco, August.

Erikson, E. H. 1980. *Identity and the life cycle.* New York: Norton.

Ferraro, K. J., and J. M. Johnson. 1983. How women experience battering: The process of victimization. *Social Problems* 30 (3): 325-39.

Fisher, W. R. 1987. *Human communication as narration: Toward a philosophy of reason, value, and action.* Columbia: University of South Carolina Press.

Gusfield, J. 1976. The literary rhetoric of science: Comedy and pathos in drinking driver research. *American Sociological Review* 4:16-34.

Husserl, E. 1964. *The phenomenology of internal time consciousness.* Translated by James S. Churchill. Bloomington: Indiana University Press.

Jakobson, R. 1960. Linguistics and poetry. In *Style and language,* edited by T. A. Sebock, 350-77. Cambridge: MIT Press.

Jameson, F. 1981. *The political unconscious.* Ithaca, NY: Cornell University Press.

Kohli, M. 1981. Biography: Account, text, method. In *Biography and society: The life history approach in the social sciences,* edited by D. Bertaux, 61-65. Beverly Hills, CA: Sage.

Lakoff, G., and M. Johnson. 1980. *Metaphors we live by.* Chicago: University of Chicago Press.

Levine, D. N. 1985. *The flight from ambiguity: Essays in social and cultural theory.* Chicago: University of Chicago Press.

Linden, R. R. 1989. Making stories, making selves: The holocaust, identity and memory. Ph.D. diss., Brandeis University.

Lyotard, J. 1979. *The postmodern condition: A report on knowledge.* Translated by G. Bennington and B. Massumi. Minneapolis: University of Minnesota Press.

Maines, D. 1989. The storied nature of diabetic self-help groups. Paper presented at the Gregory Stone Symbolic Interaction Symposium, Arizona State University, Tempe.

McClelland, D. C. 1961. *The achieving society.* New York: Free Press.

McCloskey, D. N. 1985. *The rhetoric of economics.* Madison: University of Wisconsin Press.

Mills, C. W. 1959. *The sociological imagination.* New York: Oxford University Press.

Nelson, J. S., A. Megill, and D. N. McCloskey, eds. 1987. *The rhetoric of the human sciences: Language and argument in scholarship and human affairs.* Madison: University of Wisconsin Press.

Polkinghorne, D. E. 1988. *Narrative knowing and the human sciences.* Albany: State University of New York Press.

Reinharz, S. 1979. *On becoming a social scientist.* San Francisco: Jossey-Bass.

Richardson, L. 1985. *The new other woman: Contemporary women in affairs with married men.* New York: Free Press.

———. 1988. The collective story: Postmodernism and the writing of sociology. *Sociological Focus* 21:199-208.

———. 1990. *Writing matters.* Newbury Park, CA: Sage.

Ricoeur, P. 1984-86. *Time and narrative.* 2 vols. Translated by K. MacLaughlin and D. Pellauer. Chicago: University of Chicago Press.

Riley, M. W. 1988. *Sociological lives.* Newbury Park, CA: Sage.

Rorty, R. 1979. *Philosophy and the mirror of nature.* Princeton, NJ: Princeton University Press.

Roth, P. 1989. How narratives explain. Paper presented to the University of Iowa Faculty Rhetoric Seminar (POROI), Iowa City.

Shapiro, M. 1985-86. Metaphor in the philosophy of the social sciences. *Cultural Critique,* Winter:191-214.

Shutz, A. 1962. *Collected papers.* The Hague: Martinus Nijhoff.

Stewart, J. O. 1989. *Drinkers, drummers and decent folk: Ethnographic narratives of village Trinidad.* Albany: State University of New York Press.

Taylor, C. 1971. Interpretation and the sciences of man. *Review of Metaphysics* 25:3-51.

Van Maanen, J. 1988. *Tales of the field: On writing ethnography.* Chicago: University of Chicago Press.

8

Performing the Text

MARIANNE A. PAGET

Death is the sanction of everything that the storyteller can tell.

—Walter Benjamin (1969)

She and he confronted each other across the chasm of his technical knowledge and his technical practice of questioning her. She was on the other side with her fear of her death. He could not feel; she could not stop feeling. He could not listen to her fear; she could not stop expressing her fear which he couldn't or wouldn't hear. He was the-one-who-would-not-listen and she the-other-who-was-not-heard, archetypes of an experience each of us knows.

"On the Work of Talk: Studies in Misunderstandings" was performed as theater on May 14 and 15, 1988 at Northwestern University (Paget 1988b). It was first published as a research article in a collection of papers on physician-patient communications. The work is about the erroneous construction of a medical diagnosis of a woman who was a cancer patient. It is a detailed analysis of a series of exchanges between a physician and his patient. I explore their turns at talk on her medical problems, using excerpts of their dialogue in my analysis and research report.

My analysis examined a censored topic, her cancer. How was it excluded, and how did its exclusion produce his diagnosis of depression? I documented how it happened that on three occasions he diagnosed depression for a woman he knew four or five months earlier had had an operation for the removal of kidney cancer. "I'm sure your basic health is good," he said.

I excavated the excluded topic. They never talked about her cancer operation but, instead, alluded to it in euphemisms like "scar" and "tumor." I also excavated the microparadigm of their talk. He controlled their discourse through his questioning practices. He introduced, developed, and dissolved discourse topics. He interrupted her. He censored expressions of her concern. And he ignored some of her replies.[1]

Two issues intrigued me about performing "The Work of Talk," as the performance was called. First, I would be breaking free of the odd way in which in sociology we have privileged the written text, as though the written text is the only model for how we can communicate our understanding of the life world, the only one that counts. There are several issues here. Not only has the written text been privileged as the model for our work, but the form of the text has been tightly controlled by a series of conventions that obscure the writer's relation to her work. Often, sociological texts are written in the passive voice, as if they were not socially constructed objects produced by authors perceiving and shaping phenomena.[2]

Distance, dispassion, and "objectivity" characterize the rhetoric of the scientific text. Thus social knowledge often appears as if it were without point of view, class interests, or values. Richard Brown (1987) has put this matter well:

> The use of scientific methodology does not permit the social scientist to avoid rhetorical discourse. Instead the scientist's lack of self-consciousness about the assumptions and limits of such a method of logic results in his using a naive and immoral rhetoric. (p. 88)

I will return to these issues.

Second, in performing the text I would be presenting a scientific work in an artistic context. What did this change in context and genre of presenting work imply?

"On the Work of Talk" was moved onstage almost verbatim. There were only a few deletions and no substantive changes or additions. Emilie Beck adapted the work, with my collaboration, and directed the performance,[3] which was done in the Chamber Theatre tradition developed by Robert Breen (1978), who taught this practice at Northwestern University.[4] In Chamber Theatre, literary works are adapted for performance not by creating a stage play but, rather, by moving the entire story onstage. The narrator and narrative devices like "she said" and "he said" and other conventions that arise in written texts are performed.

In Chamber Theatre, literary texts are staged. Mine was a nonliterary text, and given its aim as science, the language was rarely poetic. I used terms like discourse, utterance, speaking practices, politeness forms, and microparadigm. Onstage such language was unusual. But while I wanted to perform the work I didn't want to compromise it. In fact, performing a piece of science onstage was much of the challenge and the excitement for me. I wanted to do science onstage. I mean science with a small "s," a human science, sensitive to dialogue, social context, and life experience. There were seven characters in the performance: the narrator, the doctor, the patient, and a panel of four experts. The narrator tells the story of the work. She was not I, the author; she was Cancer. This was one of the few "fictions" created in the performance that was otherwise, I would argue, "factual."

The doctor and patient enacted the dialogue I had originally analyzed as a series of transcripts. Sometimes, they commented on what they had said or would soon say just as I had done in the original article. Sometimes, they reacted to the panel. Often, they listened to what others were saying and occasionally grimaced over what they heard.

The experts reported the science of my analysis—for example, from the play script, the following exchange between panel members #3 and #4:

Panel #4: Questioning patients is the most common method of acquiring information about illness.

Panel #3: Questions create a reservoir of usable knowledge in responding to illness.

Panel #4: In an analysis of the talk of British general practitioners and their patients, Byrne

Panel #3: and Long

Panel #4: report that patient care takes place as a series of discourse exchanges that last on the average of eight minutes.

Panel #3: They reviewed 2,500 tapes.

Panel #4: In eight minutes, physicians attempted to establish rapport,

Panel #3: discover the reason for a patient's visit,

Panel #4: verbally and physically examine the patient,

Panel #3: discuss the patient's condition,

Panel #4: establish a treatment plan,

Panel #3: and terminate the exchange.

This highly interactive stretch of my argument was not dialogue in the usual sense. These panel members commented serially, sometimes not even speaking in full sentences. Nonetheless, they communicated a series of facts about medical work and kept the argument/performance moving. Sometimes, they also "gossiped" about what was going on between the doctor and patient. Sometimes, they mimicked their dialogue or acted like a chorus. The cast said all that I had written in the original article. Thus the language of the analysis was preserved verbatim onstage. There is one rather amusing moment in the performance when Cancer says, loudly and distinctly, "I.E." and then continues with the example, "i.e., how often do you experience exhaustion?" (In this context, the use of "I.E." was incongruous and thus funny.) I mean this degree of fidelity to the text onstage.

The Mise-en-Scène

"The Work of Talk" could easily be performed as a staged reading, but because actors would not encode the text and enact it from memory I did not want to do a staged reading. In a staged reading, everyone would be holding the script, the text. I wanted to get free of the written text (even while preserving its content onstage). Also, Emilie Beck had a strong sense of how to perform the article as theater.

There were actually three texts: the written article, the performance script, and the performance which included the mise-en-scène. The mise-en-scène was very imaginative; before taking up the issue of the performance as an interpretive act, I want to describe some of the staging.

Cancer, as I said, narrated. She wore a long white dress (cancer at the level of tumor is white), carried an evening bag that she occasionally used, and wore no shoes (cancer is natural). She was both lovely and flirtatious. She would cozy up to anybody in the cast.

In keeping with the aversion to talking about cancer so common in this culture and in keeping with its censorship in the original dialogue between the physician and patient, the entire cast always whispered "cancer," with urgency and fear, when I used it in my report. Not the character Cancer. She would say her name with great enthusiasm and glee, throwing up her hands as if she was taking a well-deserved bow. The panel, by contrast, would huddle together, worrisomely. The patient was never able to say cancer. When she tried to speak it, she would swallow the word instead.

The physician and patient not only appeared and produced a lively and antagonistic dialogue about her medical problems, they danced together. They tangoed. At one point he twirled her around so fast and so long she became dizzy and lost her balance. Sometimes, as she sat on a small table, he examined or asked her questions. Once she left her seat, trying to hide behind a panelist, and he beckoned her back to the table. His mere gesture of patting the table authoritatively brought her resigned return. Thus he expressed his power over her.

At another point, the cast acted as a machine, a many-levered instrument producing work along a line. Everyone bleated or bayed a mechanical sound and moved about synchronously. The machine (the cast) surrounded the patient. Cancer sat on her lap, bobbing up and down. The cast said the following lines. They respond to and analyze a dialogue that has just taken place between the physician and patient:

Doc: HAVE NOW GOT carries strong stress, and it expresses
Cancer: across the obliqueness of the form of this utterance,

Doc: his assessment that her nerves
Doc and Panel #3 and 4: have now gotten
Doc: to the point where they suffer and need assistance
Pat[ient]: She,
Cancer: again and quite characteristically
Pat: answers his questions,
Cancer: "Yes,"
Pat: and observes that she is a little nervous, and she continues
Cancer: I-I-don't see what you mean.

These exchanges reveal how the cast can exchange roles and say each other's parts, thus reporting back the dialogue in a new dimension. Here the machine mimes the physician's oddly mechanical talk.

Throughout the performance, Cancer pays close attention to the patient. She dresses her up, coming by at one point to apply makeup and at another to give her a chocolate. The patient belongs to Cancer. Occasionally, panel members also try to help the patient. At one point, panel member #1 drops glitter on her back; at another time, she massages her back. These attentions to her back foreshadow the final moments when the patient reports that she has gone to another clinic and been told that she has cancer of the spine.

Why Performance?

I was often asked why I wanted to perform "The Work of Talk." Performance permits a live experience, the vivid present of watching and hearing a misconstrued moment of medical care. I once called it a catastrophe. Hearing the voices of the physician and patient rather than reading silently a written transcription seemed important, for such detailed written transcripts are very opaque and difficult for nonspecialists to follow. But, more important, seeing the physician and patient onstage mattered too.

While they seemed like archetypes, of the-one-who-would-not-listen and the-other-who-is-not-heard, they were by no means flat, thin creatures. I was struck by the odd familiarity of their conflicts as I listened to their tapes. They "quarreled" with each other just as women and men do. They "quarreled" over little things, not just big ones (for example, whether he would examine a particular area of her back now or later).

At one moment at the end of their first exchange, he assures her that her basic health is good and she replies, "Oh doctor I'd kiss you if I were sure you were right." She was sometimes coy and furtive, trying to catch him offguard, to learn his secret knowledge. He was not always harsh and authoritative. Sometimes he was exasperated. Once or twice he seemed concerned. She was a difficult patient. She was smart. She was afraid. She challenged him. He reacted to her character. She reacted to his. He became more rigid and ungiving as she became more upset. They were locked in their positions.

Seeing the text performed, an audience could react to complexly textured characters. The layers, the dimensions of live actors performing, would signal so much more than I could communicate in writing. There is something odd about privileging an analysis of discourse in its least robust form, a written text, exploring it in great detail while ignoring the speakers' miens and intentions. The analysis of conversation, sometimes, is completely empty of the complexity of character. Not even the content of a communication is explored or thought relevant to some investigations of turn-taking or storytelling, let alone the character of the speakers. I wanted to approach the complexity of experience: *Erlebnis,* life as lived through.

The performance was not morally neutral, nor was the original work. I had done the analysis from her point of view. When I listened to their exchanges, I kept noticing that he missed information that I heard. I believed there was something medically wrong. I sensed her fear. I began to focus on his discourse and his diagnosis. He controlled their talk, just as he controlled the diagnosis, had the power to name it "depression." Had I done the work from his point of view I would not have suspected that she was a cancer patient. I would have taken for granted his diagnosis of "depression." I would not have begun the intense, troubling investigation of their talk.

I wanted to engage the audience, to awaken them to the experience of this troubling talk and the importance of talk in medical work. The care of patients often goes on in and through discourse. A medical diagnosis is a speech act—a form of action in the world which is fateful.

With students trained in theater and performance, I could approach an artistic standard. We have a low artistic standard for performance in sociology. Usually, we ignore the aesthetics of our work when performing. We go to meetings, present papers, compressing our points because of the constraints of time, rushing our speech, apologizing for not getting everything said, and entering and exiting each other's sessions at will. We read papers written to be read silently by others; we read them on the way to publications, out loud. We give them analytic and technical—rather than expressive—readings.

Howard Becker, Michal McCall, and Lori Morris (1988) did a staged reading of a paper of theirs on theater communities. They read as authors and narrators, and they read as actors and actresses. They changed parts and moved to different positions on the stage as they read/performed different roles. The lighting changed with the changing focus of who was reading/performing. Their reading was not merely analytic but interpretive. They geared into the text, a sociological text. Thus they uncovered the performance aspect of sociological work—perhaps anti-aesthetic aspects of sociological performance would be more appropriate. Our meetings usually ignore the aesthetics of performance; their performance did not. Our meetings usually keep us in the conceptual realm, producing a conceptual and abstract science. Our meetings do not intend to invoke or produce experience but suppress involvement, emotion, and imagination —thus the brief, badly read presentations, the endless abstractions, and the boredom.

Performance enacts experience. Experience is in the present, now. For me, though they met in 1971 and I found their tapes in 1978, this physician and patient were in the vivid present, a story that unfolded and became darker and more complex as I tried to approach it, to know and understand it.[5] I wanted to make their presence felt. I wanted an audience to experience their presence, their struggle, and their humanity, their tragic conflict. Performing the text meant that the work was alive, and I also wanted the work to live.

The Real Text

The performance, that is, the performance script and mise-en-scène, in giving the text life also interprets it. What is the relation of the interpretation to the original work? This question did not trouble me. On the contrary, it intrigued me. The question seems to imply that the written text is the real text. But I did not want to privilege the written version, the article, as the real text. The written version was an interpretive act as well. It was, in fact, a

version of a series of conversations/encounters/exchanges
on the problems of a woman seeking medical care. The "real"
text was the text from life, the exchanges that I rendered in
my written analysis. What was the relation of the performance to the text from life?

The performed version was another version of the text. I
thought of the performed text as Emilie Beck's version.
Making Cancer the narrator was a stunning interpretive act
that had many implications for the production of the performance's meaning. Creating the panel was another. The
four panel members (two women, two men) had distinct
character. Each was a rather singular and one-dimensional
type. One was rather prim, like our stereotype of the librar-
ian. Another was young and precocious. He was constantly
unmasking the doctor and enjoyed it. The third was all
business and matter-of-fact, and the fourth was rather
lewd, a guy "on the make."

Excluding the author and investigator was another interpretive act. Including me as the investigator, Emilie Beck
argued, interfered with the production of a necessary atmosphere that would engage the audience. Here is one of the
conundrums of the performance. The performance made
fantastic some of the facts in order to state them. On the
other hand, the performance was faithful, very faithful
indeed to the written analysis.

I puzzled about the status of the "real" text. After the work
was accepted for publication by the coeditors of the book in
which it appeared, the in-house editor at the publishing
house tried to edit my manuscript to bring it into conformity
with her view of sociological discourse. She removed all
personal pronouns. All references to she and he, him and
her, this patient and this doctor became "the" doctor and
"the" patient. Thus the personal, gendered nature of the
exchange was lost. Presumably, I could then have brought

in the fact that this was a "male" physician and a "female" patient as a variable in the analysis. Now, in converting all local gender markers to "the" she had reified the text. She also changed the tense of my analysis, often putting the present tense into the past, further deadening the work. Finally, she wanted me to redo the transcripts, bringing them closer to written conventions for transcribing speech. Had I allowed that, the grounding of my argument would have been lost.

I fought to recover the original version and succeeded most of the time, but some of the editor's "the's" stayed and some of her changes in tense stayed. The original transcripts were used as I had done them. My point is that the published version was not quite my original version, though it came close. The performance isn't quite my version either, but it is close. Certainly, it has unusual fidelity to the text and to my language. Even so, in the process of watching the performance develop, I began to create another interpretation of the performance, which I thought of as my version.

During rehearsals (and there were many rehearsals), the cast played theater games. The games helped create the company, an ensemble in which everyone worked together. They also developed skill in communicating character and moving around onstage. Games are a common acting technique in the Chicago theater community and especially in Chamber Theatre (see, e.g., Spolin 1970). The games played included several forms of tag. One I particularly admired for its implicit aim at *communitas* had the following rules: "It" could tag you and thus you would become "it"—unless you hugged another cast member, then you were safe; however, you could only hug to the count of five, then you had to move. A number of games involved pantomime, or speaking gibberish and having a translator interpret, or acting a problem like just having learned that you have cancer. I mention these games because they really brought the cast together and were usually fun. Sometimes, as much as half a rehearsal was devoted to theater games. I noticed early on a diffuse erotic atmosphere developing. The doctor and patient could not look at each other without giggling. I became a little concerned about how these two could act as antagonists in serious conflict when they kept breaking out in laughter. At one point I thought, "My God, they're falling in love and we're going to have a musical comedy." But the doctor and patient were by no means the only cast members flirting.

The ambience of rehearsing was rarely serious because, of course, the performance text was quite serious. I rarely commented on rehearsals, the developing mise-en-scène, or the atmosphere. I came to rehearsals to learn about staging theater, not to critique the process. I was also there to help the production when I could.

The games were influential in developing the mood of the performance, and I must say that I took up the spirit of lightness too and much appreciated the many laughs I had over a work that had been nearly unbearable for me to do. I actively collaborated in Cancer's brazen performance. I thought here was an opportunity to develop a different imagery of death. Why not a beautiful woman in bare feet?

Here I want to add yet another touch of the mise-en-scène. The play opens with the panel members entering from several sides, taking their places onstage in simple classroom chairs. "One More Kiss Dear" is playing (the erotic subtext). Cancer enters from backstage right. She walks around proudly and happily, almost as if she is walking along a boardwalk. She's carrying a woolen hat that eventually she holds up knowingly. In the opening exchanges between "the real doctor and real patient," the doctor asks, "D'yuh wear a hat by preference or yer having something wrong with yer *scalp?*" Apparently, she was wearing a hat with her examination robe in the examining room. This is the hat Cancer holds. The patient enters from backstage right and walks slowly toward Cancer. Reluctantly, she takes the hat and puts it on. It is her turn. In this moment, she becomes the cancer patient and the woman-who-is-not-heard.

The performed work was not nearly as dark as the original exchanges. The erotic ambience, the youth of the cast, the difficulty, I thought, of their coming to terms with death when they were so young, Cancer's role and appearance, and the games they played affected the performance. The entire analysis was nonetheless onstage. The science, every piece of it, was performed. What did it matter if the cast played their parts somewhat differently? The doctor, for example, was far less technical and cold than the "real phy- sician." He was slightly kinky and obtuse, as though sex was on his mind (the erotic subtext again). The patient was far less angry, far more searching and earnest than the "real patient." Cancer was so high-spirited that you forgot to be scared.

I did not privilege my own knowledge of the tapes. Neither Emilie Beck nor the cast wanted to hear the tapes. They all read the original work at one point during rehearsals. What I discovered was that the play of their imaginations, and the mise-en-scène, didn't interfere with the argument onstage. Yet I had in mind a darker encounter. That I would do another performance, including creating another performance script, means that the work is evocative enough to support several interpretations without compromising the argument and analysis.

The Art of the Text

Onstage, the analysis intends an experience. Theater intends an experience. In fact, theater is a vehicle for the recovery of experience and for the play of emotion and imagination so typically suppressed in the production of social science texts.[6] The performance was not done in the tradition of realism. An assembled cast that narrates and sometimes reiterates the dialogue, dissecting it, a cast that sometimes switches roles or acts in unison like a machine, a cast led by Cancer's storytelling is not acting in the theater of realism. Yet the performance worked as theater. The dialogue reported the unfolding analysis of what "really" happened when the one-who-would-not-listen and the-other-who-was-not-heard encountered each other in a medical context. And it communicated the analysis, sometimes enacted the dialogue in real time as in documentary theater.

In my version, I would emphasize the physician's technicality. I would have him coming onstage with all sorts of medical gadgets, stumbling, thus dropping them and having them all clink and clatter on the floor. Again I would have seven characters, six would be women, the physician being the only man. I would occasionally want some of these women to size him up, look him over, his odd language and strange ways, circle around, not to ridicule him but to discover what species of man he is: Technical Man, FACTSMAN, with his gadgets, his denial of death, and loss of feeling.

I would have a second physician who would be the "real" physician's mirror and a second patient to mirror the first. They would comment on the dialogue, just as I once had and just as the panel in Emilie Beck's version sometimes did. I would have a second narrator to help report the science of the work and to support the first narrator whose anguish sometimes made it hard to present the analysis of how it happened that on three separate occasions he diagnosed depression for a woman who was a cancer patient—told her that her basic health was good.

The panel, as clever as they were, distracted from the drama of the physician and patient; they competed with the physician and patient and with Cancer for the focus of the audience's attention. The doctor's mirror, the patient's double, and the second narrator would replace the panel. Death also would be present, although in much less prominent a role. She would not narrate the performance but occasionally would speak, participating in the unfolding analysis/performance, and when she did speak what she said would carry weight. And, yes, she probably would be beautiful and young.

I would have the cast laugh through the final section of the performance. Their lines would go something like this:

2nd Phy[sician]: This analysis has not investigated this physician's intentions.

1st Nar[rator]: I suspect that he would not have chosen so cruel an outcome of his encounters with this patient.

1st Phy: In good faith, he taped their meetings as a participant in a research study. He, therefore, was no longer aware of his manner.

2nd Phy: This analysis has, however, addressed the question of how their talk developed.

1st Nar: What this physician might have intended does not seem as relevant in understanding their discourse,

2nd Nar: as how their talk proceeded

2nd Phy: and how, as a series of turns at talk on discourse topics, it shaped the meaning of her illness.

1st Phy: It was not his intentions that shaped their discourse;

1st Pat[ient]: It was his questioning practices.

1st Phy: It was not his intentions that shaped the meaning of her illness;

2nd Pat: it was his inattentions.

Death: And, in any case, it is not the intentions of physicians that are at issue here;

1st Nar: it is how a discourse process expresses and realizes the work of medicine,

2nd Nar: For the work is in the talk and the talk is a realization of the work.

1st Phy: (Beginning to laugh) The discourse of physicians and patients is controlled by physicians who, in asking questions,

1st Nar: (Laughing) "request"

2nd Phy: (Laughing) that patients respond on specific topics.

1st Nar: (Laughing) And the development of discourse topics is also controlled by physicians, who, with each successive question or request, shape the meaning of what is said.

1st Phy: (Laughing) This physician reported his diagnosis on a questionnaire called

2nd Nar: (Laughing) "Physician Questionnaire Concerning Specific Patients."

1st Nar: (Laughing) It was as follows:

2nd Phy: (Laughing) "(1) depression,

1st Phy: (Laughing) conversion symptom,

2nd Phy: (Laughing) (2) status post nephrectomy for a hypernephroma, 1971."

1st Phy: (Laughing) He also reported that he was certain of his diagnosis.

2nd Pat: (Laughing) This patient also answered a questionnaire.

1st Pat: (Laughing) Like so many physicians

1st Nar: (Laughing) she said

1st Pat: (Laughing) this physician told her that there was nothing wrong when she had

All: (Laughing and whispering) cancer,

1st Nar: (Laughing) She also said that since their last exchange she had gone to another hospital where she was told

2nd Nar: (Laughing) that she has

All: (Laughing) cancer

1st Pat: (Laughing) of the spine.

Death: (Laughing) No further information is available on this woman and her search for care.

I did not search for the physician's intention. I did not ask why he did not hear. Rather, I asked how he constructed his diagnosis. The "cause" or "causes" of his misdiagnosis I set aside. He was an anonymous participant in a research program, as was she. Although I did see a questionnaire with some information on his biography and his medical opinions, I did not have access to his identity. I couldn't question him or even see him. I could only imagine how he looked. I worked with mere voices. Perhaps this is yet another reason, more visceral than the others, why I wanted to perform the work, to see them in the flesh onstage. Onstage, they were alive. They were not shadows or voices arguing in the dark.

Onstage, I could recover more of the experience, experiment with an explanation of *why* it happened as well as *how* it happened. In my view, Technical Man is an explanation, just as the defensive denial of death so characteristic of American physicians is an explanation, just as the atrophy of feeling, "numbing," as Robert Lifton (1983) appropriately calls it, is an explanation. Also, onstage, I could adopt an ironic attitude. I could laugh. Even if it is black humor, it seems fitting.

The Implications of Performing the Text

What does performance imply? Performing the text establishes a different kind of communicative relation with the audience of research. In performing the text, I am not privileging the analytic report, separating it from the experience of life as it is lived. I am not relying on the inner eye of the reader reading an abstract text. I am privileging the *experience* of knowledge, the communicative act of showing and telling how it happened that on three separate occasions a physician diagnosed depression in a woman who was a cancer patient. Performance privileges the experience, reawakens and recovers the audience's capacity to participate and feel too.

In performing the text, the audience's attention is focused on a vast range of signifiers of meaning (makeup, dress, stage set, gender of the performers, etc.). The audience enters a performance context, comes with a different awareness of the demands of attention, comes with the intention of participating in the play of emotions and the play of interpreting signifiers of the performance. The audience does not come simply for the facts, does not presume that the performance can be summarized acutely in an abstract of a hundred words or less. The audience does not presume that it has the point halfway through the performance and thus exits. The audience is not on the way to someplace else. The audience, too, privileges the experience of performance.

As a method of reporting social knowledge, performance is complex, subtle, provocative, and dialogical. I call it a concretion (rather than an abstraction) of experience. The term concretion is Jean Arp's (1987). He called a series of biomorphic sculptures that he produced in the thirties concrete art. Concretions hug the natural world but not as exact equivalents of natural forms. They display movement, process, change, and transformation. They are expressive, sensitive, and experience near. They resonate, they seem strangely familiar, and yet they are not.

Performance represents the text in new ways. Yet it does not alter the text's argument about questioning practices among physicians, or the ways in which these practices affect the development of the diagnosis and the care of patients. Performance accounts for these practices under different sign systems. For example, suppose that the physician onstage is slightly hearing impaired rather than mechanical, abrupt, and cold. This would cast a different light on his inability to empathize with his patient. Suppose, instead of a second physician I used a lawyer who was concerned to establish that the physician was at fault—an interpretation I would not make. Suppose the patient was a black woman. That too would introduce difference. And yet each of these changes in cast would not "fundamentally" alter the unfolding text. I mean that, as a written document, the text is realized in new ways in performing it. The multiple interpretive acts of performance enhance, rather than diminish, the intelligibility of the text as a scientific account because these multiple interpretations enhance our understanding of the complexity of the reality to which the text and the science of the text allude.

Performance promises a far richer and more subtle science of culture than the analytic text can establish. But it makes different demands. It requires a narrative, drama, action, and a point of view. This work succeeded as theater because the original text had a narrator who reported dramatic events, because it contained real dialogue, and also because it had a reason to be told. The text had the moral force of storytelling, "good counsel" as Walter Benjamin (1969) called it. And it was well-received because it was imaginatively staged and acted.

The audience of the performance of a document like mine is not the same audience as the reader of the document who locates the work in a collection of papers of physician-patient communication. The audience comes to experience the performance, comes with an aesthetic sensibility, and the desire to experiment with new ways of knowing and experiencing. The performance enters into a performance tradition, in the instance of my work, Chamber Theatre and Documentary Theater. The extraordinary speed with which students in the Department of Theater and Department of Performance Studies took up the work reveals how quickly it could be assimilated to a performance tradition, even while preserving its status as a way of doing science, for the science of the work was never compromised. This also means that an art tradition can be used to do science without compromising it. Performing science demonstrates a methodic and systematic inquiry as it occurs in time. It is not a separate activity from the production of science. Performance is a genre of science (see esp. Gusfield 1981 on the rhetoric of the social sciences).

That I want to perform "The Work of Talk" again, that I want to perform other texts as well, suggests that I privilege lived experience and that I seek a richer and subtler interpretive science. But I do not wish to imply that the written text cannot invoke experience, complex contact, or an interpretively rich human science (on the contrary, see, e.g., Smith 1978, 1983; Paget 1982, 1983, 1988a, 1990; Marcus and Fisher 1986; Clifford and Marcus 1986; Van Maanen 1988). Rather, I want to suggest that many written texts mask their point of view, as if the absence of narration or of a narrative point of view demonstrated the work's merit as a scientific text. The absence of the experiencing author is a rhetorical device intending to imply that the events are plucked like fruit, right from nature.

One reason why I want the author of the text of "The Work of Talk" to appear in my version of the performance is that I want to affirm the presence of the human sciences in the performance of culture. I imagine performing texts as one genre of the human sciences, as ethnoperformance, like ethnopoetics or ethnomethodology. Ethnoperformance is native, artful, subtle, imaginative, interpretive, and dialogical. Above all, it is alive.

Notes

1. The work is a contribution to the science of talk. In the tradition of conversation analysis, it takes about an hour to transcribe a minute's worth of talk. I dealt with an hour and a half of conversation, three separate exchanges, sometimes at that level of detail. See an early notational system for talk developed by Gail Jefferson in Schenkein (1978).

2. See Steve Woolgar (1988) on the social practices of science and Joseph Gusfield (1981) on the rhetoric of science.

3. The cast members were all students of either the Department of Performance Studies or the Department of Theater: Arthur Aulisi, Andrea Dzavik, Tim Ereneta, Pat Dressel, Koren Ray, Harry Riggs, and Tracy Walsh. Lynn Hoare was the Assistant Director. The show was sponsored by the Center for Interdisciplinary Research in the Arts at Northwestern University.

4. This same theater tradition is called Story Theater by Paul Sills.

5. The tapes were from Howard Waitzkin's and John Stoeckle's study (1978) of information control among physicians (cf. Waitzkin et al. 1978). Waitzkin and Stoeckle left approximately 30 tapes at the Laboratory in Social Psychiatry at Harvard Medical School for further research. I found them in a box.

6. On performance in the Human Sciences, see Turner (1982) and Conquergood (1985, 1986).

References

Arp, 1885-1966. 1987. [Museum catalogue of an exhibition.] Minneapolis, MN: Minneapolis Institute of Arts.

Becker, H., M. McCall, and L. Morris. 1988. Performing culture: Local theatrical communities. Performed at Northwestern University Theater and Interpretation Center, Evanston, IL, January 15.

Benjamin, W. 1969. Illuminations. Edited with an introduction by H. Arendt. Translated by H. Zohn. New York: Schocken Books.

Breen, R. 1978. Chamber theatre. Englewood Cliffs, NJ: Prentice Hall.

Brown, R. 1987. Society as text: Essays on rhetoric, reason, and reality. Chicago: University of Chicago Press.

Clifford, J., and G. Marcus, eds. 1986. Writing culture: The poetics and politics of ethnography. Berkeley: University of California Press.

Conquergood, D. 1985. Performing as a moral act: Ethical dimensions of the ethnography of performance. *Literature in Performance* 5:1-13.

———. 1986. Performing cultures: Ethnography, epistemology, and ethics. In *Miteinander sprechen und handeln: Festschrift für Hellmut Geissner,* edited by Edith Slembek. Frankfurt: Scriptor.

Gusfield, J. 1981. *The culture of public problems: Drinking-driving and the symbolic order.* Chicago: University of Chicago Press.

Lifton, R. 1983. *The broken connection: On death and the continuity of life.* New York: Basic Books.

Marcus, G., and M. Fischer. 1986. *Anthropology as cultural critique: An experimental moment in the human sciences.* Chicago: University of Chicago Press.

Paget, M. 1982. Your son is cured now; You may take him home. *Culture, Medicine and Psychiatry* 6:237-59.

———. 1983. Experience and knowledge. *Human Studies* 6:67-90.

———. 1988a. *The unity of mistakes: A phenomenological interpretation of mistakes in medical work.* Philadelphia: Temple University Press.

———. 1988b. The work of talk. Adapted for performance by E. Beck in collaboration with the author. Directed by E. Beck. Performed at Northwestern University Jones Arts Residential College, Evanston, IL, May 14-15.

———. 1990. Unlearning to not speak. *Human Studies* 13:147-61.

Schenkein, J., ed. 1978. *Studies in the organization of conversational interaction.* New York: Academic Press.

Smith, D. E. 1978. K is mentally ill: The anatomy of a factual account. *Sociology* 12:25-53.

———. 1983. No one commits suicide: Textual analysis of ideological practices. *Human Studies* 6:309-59.

Spolin, V. 1970. *Improvisation for the theater: A handbook of teaching and directing techniques.* Evanston, IL: Northwestern University Press.

Turner, V. 1982. *From ritual to theater: The human seriousness of play.* New York: Paj.

Van Maanen, J. 1988. *Tales of the field: On writing ethnography.* Chicago: University of Chicago Press.

Waitzkin, H. et al. 1978. The information process in medical care: A preliminary report with implications for instructional communication. *Instructional Science* 7:385-419.

Woolgar, S. 1988. *Science: The very idea.* New York: Tavistock/Ellis Horwood Ltd.

9

The Challenges
of Postmodernism[1]

PETER K. MANNING

Goffman knew more than he could say to the rest of us.

—John Van Maanen (1988, p. 131)

The spector of postmodernism is haunting literary criticism, feminist studies, critical legal studies, architecture, and philosophy. With a few notable exceptions, postmodernist authors and their works are virtually unknown in American sociology and barely known in English sociology. Some very valid reasons sustain this dubious state. Postmodernism, a perspective that rejects the assumptions of modernism, universal truths, theoretic systems, and social progress achieved via cumulative knowledge, challenges the central assumptions of modern empirically oriented social science. These assumptions or presuppositions include its positivism, its radical ad hoc empiricism; its guise of defining (ostensively and nominally) its problems in the language of theories produced by the dead writers of the late nineteenth and early twentieth century; its aspiration to the status of a scientific profession based on the dominant paradigms and assumptions of Western European thought; its rigid clinging to a technical and methodological core (articles in the *American Sociological Review* and *American Journal of Sociology* display vividly the technique-driven character of modern sociology); and its natural-science-derived notions about the nature of theory building and the role of cumulative evidence.

Indubitably, while postmodernism is marginal to the current sociological enterprise, it elicits cautious, if not somewhat "panicky," appreciation among many serious scholars (Hassan 1988; Harvey 1989). Nevertheless, postmodernism is emblematic of salient features of modern society neglected only at our peril: its *fluidity* (vast and rapid changes are visible in temporal and spatial relations), *reflexivity* (images of the consequences of actions affect one's choices of social action) and *hyperreality* (signifiers are produced and consumed but lack precise referential functions and easily identified signifiers serving to constitute a complete sign). Difficult to define precisely, these seem to capture aspects of the family of meanings that surround "postmodernism" (see Lyotard 1984; Eco 1986; Baudrillard 1988; Featherstone 1988).

Postmodernism provides an opportunity for reinvigorating ethnographic research. The features of modern society associated with the postmodernist perspective resonate with many of the aims of ethnographic research since alterations in society alter the time and place assumptions made about culture and its description, the role of the

observer and the subject in scientific observations, and the
context-based nature of description and discourse.

Anthropology and sociology, admittedly, respond differen-
tially to the challenge. Arguably, anthropology is neither as
theoretically grounded nor as positivistic as sociology. It
relies on comparative ethnographic work. Anthropologist
Paul Stoller (1989b) observes, accurately I think, that "anthropology has one strength: ethnography, the original,
albeit imperfect product of our discipline. Despite its taken
for granted status, ethnography . . . has been and will continue to be our core contribution" (p. 138). However, the
fundamental presumptions of postivistic sociology deny the
emergent, fragile, and reflexive character of modern life,
and they do so by clinging to the putative methodological
center of the paradigm. Erving Goffman (1983) accurately
reflected, even after death, that in the absence of close and
detailed descriptions of social life sociology is in danger of
becoming an even more empty and technocratic enterprise.

Here I outline the transdisciplinary challenge represented by postmodernism. In succinct terms, this challenge
can be met by ethnographic work. Close description of social
worlds that serves to make the strange less so and the
familiar more so, cast in whatever form and emanating from
whatever narrative voice, may be the one mode of understanding the other that connects anthropology and sociology
and their humanistic mandates (Van Maanen 1988, xiv).

Roots of Postmodernism
as an Antitheory

The social roots of postmodernism are also the principal
sources of contemporary French sociology. Because many
postmodern writers are profoundly ignorant of the sociologi-

cal tradition and often eschew or ignore relevant sociological writing, postmodernist works often appear ahistorical and de trop. Nevertheless, a distinctive set of ideational themes in French social thought connects it directly to the current preoccupations of ethnographers.[2] A useful example of this is the golden thread of continuity found running between the French "Durkhemian school" of sociology (Lévi-Strauss 1945)—with its affinity for artistic ethnography, expressionism, and experimentalism—and postmodernism. Ethnographic work in Africa by Leiris, Griaule, and Rouch and the rich, excessive, and challenging experimental writings of *College de France* members, such as Bataille and Callois, both encouraged by Mauss, also inspired indirectly current postmodernist ethnography (Clifford 1988; Hollier 1988).

Postmodernism also shares many intellectual roots with American symbolic interactionism, and the postmodern challenge is consistent with the mandate of the leading school of American pragmatism. The irrational and semiconscious aspects of symbolic interactionism have an enduring tradition and share the same origins: the Bergsonian vitalism and Hegelianism craftily assembled with pragmatism by George Herbert Mead (1934). Symbolic interactionism has a long tradition of detailed description of symbolic aspects of life. It elevates to centrality the spontaneous interpretive self and the role of the situated and negotiated order and has shown a passionate resistance to formalization and systematization. A final parallel exists. Like symbolic interactionism, postmodernism is not a theory but a *perspective*. Postmodernism, as has been implied above, eschews "metanarratives" such as Marxism, Freudianism, sociology, and scientific reasoning generally. The "anti-theory" tone of postmodernism arises in part because it reflects a painful reaction to the perceived failure of rationalism and social planning in European life.[3]

Postmodernist Themes
in Ethnography

The essential features of the acutely self-conscious post-modern ethnography are summarized in several recent works.[4] To a striking degree, critical writings concern matters of form and style, the representations of representations, more than the validity or reliability of field data (Van Maanen 1988). The interested reader must act like the *bricoleur,* a modest collector (Lévi-Strauss 1966) of bits and pieces, and fragments that have appeared. Only a handful of examples of postmodern ethnography have appeared (see note 3). The development of postmodern ethnography is embedded in the oral traditions and "trade secrets" of the fields (see Chap. 1, this volume). Let us consider some general features of postmodern ethnography.

Anthropologists George Marcus and M. M. J. Fischer (1986), in *Anthropology as a Cultural Critique: an Experimental Moment in the Human Sciences,* make several useful critical points. They argue that "every individual project of ethnographic research and writing is potentially an experiment" (p.ix), and encourage the "play of ideas, free of authoritative paradigms." The word "experimental" in this context conveys several implications about ethnographic work. In an essay that both advocates and asserts by example, the authors suggest several characteristic features of this emergent literary form.

A postmodern ethnography should show a concern not only for field techniques and methods but sensitivity to a choice of available modes of representation and literary *genres* (e.g., the novel, the journalistic report, the travel log, the anthropological monograph, and the photographic essay are equally valid modes of representation of a field of events). These may be used together, and fragments and shards of events may dance in and out of a narrative. These choices should enable the investigator to develop new approaches rooted in an appreciation of the fundamental perversity and *unpredictability* of human conduct. Chance and indeterminacy, not causality or correlation, are central to explanation. One should demonstrate a willingness to write reflective and reflexive work that takes into account the subtle demands of making sense of others' conduct as well as one's own. This requires an understanding that when studying societies as wholes in a comparative fashion one should encourage systematic, often intertextual integration of the natives' and the observer's *perspectives*. This may mean playful adjustment of perspective, of subject/observer roles, or modes of presenting materials. Such new modes should not obviate an ability to set ethnographic questions and the ethnographic moment in broader political, economic, and historical perspective. Relativism and historicism remain: social *spaces,* not space as a universal or transcultural concept, are to be appreciated, and *times,* not time, are to be valued. Also required is a sensitivity to the location of culture in discourse and in the *image* or model of reality that constitutes the *experience of the other.* Much is asked of and much hope is placed in language, sociolinguistics, and semeiotics. Ironically, much is also expected of intuition and insight, knowing and reporting what is unsaid and perhaps *unsayable.* Further, it would appear that context, that which the observer brings to the object as well as the field in which the object is constituted, is critical in the analysis of the written representation of objects and in a sensitive work of deconstruction (Marcus and Fischer 1986, vii).

These points are abstracted caricatures that, if the reader does not have the context, do not help "clarify" the putative emergent modes of postmodern ethnography. Rather, one needs case materials, examples, and an analytic framework.

In what follows, I use seven dimensions (cf. Marcus and Fischer 1986; Clifford 1988; Van Maanen 1988, 1990) to trace some aspects of the evolution of ethnographic work. I characterize the work in terms of its explicitly detailed concerns and then discuss the nature of the fieldnotes and data, the perspective adopted, the role of causality and prediction in the explanations used, the literary genre(s) employed, conceptions of space and time found in the research, and the imagery or metaphoric work as they are exhibited in the text. An examination of three texts might suggest *how* postmodernism challenges sociological and anthropological visions of complex ethnographic tasks.[5]

Three Case Studies in the Ethnography of Experience

Three pieces of excellent ethnographic work on experience are the basis for identifying some of the emergent features of ethnography and facets of the challenge of postmodernism: Thomas Gladwin's (1970) *East Is a Big Bird,* Douglas Harper's (1987) *Working Knowledge,* and Paul Stoller's (1989b) *The Taste of Ethnographic Things: The Senses in Anthropology.* These research-based works illustrate the changing significance of the seven points listed above. Because rational and logical explanations and theoretic superstructures are rejected, the experiential aspect (or lack thereof) of ethnographic work (both of the investigator and the others) becomes even more critical as a basis for judging the validity of the report. These works represent different time periods or fashions or trends in the emerging forms of ethnography.[6] Finally, they are engaging, very well executed, and written, and rather easily caricatured for these purposes!

EAST IS A BIG BIRD

The Work. Thomas Gladwin, a cognitive anthropologist, spent considerable time in the South Pacific near Puluwat Atoll before taking "only two and one half months early in 1967 to do the actual fieldwork" (Gladwin 1970, Preface). The research was completed in the late 1960s and published in 1970. His topic and precise intellectual problem is succinctly well defined: how do these particular Pacific islanders manage to sail unaided by modern navigational aids across great distances to find tiny islands with relative efficiency? He writes in an admirable, sparse, elegant, and very tightly controlled prose style, shorn of unnecessary embellishment, irony, metaphor, or jargon. Gladwin presents a nonpersonal, realist tale (Van Maanen 1988). It is a narrowly constructed ethnography microscopically scrutinizing a relevant section of the people's technology and activities of interest: sailing an outrigger canoe across the Pacific by dead reckoning. His theoretical interest is in drawing parallels between modes of thinking and reasoning among preliterate peoples and lower class or poverty-status people in American society. The book is divided into six brief chapters: "A Sail in the Sun" (a metonomic gloss on the seafaring culture of this tiny atoll in the Caroline Islands), "The Way of the Voyageur" (a description of sailing), "The Canoes," "The Navigators," "Navigation under the Big Bird" (this is the central ethnographic chapter in the book), and "Perspectives on Thinking."

Fieldnotes and Data. There is no methodological appendix nor a standard sort of ethnographic methods discussion. Gladwin mentions in the text (at p. 138) that he had to promise not to reveal sufficient detail about navigation that a reader could learn it from the book and that his fieldnotes "would require a volume several times the size of this."

Gladwin spoke in Trukese, a second language to him and his informants, and recorded his fieldnotes in English. He elicited the theory of navigation seated at a table across from his informants on the atoll. "Most of the instruction was verbal." (p. 138). Much of what is reported is taken from informants' description of how they would sail from here to there on a map. He did accompany them on sailing journeys but does not linger on the differences, if any, between the elicited logic of navigation and its practice.

The Perspective. The writing is cast in the third person; "Already distant, a canoe is sailing away. Its sail accents the scene, a white cockade bobbing over the waves, impudent and alone on the vast ocean" (p. 1) or "one gets the inescapable impression . . ." (p. 41). The analysis is stripped of quotes, of native language, of symbolic representations in the native tongue, and of the views of the natives, except as incidental to the narrative.

The Participation of Others (Subjects). On the frontispiece, Gladwin dedicates the book "To my 'coauthors' Charles Bechtol, Hipour, Dick Neisser and Seymour Sarason" but makes very little other reference to informants or cultural involvement except in his chapter on the navigators. Pictures of his key informants are included but none of the author in situ. The author's self makes rare and darting entrances and exits.

Causality and Prediction. Gladwin argues that the theory of navigation he elicited is almost mechanical, based on dead reckoning, the varying positions of stars on the horizon, and marvelous memory for concrete detail (this mode of navigation is summarized in chapter 5). A long quote (p. 220) on navigation and the two "qualities" serving "to characterize it logically" is very revealing:

It is on the one hand comprised of systems of explicit theory, and on the other hand works with a limited array of prede- termined alternatives of acceptable input and output. . . . Puluwat navigation (and canoe design) can be said to be cast in theoretical terms because it is explicitly taught and conceptualized as a set of principles governing relationships between phenomena. The phenomena are sometimes directly observed but at other times are only inferred, as is the case with star-compass bearing when the course star is not in a position to be directly observed. These relationships and these inferences are unquestionably abstractions. . . .

   The second characteristic, that all inputs of information and outputs of decisions are . . . prepackaged or predetermined, means that within the navigation system there is little room or need for innovation. Navigation requires the solution to no unprecedented problems. The navigator must be judicious and perceptive, but he is never called upon to have new ideas, to relate things in new ways.

In microcosm, the argument is that by describing logically how navigators use a few abstract concepts in a closed system of reasoning the author produces a social world that is determinant, causal, predictable, and elegant. Like the navigation system itself, it is parsimonious. The writing mimics with great beauty the simple, adequate theory that explains Puluwatan navigation.

Genres. The book is printed on glossy paper (232 pp. plus bibliography and index) with wide margins, illustrated with photos taken by the author of canoes, of the atoll, of the leading characters (all but one of them men, who are sailors and navigators), and contains a few maps and diagrams, footnotes, a bibliography, and an index. The pictures complement the text but, unlike the maps and diagrams, are not necessary to carry the burden of the argument. This is a scholarly monograph.

Space and Time. Interestingly, Gladwin takes pains to instruct the reader that the native means of navigation is easily described in English, follows the logic of dead reckoning used by all sailors (one supposes), and is a closed, invariant operation based on memory and logic that is unequivocally scientific, rational, and reproducible. There is no tension between the natives' point of view and that of the writer. One can map the native theory on the Western mode of navigation with instruments without difficulty or exception. No translation or back translation is used nor needed.

Imagery. Gladwin writes evocatively, with a grasp of language's uses and power, a marvelous turn of phrase, and an admirable precision of expression. The root imagery or metaphor is the mechanical and deterministic metaphor of natural causation, science, and the metaphor of concrete knowledge assembled to accomplish repetitious, useful and necessary, core activity critical to the culture. The text contains no irony or parody, the hidden shocks of "stumbled upon" insights, nor confessions of errors in fieldwork strategy or tactics. In short, this is realistic, to-the-point, nononsense, and very powerful analytic anthropology.

WORKING KNOWLEDGE[7]

The Work. Douglas Harper, a sociologist trained by E. C. Hughes in the University of Chicago "work and the self" tradition, encountered the hero of this work, "Willie," because Harper has a Saab often in need of repair. Willie is the mechanic/repairman in the local area of upstate New York where Harper taught and lived at the time. Begun in the early 1980s, the book was published in 1987. This is adventitious ethnography, resulting when Harper found he

needed repairs to his Saab. Harper writes in the introduction, "Now, ten years later [after first meeting Willie], I
wrote about the man's work and how that work fits into the
'web of group life.' " Harper includes a methods section (pp.
9-14), but his focus is not on methodology but on Willie's
mode of work as a *bricoleur* (via Lévi-Strauss) and his
relationships to the community in this isolated rural area,
or what Harper terms the "ecology of Willie's life" (p. 9). He
uses photos extensively. The book is a "coffee table book,"
almost a folio size, and contains acknowledgments, an
introduction, two sections entitled "The Nature of the Work"
and "Contexts of Work," and an epilogue. It also contains
notes, references, an index, and photos and line drawings
by Suzan Harper to whom the book is dedicated.

Fieldnotes and Data. The author took numerous photographs of Willie at work and then selectively used them for
elicitation and also took three hundred pages of fieldnotes
and observations made of Willie at work. Harper includes
very clear drawings illustrating some of Willie's repair
techniques. Harper uses compressed vignettes and stories
of events to capture social processes, such as the "green-
house story" in which Willie rescues Sue's (Harper's wife)
seedlings in the midst of a winter storm and then refuses to
accept any pay for it.

The Perspective. Harper elides his ideas with Willie's,
aiming to refine a theoretic perspective that combines a
community/work study with an analysis of the connections
between human thought, action, and feeling. He quotes
admiringly from Henry Glassie, an anthropological ethnographer, and borrows Glassie's term "ecology of consciousness" as a synecdochical representation of his own intellectual aims in doing the book (p. 14). Both he and Willie

speak American, and the field notes and observations were recorded in American. He quotes at length from Willie, includes dialogues between himself and Willie, and concludes with several selected stories or vignettes featuring Willie's problem-solving acumen.

The Participation of Others (Subjects). Willie cooperates in the research exercise after having been shown Harper's (1982) photographic essay on the railroad tramp. "The book now includes Willie's voice and mine, both moving from analysis to narrative" (p. 13). This ellision of two voices is rendered, however, in a third-person or first-person-singular voice, Harper's, although long quotes from Willie describing his jobs are presented. Interviews are reproduced as "Doug" and then "Willie" dialogues. What Willie does is more engaging than his words. His remarks are often laconic, elliptical, and highly contextualized bits of "folk wisdom." It is not clear just how a reader is to interpret these epigrams.

Causality and Prediction. Harper's description of the work and technique, the lifestyle, and the moral order of upstate New York, has a distinctly Heideggerian flavor. This is well conveyed in Harper's descriptions of work and technique and his rendering of the moral order that emerges. Harper admires Willie and sees him as emblematic of aspects of a lifestyle they partially share. They work jointly on projects. Work and the self, the moral community, and the ecological order are found to be in some nuanced balance. Here, in this remote part of the United States, the ecosystem produces a set of moral contingencies in the work. Workers cope with these matters, as E. C. Hughes (1958) taught us, in the here and now, establishing trust, and working out a mandate. Willie stands behind his word with his work and his work with his word. Predictability comes in this low-level, dyadic, and reproducible response to a relatively simple face-to-face community. When available, trust provides the basis for these kinds of relationships, while ingenuity stands ready as a resource for coping with the failure of a deal or the temporary collapse of mutual trust.

Genres. Harper uses field observations, interviews with Willie, and a "photo elicitation" technique. This approach, borrowed from John Collier, uses photographs selected to illustrate a "general theme," as generalized stimuli to elicit comments and reactions from a key informant. These elicitation sessions were rather lengthy, taking from two to four hours (p. 12).

Space and Time. The space described is the limited and constrained moral universe of the rural north country of upstate New York. It is little touched by mass culture (p. 3). While it presently includes a set of known and overlapping social worlds and networks, it remains a shrinking universe: "Willie's world shrinks as even the North country modernizes" (p. 200) and "What is Willie's place in this new age?" (p. 200). Space and time are not collapsed into a single vertiginous swirl; atemporal angst (my term) has not overtaken Willie. Yet he is archaic. Harper ominously suggests that in the case of new technologies "even Willie's hand, ear and eye, cannot fathom their workings" (p. 200). Loss of control and understanding of a moral universe leads to alienation, but being a part of a dying world, Harper interpolates, produces despair and feelings of loss.

Imagery. The imagery and metaphor are moral. The language occupies a space where aesthetics and ethics cohere and produce mutually sustaining consequences. Willie strikes one as a kind of beatific saint, a rural icon of reliability, individuality, self-sustaining courage, and skill: a model of the American entrepreneur. Veblen and C. W. Mills celebrate him. Working against the odds, nature, and the weather and against the vicissitudes of human conduct in a deteriorating, blighted, and poverty-stricken region, he ingeniously copes. Without a consistent salary, yet embedded in and dependent on the monetary urban economy that sustains him—his clients and neighbors—Willie is a folk hero of nineteenth-century proportions.

THE TASTE OF ETHNOGRAPHIC THINGS

The Work. Paul Stoller, a sociolinguistically trained anthropologist and Africanist, has worked periodically among the Songhay people in Niger for over eleven years. This book of essays on the Songhay was preceded by two ethnographic reports on sorcery and a dissertation on communicational patterns (Stoller 1989a; Stoller and Olkes 1987). His research is organized around a humanistic thesis that entails a quest for integration of the senses. He argues persuasively for integrating feelings, thought, and action in fieldwork and ethnographic writing, or the "representation of the other." Stoller characterizes most ethnography as "realistic" (Marcus and Cushman 1987): objective and distant, omitting the feelings and perceptions of the observer as well as the sensate worlds (the senses hearing, smell, touch, and sight) of others. He reports his materials in an uneven style, which varies in richness, detail, and sensual content and adheres for the most part to what he calls the representational conventions of realist anthropology. (These essays are written in the style and adopt the format of articles published in anthropology journals in which these essays were originally published.) A slim book of 156 pages, it has nine chapters set in four sections on taste, vision, sounds, and the senses in anthropology.

Fieldnotes and Data. Stoller is rather vague on the nature of his fieldnotes and does not explicitly discuss his field method. He illustrates his book with photos (one of himself), writes long vignettes, and mentions using a tape recorder. The analysis includes long quotes, stories and vignettes, reported dialogues, quotes from other scholars, a list of films, and photographs and figures (maps of the village in which Stoller lived). He also gathered a useless language survey whose responses revealed to him that people lie, even to earnest, well-intentioned fieldworkers. Stoller worked with several key informants and used full participant observation, including undertaking training in and becoming a sorcerer himself. He tries to integrate in his writing various sense data and shows successfully how senses reflect and illuminate the nature of the social organization of the Songhay.

The Participation of Others. Periodically, the text is "dialogic," shaped by interactions between informants or "the other" and the observer. For the most part it is a series of analytic exercises no one from this village could or would understand if they could read. He works closely with his coauthor, Cheryl Olkes, to whom he dedicates this book. Several of the illustrative photos reproduced in the volume are attributed to her. He notes his debts to his sorcery teachers and other key informants. His key informant, a man whose funeral at age 106 prompted Stoller to return to Niger, is prominently pictured and features dramatically in many of the tales. He depicts himself in his relationships as warm and likable. His self stalks the book and his face pops up in a dramatic picture (circa 1976) leaning on a Citröen in trousers with elephantine bottoms. In the text near the photo, he discusses images of fieldworkers and how he was cast by some of his informants as "the son of Rouch" (the picture's caption), a French ethnographer and cineast. The picture, one assumes, shows Stoller as he sees himself as seen by his others. A further reflexive note: the photo is attributed to Cheryl Olkes. Her picture is not included.

The Perspective. The book is written from three perspectives: thirdparty reporting—"In 1984, Paul Stoller, an anthropologist . . ." (p. 15); first-person narrative—"I was lucky because I discovered early in my fieldwork that people were lying to me" (p. 127); and the observer as writer— "According to John Dewey . . ." (p. 152). He struggles with the notion that emotions and feelings about experience should penetrate "in side" so that the other is part of the self (my words). Stoller remains present in the essays, whatever the content, and he inserts his voice from time to time to rescue the text, to place himself in the narrative, and to include his reactions, impressions, and feelings. His brief chapter on the semiotic significance of the Songhay bush taxi is especially rich. The author rather sadly asserts that he has failed to develop an adequate style, one in which anthropological writers allow the events of the field to "penetrate them" (p. 54). He then claims, given his intense field experiences, that he will have to develop "a different mode of expression, a mode in which the event becomes the author of the text and the writer becomes the interpreter of the event who serves as an intermediary between the event (author) and the readers" (p. 54).

If language shapes the senses, Stoller does not help the reader to cogitate on that. He mentions speaking in French or in Songhay to someone, but the text is always rendered in English, so one does not always have a sense of the actual language of communication. His primary language in the field is Songhay, and he reports himself as a quite competent speaker.

Causality and Prediction. Magic and sorcery are the subjects of much of his research, and he reports his experiences very candidly, including his own possession experience (p. 46). The Songhay live in series of life-worlds characterized by determinant results, whether orchestrated by sounds, beliefs, or material objects, yet Stoller sees the world as highly contingent, problematic, and full of detours, meanderings, playful false leads, and the free play of words. Songhay metaphors work, in the same sense that magic or sorcery work, by tapping the power of belief and of nonreferential or expressive discourse (p. 144). He rejects the logic of binary reasoning (inside vs. outside, emotion vs. reasoning, art vs. science, appearance vs. reality; see p. 139) and seeks to reproduce sensate experiences. Ideally, he seeks an integration of thought and feeling and "to blend science and art" (p. 139). He presents his field experiences as somewhat aleatory, subject to mistakes and misunderstandings, and not a quest for logical or aesthetic closure or certainty.

Genres. The book is stylish in a conventional anthropological fashion. In spite of his protestations and nominal rejection of these conventions, he rigidly adheres to them in this book. He employs several kinds of pictures, objective representations, footnotes, full and accurate references, margins, and textual presentation conventions. He speaks admiringly of Lieris's text, *Afrique Fantome,* a hastily written first draft exercise in magical writing, but writes with care and restraint and produces an error-free text. He is planning to film a documentary on the culture of the

Songhay for English Granta television (P. Stoller, personal communication, October 1990).

Space and Time. Stoller struggles, sometimes with flashes of brilliance, with representing the concept of space. He seeks to limn perception of space and the central Durkheimian question of the nature of the connections between conceptions of space and time and social organization. Stoller candidly reveals his own initial misperceptions of the village based on the colonial model of spatial relations and social status and how he learned to see space as a social construction and a vehicle for the organization of other symbolic materials. Space is used by actors and groups to maintain power positions. He uses only European clock time when referencing time ("In 1984, . . ." or "On Saturday . . .") rather than native conventions and rarely uses native terms or categories. When he does, he brackets the Songhay words as a gloss after the English word or phrase.

Imagery. Stoller speaks imaginatively and skillfully, using synesthesia repeatedly to show how the senses work in social relations. He speaks of "hearing the spirits" in a ceremonial music performance. He shows how certain sounds are taken to be the signs of the presence of the spirits. A story in which taste in both senses of the term indicates sociality is a highlight of the book. A bitter and offensive sauce served to guests represents social relations, sustains them, and reproduces in microcosm the bitter taste of a feud that sustained soured feelings. His analysis of the metaphoric features of Songhay interactions is rather vague, done in English, and not very revealing. The imagery here is that of the inner and introjected nature of the experience of the anthropologist. He claims that since experience is located "within" the anthropologist, the story of the "taste of ethnographic things" necessitates rich, multilayered, variously metaphoric, sensate and nonreferential discourse. Like most anthropologists, he reduces sight to secondary status, opting to emphasize other senses, especially hearing and taste in his writing.

Comment

These three works illustrate many interesting and suggestive themes that echo the challenges issued by postmodernism. Any single representation of a set of books, much like a book that is selectively constructed from a massive sheaf of fieldnotes, is perhaps unfair, but it does sensitize one to some significant changes in the style and content of ethnographies. These three studies do not a random sample make, but they reflect current trends and influences of the current experimental moment. As a way of closing this discussion, this comment is organized around the subheads used above. The conventions used to assess ethnographies are changing, even as ethnographies and ethnographers change.

In spite of an interest in *experience* and its central role in ethnography, written words organized by linear logic prevail in these three books. Words are the dominant mode of expression, and Western thinking and categories are employed to sort out and define the work studied whether it be navigation, repair, or the organization of sensual experience. The logic used gives rise to generalizations that claim implicit cross-cultural validity rather than being restrictive and local. All three books are about work and use illustrative pictures, stories, and diagrams.

Clearly, the experiential dimension conveyed by these texts cannot be fully captured in words. Perhaps the mode of text presented to the readers makes such limits certain.

One cannot smell the salt breezes or freshly caught tropical fish nor the reek of pyramids of rotting garbage in the roads in Niger, cannot hear the crashing of waves against the bow of the outrigger nor the sounds of complex Songhay chants. The reader cannot hear but can only imagine the hiss of Willie's welding torch cutting into yet another unforgiving Saab. We do not see the stars in a dark, clear velvety southern sky nor image the details of star-compass bearings. These books are representations of experience, but reading them is much like reading any other book. They echo the claims of structuralism that suggest some "deep code" exists and permits us to translate from one form of communication to another.

Culturally differentiated times and spaces are noted and valued, but Western time and space are discussed in English.

Only Stoller asks himself the primary epistemological question: Are they lying? He collected a language survey and found that his respondents had lied to him. If language is problematic, and deeper meanings are to be plundered, how does one decipher reality or find the truth? The reality observed here nevertheless was penetrable, coherent, understandable, and reproducible. Postmodernism questions such confident claims or views them as irrelevant. Neither Gladwin nor Harper directly address the question of the nature or basis for the reported reality, but each affirms and appreciates its texture and existence. Underlying Gladwin's reality is a cognitive structure somehow geared to the physical universe, whereas Harper's reality reflects a posited techno-moral structure. Stoller, however, refuses to accept Platonic reality and convincingly describes the existence of many realities, multiple social worlds, and various epistemologies. Unfortunately, he does not always explicate them well in these essays.

Stoller displays a healthy and playful contempt for unidimensional imagery and advocates (implicitly) the value of trying out various modes of experiencing the other. Of all the works, only Gladwin's does not use social-cultural causation as a metaphor. His metaphoric vision involves mapping physical causation onto social and psychological space. Puluwat navigation is a form of local knowledge based on a closed logical system, mechanical and invariant, a known set of problems and inferences. These shape the known and available solutions. While navigating these islands, certain conventions are used, and no new or unanticipated problems arise. Classification and categorization of the relevant information, along with deference to tradition and the belief in the infallibility of the navigators, accomplishes the work. Reclassifying, innovation, or improvisation are not needed in Puluwat navigation. Chance and indeterminacy are coped with variously in these settings and by the authors, but there is a sense in which rational decisions produce coping styles unaffected by the imagery and the rhetoric of pseudocausality used in Anglo-American society. Yet certainly the overlapping and mutually reinforcing models of moral and physical causality found in Puluwat, in upstate New York, and in Niger provide a satisfying degree of cohesion and integrity in social action.

The several ironies woven into these books illustrate the complexity of postmodernist ethnographic work and the challenge it represents. The notions used by these authors to gloss the idea of causality and predictability are revealing. The navigatory system described in Gladwin's (1970) *East Is a Big Bird* is a local logic based on the present star positions as seen from the atoll and their movements, it employs space/time calculations relevant only to the Caroline Islands, and procedures, modes of thinking and acting, are given by a precise set of clues read from the skies, the sea, and the wind. The local character of the knowledge is not the sort associated with postmodern, atemporal, or spatial knowledge but, rather, is spatially and temporally grounded and rooted. It is a locally constructed and known map that reflects accurately the physical and natural causation manifested in the sea and environs. The logic of Willie's work is also local but not in the sense suggested by postmodernism: local, timeless, and in a constructed social space, built from amassed floating signs. To the contrary, it is based on calculated and well-calibrated interpersonal trust, close dyadic relations, and the intersection of history and biography. Willie's thinking and acting are products of the locale. They are pragmatic and produce a kind of Zen harmony between Willie himself, machines, and their owners. Stoller's essays strike the most universal themes. He seeks modestly to convey *the invariant universals of the human experience,* feelings of pleasure, of fear, of laughter, but he does not find them in the culturally sanctioned forms of experience but in the senses and sensate equivalences found "inside" people. Reports of these sensate experiences, in turn, are based on modes of interpenetration of the experiences of the observer and the observed. How one moves from one to the other is a process he does not clearly explicate.

Other ironies remain. The texts are rendered entirely in English and, with the exception of a few photos, the weight of the argument is carried by the written word of an author (logocentrism reigns). Actors' categories are not employed; the subheads are all jargon and variants thereof. How is it that the unsayable, the deep structure of human lives, is conveyed by such words, and how do words capture that which cannot be written?

The authors of these books are variously presented and present. Both Harper and Stoller speak with, from, and behind their characters to an extent that makes it difficult to see who is the other. If something is inside, it can be known only in actions, in displays of words, in language games. Thus the "inside/outside" metaphor breaks down when the "meaning" of the reported experience provided by context is begged (Needham 1973). Put another way, one might ask by what conventions could one assess the validity of these books?

The degree of fluidity and reflexivity in these works is also ironically conveyed. For example, the Puluwat navigators use the logic of space-time universals, yet can only navigate in areas they know or have previously navigated. Sailing only a few hundred miles to the east or west, they confront profound problems. Because they do not know where they have been they do not know where they are going (Gladwin 1970, chap. 6). Could Willie work among the Songhay in Niger? He could manage the required technical tasks, but the moral environment or context he assumes and perhaps even requires would be absent. Would he be a pathetic lost figure like Stoller, wandering about inquiring about people's mechanical skills? Stoller is the featured other in his book: it is about himself, a growing and learning scholar, and his responses speak a generality transcending language or symbolization. His being speaks to us, but we do not know exactly what it says. Like magical writing or the automatic writings of Swedenbourgians, we only know and write what we have been taught: the text may speak to us, but we must be able to create an informed context within which to view it.

That point carries us directly to an acknowledgment of the fundamental constraints of the modern world: those of income, race, class, and gender. These books contain snapshots, pictures of men's work, taken of men as viewed by men for men, and work that is imbued with men's risks in those cultures: sailing, repair, and sorcery. These books contain delightful stories seemingly unrelated to the massification of imagery, decline in the power of metanarratives, and the structural constraints of modern society. These all seem shadowy figures and serve as a mere background for the analyses.

These works are good to think with. They stretch the imagination and challenge the intellect. Does the postmodernist perspective allow ethnographers to superimpose "their worlds" on "ours," to create a dialogue or compose a social portrait that is the literary equivalent of Picasso's fractionated, gross, purple, multiheaded beach dwellers of the 1930s or the anguished faces of the tragic inhabitants of an imaginary *Guernica?* Not yet, but stayed tuned.

Notes

1. This chapter was originally prepared for presentation in a session on symbolic interactionism chaired by Anne Rawls at the August 1990 annual meeting of the American Sociological Association in Washington, DC. Its content owes a great deal to John Van Maanen's creative work and our conversations over the years on topics both worthy and unworthy.

2. I consider here such matters as the disillusionment with rationality and its failure to cope with and control irrational forces (Rabinow 1990); the surrealistic and antirational forces at play in French art, music, and social science (e.g., the writings and works of the surrealists); the concern with the paradoxes of "rational people in an irrational world" in which the spinning vortex of time/space conflation confronts people with themselves (in the form of existentialism and phenomenology); the growth of mass media, especially of television and films, and the media's disconnected, powerful forces that reverse time, interdigitate the past and the present, obliterate history, and predispose modern citizens to see themselves only in contrast with the "cold" cultures of preliterate peoples; and finally, the elevation of experience, especially unreflective or semiconscious feelings, over cognition, memory, and logical reasoning. In addition, a long tradition in French thought, connected to the Hegelian

and Neitzchean philosophies, contains a tendency to prefer aesthetics to ethics (Descombes 1980; Harvey 1989). These trends suggest that the unsayable or the unspeakable attains eminence or at least competes not unequally with words (written or spoken) as a central source of knowledge. Surely, that is a paradox worthy of exploration.

3. For example, at each point after a crisis in the French state (e.g., in the late nineteenth century, after the Franco-Prussian War, after World War I until 1939, and the period immediately after World War II when Sartrean existentialism arose), the response of French intellectuals was to seek alternatives to the stifling dominant rationalities, whether they be Marxian, Hegelian, or evolutionary positivism. In its present extreme guise, French irrationalism, in the writings of Delueze and Guattri and Baudrillard, explicitly rejects holistic and logical explanations and valorizes instead minisegments of life, fleeting glances of language games, metaphoric and figurative tales, fragmented selves, and dislocated experiences, critically making acontextual or "deconstructing" embedded arguments to reveal both the nature of their embeddedness and their sterility.

4. I include here, for example, the works of Marcus and Cushman (1987), Marcus and Fischer (1986), Clifford (1988), and Van Maanen (1988, 1990) and the works of Dan Rose (1989, 1990), Renato Rosaldo (1989) Jonathan Dorst (1989), and Dean MacCannell (1986).

5. The aims of ethnography are easily distinguished from those of the dominant positivistic paradigm stated in the first paragraph of this chapter.

6. The "new ethnography" movement, associated with the work of Roy D'Andrade, Kim Rommney, Duane Metzger, Ward Goodenough, Charles Frake, and Harold Conklin, was based on premises that the logic of thinking was universal in character and that the structure of human thinking could be elicited and shown to pattern the symbolic worlds of preliterates as well as modern citizens (see Manning and Fabrega 1975).

7. I am much indebted to John Van Maanen's (1990) perceptive and sympathetic review of Harper's *Working Knowledge* in *Human Studies*.

References

Baudrillard, J. 1988. *Selected writings*. Edited by M. Poster. Stanford, CA: Stanford University Press.
Clifford, J. 1988. *The predicament of culture*. Cambridge, MA: Harvard University Press.

Descombes, V. 1980. *Modern French philosophy*. Cambridge, UK: Cambridge University Press.

Dorst, J. 1990. *The written suburb*. Philadelphia: University of Pennsylvania Press.

Eco, U. 1986. *Travels in hyperreality*. New York: Harcourt Brace Jovanovich.

Featherstone, M. 1988. *Postmodernism*. London: Sage.

Gladwin, T. 1970. *East is a big bird*. Cambridge, MA: Harvard University Press.

Goffman, E. 1983. The interaction order. *American Sociological Review* 48:1-18.

Harper, D. 1982. *Good company*. Chicago: University of Chicago Press.

———. 1987. *Working knowledge*. Chicago: University of Chicago Press.

Harvey, D. 1989. *The condition of postmodernity*. Oxford, UK: Basil Blackwell.

Hassan, I. 1985. The culture of postmodernism. *Theory, Culture and Society* 2:119-32.

Hollier, D., ed. 1988. *The college of sociology, 1937-39*. Translated by B. Wing. Minneapolis: University of Minnesota Press.

Hughes, E. C. 1958. *Men and their work*. Glencoe, IL: Free Press.

Lévi-Strauss, C. 1966. *The savage mind*. Chicago: University of Chicago Press.

Lyotard, J. F. 1984. *The postmodern condition*. Minneapolis: University of Minnesota Press.

MacCannell, D. 1986. *The tourist*. New York: Schocken.

Manning, P. K., and H. Fabrega, Jr. 1975. Fieldwork and the "new ethnography." *Man* (n.s.) 11:39-52.

Marcus, G., and G. Cushman. 1987. Ethnographies as texts. *Annual Review of Anthropology* 11:25-69.

Marcus, G., and M. M. J. Fischer. 1986. *Anthropology as cultural critique*. Chicago: University of Chicago Press.

Mead, G. H. 1934. *Movements of thought in the nineteenth century*. Chicago: University of Chicago Press.

Needham, R. 1973. *Belief, language and experience*. Oxford, UK: Basil Blackwell.

Rabinow, P. 1990. *French modern*. Cambridge: MIT Press.

Rosaldo, R. 1989. *Culture and truth*. Boston: Beacon.

Rose, D. 1989. *Patterns of American culture*. Philadelphia: University of Pennsylvania Press.

———. 1990. *Living the ethnographic life*. Newbury Park, CA: Sage.

Stoller, P. 1989a. *Fusion of the worlds*. Chicago: University of Chicago Press.

————. 1989b. *The taste of ethnographic things*. Philadelphia: University of Pennsylvania Press.

Stoller, P., and C. Olkes. 1987. *In sorcery's shadow*. Chicago: University of Chicago Press.

Van Maanen, J. 1988. *Tales of the field: On writing ethnography*. Chicago: University of Chicago Press.

————. 1990. Escape from modernity. *Human Studies* 13:275-84.

About the Authors

Michael Agar currently divides his time between teaching linguistic anthropology at the University of Maryland at College Park and consulting with Ethknoworks in Takoma Park, Maryland. His latest book, *Language Shock: Understanding the Culture of Conversation,* was published in 1994 by William Morrow. He is currently working on two projects. One is a forty-country study of leadership conducted by the Wharton School; the other is a project to incorporate ethnographic approaches into national and international epidemiology panels concerned with drug and alcohol use. His chapter in this book reflects his ongoing concerns with the relationship between truth and beauty.

Eyal Ben-Ari is Senior Lecturer in the Department of Sociology and Anthropology at the Hebrew University of Jerusalem. An anthropologist by training, he is interested in the interrelationship between cultures and organizations. He has carried out fieldwork in Japan (on white-collar suburban communities and preschools), Singapore (among Japanese business expatriates), and Israel (in a military unit). His most recent book is *Changing Japanese Suburbia: A Study of Two Present-Day Localities* (Kegan Paul International, 1992).

Gary Alan Fine is Professor of Sociology at the University of Georgia. His most recent book is *Kitchens: Structure and Culture in Restaurant Work* (tentative title) to be published in 1995 by University of California Press, and he is editor of *A*

Second Chicago School? Midcentury Sociology of the University of Chicago, also due out in 1995 from University of Chicago Press. He is currently working on a study of attitudes toward environmental leisure.

Jean E. Jackson is Professor of Anthropology at the Massachusetts Institute of Technology. Her publications include *The Fish People: Linguistic Exogamy and Tukanoan Identity in Northwest Amazonia* (Cambridge, 1983) and several articles on the politics of culture in the indigenous rights movement, including "Is There a Way to Talk About Making Culture Without Making Enemies" (*Dialectical Antropology* 14, no. 2, 1989), "Culture, Genuine and Spurious: The Politics of Indianness in the Vaupés, Colombia" (*American Ethnologist* 22, no. 1, 1995), and "Preserving Indian Culture: Shaman Schools and Ethno-education in the Vaupés, Colombia" (forthcoming in *Cultural Anthropology*). She has also published several articles reporting on research on chronic pain treatment and is finishing a book entitled *Camp Pain: Building Community and Rebuilding Self at a Chronic Pain Center.*

Peter K. Manning is Professor of Sociology and Criminal Justice at Michigan State University. Author of several books and articles on policing, he has written *A Communicational Theory of Policing* (forthcoming). His current research includes a dramaturgical analysis of loyalty in private security, work on postmodern ethnography (with Betsy Cullum-Swan), and fieldwork on the politics of promotion in a large urban police department.

Daniel D. Martin is a doctoral student in sociology at the University of Minnesota. He is presently working on his dissertation, a critical analysis of the holistic health movement entitled "Rationalization and Reenchantment: Modernity, Meaning and Healing Among Holistic Health Practitioners."

Marianne A. Paget died of cancer on December 22, 1989. At the time of her death, she was a Research Associate in the Department of Sociology at Brandeis University and a Visiting Scholar in Law and Social Science at Northwestern University. Her final writings explore silences about medical errors. A collection of her work—including this chapter—appears in *A Complex Sorrow: Reflections on Cancer and an Abbreviated Life,* edited by Marjorie DeVault (Temple University Press, 1993).

Laurel Richardson is Professor of Sociology at Ohio State University. Her interests are in poststructuralist theory, narrative, and qualitative research. She is author of six books, including *Writing Strategies: Reaching Diverse Audiences* (Sage), *Feminist Frontiers* (McGraw-Hill), and *Gender and University Training* (SUNY Press). Her recent articles appear in *Sociological Quarterly, Journal of Contemporary Ethnography, Symbolic Interaction, Studies in Symbolic Interaction,* and *American Sociological Review.* She is working on a manuscript, *Texts of Illegitimacy,* which focuses on alternative representations of social science. Her goals are to problematize the narrative structures through which social science claims authoritative knowledge, to write more interesting sociology, and to find methods that increase the probability that readers chose to become writers/tellers of their own lives.

John Van Maanen is Erwin Schell Professor of Organization Studies in the Sloan School of Management at the Massachusetts Institute of Technology. He has published a number of books and articles in the general area of occupational and organizational sociology. Cultural representations figure prominently in his studies of the work worlds of patrol officers on city streets in the United States, police detectives and their guv'nors in London, fishermen in the northeast Atlantic, and, most recently, park operatives in Disneyland at home and away. He is author of *Tales of the Field: On Writing Ethnography* (University of Chicago Press, 1988).

Harry F. Wolcott is Professor Emeritus in the Department of Education and Anthropology at the University of Oregon in Eugene. His ethnographic studies include *A Kwakiutl Village and School,* reissued with a new "Afterword: 25 Years Later" in 1989; *The Man in the Principal's Office: An Ethnography,* reissued in 1984; *The African Beer Gardens of Bulawayo* (1974); and *Teachers versus Technocrats: An Educational Innovation in Anthropological Perspective* (1977). His most recent publication is *Transforming Qualititative Data: Description, Analysis, and Interpretation,* published in 1994 by Sage.